Postsocialism

.

Postsocialism

Politics and Emotions in Central and Eastern Europe

Maruška Svašek

Berghahn Books
New York • Oxford

First published in 2006 by
Berghahn Books
www.berghahnbooks.com

©2006, 2008 Maruška Svašek
First paperback edition published in 2008

Library of Congress Cataloging-in-Publication Data
Svašek, Maruška.
Postsocialism : politics and emotions in Central and Eastern Europe / Maruška Svašek
p. cm.
Includes bibliographical references and index.
    ISBN 978-1-84545-124-0 (hbk., alk. paper)
    ISBN 978-1-84545-534-7 (pbk., alk. paper)
1. Post-communism--Europe, Eastern--Psychological aspects.
2. Ethnopsychology--Europe, Eastern. 3. Emotions. I. Title.

    HN380.7.A8S89 2005
    306.0947--dc22

    2005055851

British Library Cataloguing in Publication Data

A catalogue record for this book is available from the British Library

Printed in the United States on acid-free paper

ISBN 978-1-84545-124-0 hardback
ISBN 978-1-84545-534-7 paperback

Contents

Introduction

Postsocialism and the Politics of Emotions

Maruška Svašek

A second month has gone by since I was torn from you, from our home, from our Sarajevo. I have learned in this short but for me so long time what sorrow, loneliness and nostalgia mean. And suffering, real suffering.

Woman, late 20s, Sarejevo. In: Mertus et al. (1997: 93)

People are insecure, and there is so much conflict about every little thing: over land, over anything that a person gets –there are accusations about how he got it, and then he gets mad at the accusers and soon whole families are not speaking to each other.

Woman, 50, Bulgaria. Quoted by Creed (1999: 228)

Oh, we had fun at work. We laughed a lot together. That is to say, the work was really hard, physically hard, you know? But we looked after each other. If one girl was ill, we others would cover for her, do her work, so the director wouldnt know. Oh, and we went out together after work – sometimes for tea and cakes and sometimes – you know? – for vodka. Now? No, I don't see any of them any more. It costs too much to go into town. And I have no money to go out. And what would we talk about now? I'm embarrassed.

Woman, 40, Poland. Quoted by Pine (2002: 104)

Introduction

This book intends to demonstrate that emotions are inherent in political dynamics. It opens up a theoretical debate on the significance of emotional dynamics to political processes in the context of postsocialism, and offers intruiging ethnographic analyses that explore the dialectics of emotional and political change and continuity in Bulgaria, Croatia, the Czech Republic, Poland, Romania, Russia and Slovenia. While some chapters analyse small-scale dynamics on the level of village politics, others investigate political relationships in rural areas, border regions, towns and cities. A number of chapters have a broader scope, and explore local reactions to and participation in globalising processes, including migration, remigration and European Union enlargement.

From the perspective of emotions, postsocialist Europe is a fascinating area of research. As the above quotes suggest, in many parts of the region the tumultuous political and economic developments have generated strong feelings, ranging from hope and euphoria to disappointment, envy, disillusionment, sorrow, loneliness and hatred. Over the past fifteen years, the region has attracted the attention of an increasing number of scholars from different disciplines who have analysed various aspects of what has become known as 'the transition' or – theoretically more apt – rather diverse transformation processes (Berdahl 2000: 2–3; Bryant and Mokrzycki 1994: 3–4; Stark 1992: 22). Most of them, however, have focused narrowly on the economic, political and social dimensions of this process, and have paid little or no attention to emotional dynamics.

This lack of interest in emotional processes can partly be explained by the rather persistant idea that 'reason' and 'passion' are mutually exclusive categories, and that 'true politics' are (or should be) a process of *rational* decision-making. The myth of pure rationality has been propagated for centuries in different forms by influential Western philosophers. Plato (*c*.429–*c*.347 BC) imagined reason as a charioteer who dominated the unruly passions, represented as wild horses. Philosophers such as Kant (1724–1804) and Hegel (1770–1831) equally contrasted rational action to uncontrolled, passionate behaviour, and saw reason as a way to obtain freedom and to attain moral truth. In this view, reason was the foundation of sound politics, whereas passion threatened the moral and societal order.

The reason-versus-passion tradition has been criticised by a philosophical countercurrent, represented by scholars such as Aristotle (died 322 BC) and Hume (1711–76). Aristotle was interested in the ways in which emotions could be manipulated, and thus become powerful means by which orators, politicians and others influenced people (see Lyons 1980: 33). In *Rhetoric*, he defined emotions as 'all those feelings that so change men as to affect their judgements' (Aristotle 1941: 1380), thus undermining the belief in politics as a purely rational sphere of action. Instead, Aristotle defined politics as an interpersonal process in which knowledge of other people's emotional behaviour was vital.[1] Centuries later, Hume argued that 'reason is the slave of passions, and can aspire to no other office than to serve and obey them' (Hume 1739, quoted by Blackburn 1994: 319).

Sceptical about the power of reason, and regarding 'passions' as the core of all human action, he believed moral thought to be the expression of naturally evolved sentiments, which therefore ensured cooperation within societies (Blackburn 1994: 180). In line with the perspectives of Aristotle and Hume, this book argues that a focus on emotions is vital to the understanding of political processes.

This introductory chapter will first discuss some of the anthropological underpinnings of the main argument of this book, i.e. that emotions are intrinsic to politics and political change. Secondly, it will introduce the individual chapters and relate them to other relevant studies, structuring the account through a discussion of what can be loosely regarded as 'types' of emotional processes, including hope and joy, disappointment and nostalgia, mistrust and fear, and anger, hatred and xenophobia. These emotions have been produced, felt, objectified and politicised in specific ways in distinct postsocialist contexts.

A number of other themes weave through the chapters that follow. An important topic that connects the first four contributions is the influence of rapid economic change on people's everyday lives and political outlooks. While the first two chapters unravel the emotional impact of economic restructuring and marginalisation, the major theme in the second two chapters is the emotional dynamics of changing property relations.[2] In Chapter 1, Patrick Heady and Liesl L. Gambold Miller examine feelings of nostalgia in rural Russia in the context of economic transformation and social change. Dimitrina Mihaylova explores experiences and discourses of social suffering among the borderland Pomaks in Bulgaria in Chapter 2. Filippo Zerilli's Chapter 3 discusses the conflicts between tenants and owners that have arisen as a result of the privatisation and restitution of residential property in Bucharest. In Chapter 4, I explore the dialectics of emotions and moral and political justifications in the context of changing property relations in a small Czech village.

Carolin Leutloff-Grandits' Chapter 5 also deals with changing ownership, but here the changes are an effect of ethnic tensions and the violent break-up of Yugoslavia. Focusing on postwar Croatia, she looks at the ways in which emotional memories and judgements have influenced the claims for housing and property by Serbs and Croatians in the town of Knin. The major focus of Leutloff-Grandits' chapter is the upsurge of nationalist sentiments in the postsocialist context, an important theme that is also central in the two chapters that follow. In Chapter 6, Zlatko Skrbiš analyses an emotionally powerful nationalist myth about the origin of the Slovenian nation, and his contribution focuses specifically on ways in which migrants contribute to it. In Chapter 7, Justine Golanska-Ryan compares the strategies utilised in two campaigns against Polish European Union membership, demonstrating that the reinforcement of nationalist sentiments has been an important political tool.

Political rivalry is a second important theme in Golanska-Ryan's analysis. This topic is also explored in Chapter 8, in which Birgit Müller examines the politics of envy, resentment and hatred, as played out in a fierce struggle for power in a Czech village. Müller demonstrates that a lack of agreed-upon rules of behaviour, and the absence of relations of trust within the political arena have been a major stumbling block in local politics. The political dynamics of trust and mistrust is the major focus in Chapter 9. In this chapter, Don Kalb and Herman Tak critically explore the perceptions of citizens from Wroclaw of local and national policy makers during and after devastating floods in southern Poland. Their study shows how disappointement and anger with the malfunctioning of state institutions and the incompetence of regional representatives has generated widespread feelings of mistrust amongst the population, a phenomenon also common in other postsocialist states, as is apparent in the other chapters.

In her Afterword, Alaina Lemon rightly suggests that even though it is worthwhile to focus on the interface of politics and emotions, it should not be forgotten that emotions cannot be understood by a focus on political processes alone. In line with her argument, it is not our aim to propagate a perspective that reduces 'emotions' to 'politics' or vice versa. Instead, we aim to provide insights into how emotions have been actively politicised (see all the chapters), and in some cases, depoliticised (see, in particular, Chapter 5) in different postsocialist settings.

Relevant Anthropological Debates

Biology and Culture

The contributions address issues that are central to the anthropology of emotions, an area of study that has grown considerably since the late 1970s (for a discussion of the main debates in emotion theory, see Leavitt 1996; Lutz and White 1986; Lyon and Barbalet 1994; Harré and Parrot 1996; Milton and Svašek 2005; Plutchik and Kellerman 1980). Anthropologists working in the field have developed sociocultural theories that have challenged traditional biological and psychological approaches to emotions, thereby introducing a perspective that acknowledges the *political* dimension of emotional processes.

Biological theories, inspired by the work of Charles Darwin, have in most cases regarded emotions as adaptive physical processes that have developed as an inherent part of human evolution. The psychologist Paul Ekman (1980), also inspired by Darwin, compared people's facial expressions in thirteen different cultural settings, and claimed to have found evidence for cross-cultural universals, which in his view were generated by biological forces. From an anthropological perspective, however, the notion of humans as a 'biological species' is too limited because it disregards or simplifies the significance of cultural and political complexities in human life. It is thus not surprising that Ekman's work has been criticised by numerous anthropologists, including Michelle Z. Rosaldo (1983) who accused him of assuming the existence of physiological universals and then simply 'adding culture'.[3]

Rosaldo (1983), Lutz (1988) and other cultural constructionists have argued, by contrast, that cultural forces are constitutive of emotions, and affect the ways in which physical phenomena are felt, perceived and conceptualised. In their perspective, culture is an active force that affects the ways in which humans experience, express and manipulate emotions. Consequently, as power distribution is inherent in cultural process (for example in terms of age, gender, kinship, class or ethnicity), domination, resistance and cooperative sociality are at the core of many emotional processes. As this book will demonstrate, the politics of emotions are effective on many (at times tightly interrelated) levels of social interaction, from the dynamics of everyday family life to the dynamics of local, national and global political processes.

Cultural constructionists, however, have tended to overemphasise the cultural particularity of specific emotional discourses and practices (Milton and Svašek 2005). Despite cultural particularities, human beings in different parts of the world are confronted with certain types of emotionally-evocative situations that are comparable, such as confrontations with 'danger', 'loss', 'power difference' or, in the case of postsocialist Europe, with rapid economic and political change. Evidently, what or who is regarded as dangerous, precious, or powerful differs in distinct sociocultural settings and historical periods, and – again referring to postsocialist Europe – the emotional impact of economic and political transformation can be extremely diverse. Consequently, a sensitivity to contextual specificity is highly necessary, yet without losing sight of connecting links and broader similarities.

Obviously, one has to be cautious when using specific emotion terms in a comparative perspective because, as pragmatic normative tools, they tend to project rather specific images of what emotions are, and how one should behave in particular emotionally-evocative situations. The English concepts of 'fear' and 'grief', for example, are used by English speakers to label a number of *different* experiences of 'danger' and 'loss' that may be quite specific. 'Fear of the dark' and 'fear of losing one's job', for instance, are rather distinct feelings, and the latter is much more likely to be politicised than the former. At the same time, emotion terms tend to reproduce culturally and historically specific norms of emotional behaviour, which makes their translation into other languages a somewhat problematic exercise (Wierzbicka 2004).[4] As the contributions to this volume demonstrate, it is therefore crucial to firmly place emotional discourses and displays in the historical, cultural, political and linguistic contexts in which they are conceptualised, framed and experienced.

The Individual and the Social

Many psychologists have perceived emotions primarily as intrapsychic phenomena, paying little attention to political processes that affect emotions in real-life settings. They have attempted to understand emotions through experiments with individual participants in controlled environments, an approach that has been rooted in a belief in scientific objectivity, and that differs radically from the now dominant paradigm in anthropology which emphasises reflexivity and the subjective nature of knowledge production (for exception, see, for example, Whitehouse 2002). Like most anthropologists a number of innovative psychologists have criticised the common psychological tradition of laboratory-based experiments on emotions. Brian Parkinson, for instance, has noted that the emphasis of psychological theories on internal generative mechanisms 'artificially isolates emotional experience from the ongoing social context within which it is often intrinsically linked' (1995: 24).

The *social* dynamics of emotional life has been the main focus in most anthropological research in the past four decades, and this perspective has provided valuable insights into the political dimensions of emotional interaction (see below).[5] Recently, some anthropologists have suggested that not all human experiences can be understood by a focus on 'the social', and that 'the individual' should come back into the analytical framework (Milton 2005 and Josephides 2005). Abner Cohen (1994) convincingly argued that not all social norms, including those that regulate emotional display, are fully internalised by individuals (the latter conceptualised as self-conscious beings who have the ability to critically reflect on their own and other people's behaviour). From a different theoretical perspective, phenomenology-inspired studies have acknowledged that individual humans have internally-felt, bodily emotional experiences that, at least to some extent, create a sense of physical separation (Casey 1987).

Accepting that individuality and sociality are dialectically related processes, one of the major challenges for the study of emotion, then, is to provide an understanding of emotions as forces that bridge 'the individual' and 'the social' (cf. Leavitt 1996; Overing and Passes 2000; Svašek 2005a). Even though the chapters in this book do not explicitly theorise this issue, their focus on the interface of emotional and political processes does provide interesting examples of how people in Central and Eastern Europe have been politically motivated and manipulated by hope, disappointment, joy and fear – not as isolated respondents reacting to emotional triggers, nor as collectivities fully determined by shared norms of emotional behaviour, but as positioned, socially embedded, thinking and feeling individuals.

Politics, Emotions and Discursive Power

The most prominent anthropological approaches have defined emotions as functional realms of action, as culturally specific narratives, as evaluative judgements and learning devices, as embodied experiences, and as ideological discursive practices. Directly or indirectly, all have been interested in issues of power and authority.

The theme of politics has been of major importance in the work of poststructuralist anthropologists inspired by the work of Michel Foucault. In an edited collection, entitled *Language and the Politics of Emotion*, Lila Abu-Lughod and Catherine A. Lutz (1990: 15) pointed out that 'emotional discourses are implicated in the play of power and the operation of a historically changing system of social hierarchy'. Consequently, emotional discourses (for example about increasing poverty in postsocialist states, see in particular Chapters 1 and 2) and discourses of emotion (for example the discourse of *machat* among the Pomaks, see Chapter 2) may establish, assert, challenge or reinforce power and status differences. In other words, emotions are not only used by those in power to persuade and dominate the less powerful, but they *also* provide loci of resistance, idioms of rebellion, and the means of establishing complementarity with status superiors (ibid.).

Arjun Appadurai, who defined emotions as 'discursive public forms' (1990: 93), pointed out that in Hindu India, 'praise' (*stōttiram*) is a pragmatic performance in which relations of reciprocity are created between superiors and inferiors.[6] Other discourse analyses of particular emotion terms have similarly shown that emotions shape social life, and provide a moral framework in which power relations are being discussed and played out (see, for example, White 1990).

Body Politics, Embodied Sociality and Embodiment as Culture

More recently, a growing number of influential scholars have argued that discursive perspectives reduce emotions to processes of meaning construction, thereby largely ignoring the sensual, bodily dimensions of emotional experience. Studies of discursive formations of emotions, they noted, should therefore be complemented with the analysis of what has been called 'the body politic', practices of 'embodied sociality', processes of 'embodiment' and the interplay of 'meaning' and 'feeling'.

'The body politic' (cf. Scheper-Hughes and Lock 1987) refers to the regulation and control of bodies in social and geographical space, and the concept is highly relevant to the argument of this book because it draws the attention to the embeddedness of individual humans as physical (and thus emotional) beings in fields of power. Regimes of power and knowledge that contruct human subjectivity and reproduce political inequalities are partly effective *because* they regulate bodily movement (Foucault 1979, 1980).

Similarly emphasising the importance of bodily processes in the enactment of power, Lyon and Barbalet (1994: 48) argued that '[e]motion activates distinct dispositions, postures and movements which are not only attitudinal but also physical, involving the way in which individual bodies together with others articulate a common purpose, design, or order'. In Lyon and Barbalet's perspective, bodies are not only subjected to forces beyond their own control, as pointed out by Foucault, but they also function as active intercommunicative social agents, engaged in emotional and political interaction. This implies that emotions are neither completely personal inner feelings, nor purely externally imposed dispositions, but experiences of 'embodied sociality' that are essential to individual human agency (Lyon and Barbalet 1994: 48). This approach helps to explain how individuals employ conscious and unconscious bodily behaviour to express and negotiate emotional meanings that may be politically relevant.

Thomas Csordas (1990; 1994) introduced the concept of 'embodiment', criticising theories that have understood human experiences as *either* 'culture' *or* 'nature', reducing emotions to cultural meaning or bodily feeling (see also Leavitt 1996) . In Csordas's theoretical model, pre-objective, multi-sensory experiences are objectified and internalised in a process of embodiment, defined as 'the existential ground of culture and self'. In this perspective, culture is always embodied and never opposed to nature, and feeling and thinking bodies are not influenced by, but formative of culture. Embodiment is then potentially a political process. Tracey Heatherington (2005), for example, clearly showed that, as part of local resistance against the establishment of a nature park in Sardinia, embodied experiences of the common lands were objectified as indexes of authentic culture. This emotional perception and experience of local identity thus justified the political protest.

Euphoria and the Politics of Hope, Desire and Joy

In the above sections, I have introduced a number of anthropological debates and perspectives which claim that political processes are inherently emotional. In the remaining part of this introduction, I shall explore the dialectics of politics and emotions in postsocialist communities by discussing various 'types' of emotions, starting with a discussion of what may rather crudely be called 'positive emotions'.[7] What I have in mind here are the 'uplifting' emotional processes during and immediately after the end of state socialism, which expressed and reinforced the widely shared expectations that everything would now change for the better.

There is no doubt that the collapse of the state socialist regimes, and the prospect of freedom and democracy, put many East and Central Europeans in a state of euphoria, at least during and immediately after the political turns. Large groups of people were overwhelmed by joy, believing that the quality of their life would drastically improve by the introduction of democracy and the market economy. Enthusiastic Western journalists and involved scholars came up with imaginative metaphors to describe the jubilant mood. Timothy Garton Ash (1990: 62), for example, called the opening of the Berlin Wall on 9 November 1989' 'the greatest street-party in the history of the world'. This image of happy smiles and joyful songs and dances brings home the physical, multi-sensual dimension of emotions, as well as their infectuous potential, also known as 'emotional contagion' (Parkinson 1995: 183).

Longing for Freedom

There were numerous reasons for people to welcome the end of state socialism. Those who had suffered persecution – individual dissidents as well as members of particular ethnic and religious groups – welcomed the promise of political liberty. Artists and intellectuals who had worked in the 'grey zone' between official and unoffical culture, for instance, strongly believed that democracy would bring the creative freedom they had longed for (Svašek 1997). Their feelings of joy projected a strong dissatisfaction with state socialist politics, and expressed moral concerns for individual liberty. This corresponds with Renate Rosaldo's (1984) view that emotions are moral forces, which can be used to control and criticise social and political action.

In a somewhat different vein, suppressed minorities all over Eastern Europe expressed the hope to be able to express their ethnic, religious or national identities in an atmosphere of tolerance. In this case, moral discourses of joyful, intra-ethnic belonging were emphatically politicised. Some ethnic groups, such as the Latvians, the Lithuanians and the Slovaks, established their own national states, stressing the positive experience of ethnic unity. The fact that this happened in a relatively peaceful atmosphere demonstrates that nationalist sentiments are not always dominated by inter-ethnic anger and hatred. Skrbiš, in this volume, demonstrates that performances of Slovenian nationalist identity have produced emotionally rewarding experiences of belonging. He also shows, however, that enactments of ethnic belonging have projected notions of Slovenian ethnic superiority, which implies that positive feelings of ethnic pride can easily coexist with or transform into feelings of disrespect for others. Numerous studies of the break-up of Yugoslavia have zoomed in on this dark side of nationalism by exploring the dynamics of hatred and violence (see below).

It is important to note that nationalist feelings had not completely disappeared under socialism. Katherine Verdery (1996: 102) has pointed out that '[i]nstead of nudging national sentiments in a new direction ..., socialism strengthened them in ways that were not readily apparent until the changed political circumstances of the "transition" gave them new space' (see also Bringa 1995 and Denich 1994). In the postsocialist era, the politicisation of nationalist feelings has responded to and reinforced people's hope for a better future, and has been used as a strategic method by politicians who desire to gain influence and power (see, for example, Chapter 7 on the importance of nationalist sentiments in campaigns against Polish EU membership).

Longing for Prosperity

Another reason why people were euphoric at the time of the 'revolutions' was that they expected a much higher, 'Western' level of prosperity. Their perceptions of Western living-standards were, however, extremely exaggerated. As Verdery (2003: 364) noted,

> [p]eople in socialist countries built up a great illusion, a myth of the West, which they saw as a land of unimaginable prosperity in contrast to their lives in socialism – constrained, modest, and often grim. The collapse of the socialist system led them to expect that now, overnight, their lives would become like those in their myth, and westerners fanned this hope.

In some cases, the desire for more wealth was also coloured by feelings of inferiority. East Germans, for example, who knew (by means of infrequent visits, presents from West German relatives, or West German television programmes) that West German products were generally of a much higher quality than their own, longed for equality with the 'superior' West Germans (Borneman 1991: 33; see also Veenis 1999). Not surprisingly, their hope for equal access to quality consumer goods was exploited by politicians who favoured the unification of Germany.

The new postsocialist governments and their advisors reacted to the widespread desire for increasing wealth by promising rapid economic improvement. Western neoliberal economists who propagated individual ownership predicted, for example, that a policy of active decollectivisation in Russia would ensure that by the end of the 1990s around 50 percent of Russian farmland would be in the hands of relatively prosperous private farmers. Ten years later, the actual figure was no higher than a disappointing 8 percent (Visser 2003: 197–98).

Certain groups of people have clearly profited from the economic changes, and have marked their socioeconomic status through 'conspicuous consumption' (Veblen 1953). In Russia, for example, prosperous businessmen have celebrated their success by building grandiose villas in architectural styles that hint both at a preSoviet aristocratic past, and at the efficiency of contemporary European business elites. Those less successful have judged the behaviour of the wealthy 'New Russions' through a mixture of envy and contempt (Humphrey 1997).

Postsocialist consumption behaviour has also resulted in feelings of mutual rivalry among people in similar economic positions, and the material changes have brought conflicting feelings of longing and estrangement. In a study of postsocialist East German consumption, Milena Veenis (1992: 83) noted that '[d]esire and disappointment go hand in hand, and although most people ardently long for even more things, they nevertheless experience the equation of personal worth with material possessions as an extremely estranging development'.

Disillusion and Nostalgia

More than a decade after the 'end of communism', the initial feelings of hope for a better future have, in many cases, been replaced by disillusionment and scepticism. Widespread unemployment, new class differences, poverty, corruption scandals, disagreements about the restitution and appropriation of state property, and the economic advantages taken by the old nomenklatura have generated increasing distrust in the new 'democratic' states (Kalb et al. 1999).

The 'morning after' effect has evoked emotional responses among the majority of the economically less successful populations in all postsocialist countries, and in Hungary, Poland and the Czech Republic, dissidents-turned-politicians have had to admit that their initial ideas about the creation of a new moral order were naïve (Bauman 1994: 28). Those who, influenced by Western economic advisers, believed in the neo-liberal promise of a rapid transition to an ideal market economy have discovered 'that the idea of an unproblematic self-regulating market is utopian' (Bryant and Mokrzycki 1994, referring to Polanyi 1944: 3). By 1993, it had become clear that 'freedom' had a different face from what many had thought. In Prague, Czech artists frequently told me that they felt they had moved 'from the zoo to the jungle'.

The harsh confrontation with postsocialist reality has often caused people to look back with nostalgia at the socialist past. In the former GDR, the sudden domination by West German values and power within a unified Germany has evoked disorienting feelings of loss of identity. This has produced what has become known as 'ostalgia', a desire to re-experience oneself as a GDR citizen through the consumption of GDR products, and by seeing television programmes which strongly idealise life under communism. In the Bulgarian context, villagers miss the socialist emphasis on folklore and workers' rituals, which in practice produced feelings of local and national belonging (Creed 2002). In the rural areas, nostalgic memories of 'past ritual glory' painfully contrast with present-day experiences of ritual decline. Ritual decimation has generated 'a loss in dignity and selfworth, a decline in the quality of life, and a change in notions of village identity' (ibid.: 70).

In Chapter 1, Heady and Miller analyse Russian nostalgic feelings in a number of rural settings in the context of rapid economic change. Due to the transition from collective to invidivual forms of economic organisation, they argue, it has been hard for many people to form and maintain economically significant affective relationships. Referring to James Scott's concept of 'moral economy', the analysis introduces the term 'emotional economy' to outline the emotional function and significance of work relations. The latter term stresses the social dynamics of emotional processes, and helps to explain that the Russian feelings of nostalgia are not simply to be disregarded as a longing for mythical times gone by, but stem from real emotional decline and loss of social anchorage.

By contrast, in post-Yugoslavia, nostalgic pan-Yugoslav discourses have strongly criticised the break-up of the republic. Some writers and intellectuals who felt at home in a multi-ethnic republic (in which they could move freely across ethnic boundaries), lack a sense of belonging in a divided Yugoslavia. In their case, nostalgia has taken the more specific form of 'yugonostalgia', a feeling of loss and longing that is combined with the experience of homelessness and forced migration (Jansen 1998; see also Leutloff-Grandits, Chapter 5). The yugonostalgic counter-discourse has helped post-Yugolav writers to 'develop the nomadic aspects of identity that were there already', but has failed to make real political change (Jansen 1998: 105–6).

Anger and Outrage

In numerous cases, feelings of loss and nostalgia have led to anger and outrage, empowering people to take public action.[8] Polish peasants, for example, who had been much better off during the last decade under Socialism, were extremely disappointed in the economic reforms introduced by the post-1989 Solidarity government (cf. Bauman 1994: 22; Kocik 1996). The new policies, also known as 'shock therapy' (projecting the image of a mental patient who simply needs to be shocked back into 'normality', see Verdery 1996: 205, and Lampland 2002: 32), included production constraints such as 'higher costs of production resources, uncertain demand for agricultural outputs, and increased the arbitrariness of business transactions' (Zbierski-Salamek 1999: 202). If anything, the peasants were shocked into fury, and voiced their outrage during mass demonstrations in 1990 by organising road blocks, occupying government buildings, and dropping tons of potatoes in front of the Ministry of Agriculture.

In 1995, the Hungarian government faced similar angry protests when it presented a proposal to restructure the welfare system. As Lynne Haney (1999: 151) described: 'When the doors opened, a stampede of women rushed into the [welfare] office. Their emotions ran high, fluctuating between anger and fear. "I cried when I heard the news last night", one female client remarked'. The women were furious and upset because they expected that a new liberal welfare regime would give them enough space to pursue their own interests.

If we want to know more about the political impact of public protests, it is necessary to deal with the issues of agency and institutional power, and look at the ways in which willing influential political actors are able to translate emotional and moral claims into effective legal and policy changes.

The Pomak tobacco producers in Mihaylova's analysis (see Chapter 2) organised a strike to protest against the low prices paid for their products by the Bulgarian state, and a number of pragmatic politicians (who were, in Mihaylova's view, more interested in their own political careers than in the fate of the Pomaks), eventually responded to their action. This means that the strikers performed strategic acts of 'social suffering' that were, eventually, succesful. The analysis does not only show that the discourse of *narodno stradanie* was carefully played out in a well-thought-out 'emotional performance'. It also emphasises the importance of the bodily dimensions of Pomak marginality to their experience of suffering, which suggests that embodied feelings can strongly drive people to decide to take political action.

Zerilli's analysis of 'sentimental dramas' inherent in the Romanian restitution process (see Chapter 3) explores the ways in which tenants and new house owners have transformed personal emotional experiences into competing political discourses and angry protests in the context of changing national and transnational laws. The case makes painfully clear how one person's loss can be another person's gain, and shows that emotional performances have been played out for national and transnational audiences, including the European Commission.

The theatrical metaphors of emotional *performance* and sentimental *drama* acknowledge that people are able to hide or exaggerate their feelings, and that they can play emotional roles with the intention of creating a certain effect in their intended public. Evidently, people are not completely free to create and perform emotional dramas of their own choice. As Parkinson noted, emotional roles are partly constrained by institutional and cultural pressures, and the 'enactment of institutional and cultural scripts about emotion depends crucially on the allocation and renegotiation of roles, and on the stage-setting that has been done behind the scenes before the acting ever takes place' (Parkinson 1995: 202; see also Goffman 1967).[9]

Mistrust and Trust

In *Trust in Modern Societies*, the sociologist Barbara A. Mitszal (1996: 177) argued that '[s]ince we are always faced with "the unknowability of others" (Simmel 1950), and since they are free to act against our interest, believing in others' good will involves the element of risk'. Trusting someone or something is thus an emotionally ambiguous project, in which feelings of safety that are inherent in a trusting relationship are always threatened by the possibility of insincerity and betrayal. Under communism, without the freedom of choice and the option to openly question the political system, 'trust in political leadership' was mainly a matter of stage-setting and played conformity, and 'the main structures of trust were the continuation of pre-state socialist culture and were based on non-market ties of reciprocity and mutuality (Mitszal 1996: 196). As a result, many citizens defined themselves as real but silenced beings who were oppressed by a fake and corrupt state, even if they actively participated in the perpetuation of the system through party membership, through work as state representatives (from primary schoolteachers to high-level bureaucrats) or through active involvement in political nepotism and professional favouritism (Svašek 2002). A strong lack of trust in the state thus characterised East and Central Europeans at the time of the 1989 revolutions, and one of the main challenges for the new authorities was to tackle this problem.

Yet after an initial period of optimism in the early 1990s, when many citizens believed that the political change to democracy would restore their faith in government politics, an increasing number of people began to lose confidence in their new political leaders. Disappointed and worried by rising unemployment, continuing political nepotism, and other consequences of uncivil mismanagement, they once again doubted the trustworthiness of 'the state'. On numerous occasions, local, regional and national officials have come under fierce attack. In Poland, for example, inhabitants of the city of Wroclaw spread anti-state rumours when their city was flooded in 1997. In Chapter 9, Kalb and Tak argue that these rumours were a vehicle of public fear, and expressed a strong distrust in the authorities. As the chapter shows, political rivalry between different governmental agencies had weakened their effectiveness. Unproductive competition was in part a legacy from state socialist times, because overcentralisation had caused a lack of communication between the various official bodies reponsible for the waterworks. Interestingly, after the flood, public representations of the event reactivated two powerful myths of Polish identity: the myth of the whole nation's fight against 'alien agressors', and the earlier-mentioned 'people against the state' image, which had been an important justification for the turn to democracy.

The myth-producing dynamics of social memory can clearly transmit feelings of trust and mistrust over long time periods. In an analysis of the Bulgarian privatisation process, Christian Giordano and Dobrinka Kostova (2002) revealed how Bulgarian urban powerholders who attempted to restore the old system of smallholder agriculture after the end of state socialism (closing their eyes to present-day social and economic realities), were strongly motivated by a tradition of urban–rural mistrust that originated in the Ottoman past. Stirring up memories of mutual distrust is also a sound strategy when it comes to the production of fear of outside influence. In the Polish campaigns against EU membership, the political spokesmen reinforced existing feelings of insecurity and mistrust in the government through emotional narratives of past Polish victimhood. They portrayed the European Union as an aggressor that would threaten Polish national identity, and sketched the present government as a traitor. (see Golanska-Ryan, Chapter 7)

Strong doubts about foreign influence were also expressed when a Dutch investor started buying property in a small village in West Bohemia, as discussed in Chapter 4. The analysis shows that conflicting claims to ownership justified very different moral discourses of self and society. Czech villagers, Sudeten German expellees and the Dutch investor all had different ideas about the future of the community and their own position in it. Yet while some Czech villagers strongly feared the growing influence of the Dutchman and mistrusted his vision, others welcomed his presence because of the job opportunities he offered.

Mistrust can also express and reproduce ethnic tensions, as shown by Leutloff-Grandits in Chapter 5. She explores the emotionally loaded conflicts over property and housing rights that arose when Serbian house owners, who had left Croatia during the war as refugees, returned to claim their possessions, and found them occupied by new, uncooperative Croatian settlers. Her analysis shows that the claims by Serbs and Croats alike were initially influenced by emotional judgements based on group-specific war-experiences and mutual feelings of mistrust, which had been deepened by Croat nationalistic political propaganda. Yet prewar convictions and experiences became increasingly influential, and came into conflict with nationalist propaganda.

In the former Soviet Union, the combination of a lack of trust, a demand for protection by new property owners, and a supply of unemployed former Red Army soldiers and other willing 'protectors', has led to the emergence of the now globally active Russian Mafia (Mitszal 1996: 196). This clearly demonstrates that the politics of trust and mistrust has local, national and transnational dimensions.

Fear and Hatred

The Dark Side of Nationalist Sentiments

One of the characteristics of postsocialist politics has been the widespread display of nationalist feelings, and this – often worrying – development provides urgent professional and political reasons for examining the politics of nationalist sentiments. In the past twelve years numerous nationalist parties have been established, and some have gained a considerable amount of political power. Also, nationalistic members of ethnic minorities in several countries have created strong links with members of their own ethnic group in neighbouring states, and have questioned or moved existing state boundaries. Wars have been fought in the name of nationalism, and nationalist extremists in several countries have intimidated and killed Gypsies and non-European students and refugees whom they regard as 'polluting threats' to the nation. In some countries, people have expressed anti-Semitic feelings.

It is common practice for nationalist politicians to select and incorporate particular historical narratives and emotional memories into their political discourse as a rhetorical device to evoke and strengthen nationalist sentiments. In general, it is of strategic importance to politicians to influence people's perception of self, and memories that 'almost automatically' stir up feelings often have a strong impact on people's self-perception. Self, in this context, must be understood as a personal *and* a political identity. The most effective nationalist symbols collapse the distinction between the personal and the political, and portray the nation-state as a loyal kin group and an identity/place category with natural connections between blood and soil (Svašek 1999, 2000; Verdery 1999b). Those who are not included in the nation are automatically defined as polluting outsiders.

In a recent publication, Ger Duijzings (2000) pointed out that 'the suffering nation' can be a powerful nationalist image. In the run-up to the Yugoslav conflict, Serb nationalists used the Kosovo myth and references to the Second World War to reinforce the notion of Serbs as a nation of victims. The myth referred to the battle of Kosovo in 1389, when the Serbs had been defeated by the Ottoman Turks. The fate of the Serbs during the Second World War also served as an emotional narrative that stirred up vivid memories of suffering, both on a personal and a national scale (ibid.: 197). Second World War traumas have been played out by nationalist politicians in different postwar contexts (Bowman 1994; Hayden 1994; Jansen 2002, 2004).

One could give many other examples of the incorporation of references to a past of collective suffering in contemporary nationalist discourse. Czech Communists and Republicans constantly remind their audience of anti-Czech Nazi crimes in an attempt to block interregional cross-border cooperation with the Germans. In 1994, for example, the journalist Jiří

Frajdl stated in the Communist newspaper *Halo noviny* that the Euroregion Egrensis 'set up in 1992' was 'an old Nazi plan', a conspiracy between pro-German Czechs and anti-Czech Germans (cf. Svašek 2000).

In other cases, cross-border links have been strengthened by nationalist members of ethnic groups. Macedonians, for example, began questioning the border-lines between Macedonia, Bulgaria, Greece and Albania in 1989. In October 1989, supporters of the Skopje football team used the emotional context of a football match to propagate the political idea of a single Macedonian nation by shouting slogans, such as 'We fight for a united Macedonia'. In February, tens of thousands of nationalists demonstrated in Skopje to celebrate their shared identity, and to protest against the 'perceived oppression of Macedonians in Bulgaria, Greece, and Albania' (Poulton 1995: 173).

In this volume, Leutloff-Grandits (Chapter 5) shows that in the postwar Croatian town of Knin, memories of inter-ethnic aggression have evoked nationalist sentiments that have reinforced processes of ethnic identification. Yet, as noted earlier, the chapter points out that memories of pre-war friendly inter-ethnic neighbourhood relations also influence people's judgements and behaviour. Those memories 'resist the politicised reading of the past', and are at odds with the official nationalist propaganda. Consequently, such narratives and emotions have remained part of a hidden, private discourse.

Skrbiš (Chapter 6) approaches the dialectics of politics and nationalist sentiments from a theoretical perspective that incorporates economic metaphors. Inspired by Pierre Bourdieu's notion of social capital, he introduces the term 'emotional capital', and argues that the Venetological theory about Slovenian origin, which was developed by nationalist Slovenian pseudo-historians during the late 1980s, both generated and exploited such capital. Emotions are here regarded as valuable assets that can be employed by socially situated individuals to gain power and authority. In the Slovenian case, the capital consists of anti-communist, pro-religious, nostalgic sentiments that have been reinforced and transferred through particular diasporic discourses and practices.

As Skrbiš shows, certain groups of Slovenians have used the emotional capital to identify themselves as 'superior' Venets in opposition to the 'inferior' Slavs. The discourse must be firmly placed in the context of post-Cold War developments, since the Venetological theory effectively accuses the Slavic Serbs and Croats of responsibility for the outbreak of inter-ethnic violence in the former Yugoslavia. At the same time, the theory is an attempt to undermine the authority of mainstream Slovenian historians, and accuses them of communist distortion.

The concept of 'emotional capital' is indeed useful in any consideration of the dialectics of politics and emotions. It draws attention to the ways in which people actively manipulate particular sentiments for political reasons, and points out how they may use this ability as a form of 'investment'. As noted earlier, political parties in various postsocialist countries have capitalised on the disillusion of disappointed citizens, and have used this emotional capital to gain political power.

As a metaphor, 'emotional capital' may, however, wrongly suggest an image of people as overtly conscious beings who simply decide to 'spend', 'exploit' or 'invest in' particular sentiments. Even though this may often be the case, people can also feel overwhelmed by emotions, and experience emotions as bodily feelings over which they have no mental control. Well-known sayings in different languages refer to the experience of emotions as bodily changes, as in the English sayings 'being blind with rage' and 'feeling shivers down the spine' (see Leavitt 1996). Certain physical changes are, of course, not just metaphors, but are measurable and are related to physiological changes. An increasing heartbeat, for example, is related to an increasing level of adrenaline. Some anthropologists with an interest in politics and emotions have recently included a focus on physiological processes in their theoretical framework. Karen Lysaght (2005), for example, has examined how fear, as embodied feeling, can influence human consciousness, and affect the spatial behaviour of fearful Catholics in the streets of Belfast. Such a perspective could also be used to analyse the impact of fear in postsocialist Eastern Europe, in particular in cases of inter-ethnic violence and racist threats.

Racism and Xenophobia

Discourses of national belonging often include notions of ethnic purity, and make rigid distinctions between pure selves and polluting others. As Verdery suggested, such views were easily adopted in postsocialist Europe because

> [m]any East Europeans are used to thinking in terms of secure moral dichotomies between black and white, good and evil. For those who also understand democracy not as institutionalised disagreement and compromise but as consensus ... a powerful longing for a morally pure unity can easily solidify around the idea of the nation and the expulsion of polluting aliens: those who are not of the 'People-as-One'. (Verdery 1996: 94)

In Hungary, for example, anti-Gypsy, anti-Semitic and other xenophobic sentiments have been propagated by the right-wing nationalist politician

István Csurka, who established the Party of the Magyar Truth/Justice and Life (*Magyar Igazság és Élet Pártja*) in 1993. The party name is identical to the name of one of the old fascist political parties of the 1930s, and skinheads who are also party members talk of themselves as 'Hungarists', another word created by the fascist movements of the 1930s. The party aims at spreading fear by picturing non-Magyars as a threat to the nation, and refers to socialism, communism, liberalism and globalisation as chapters in a 'world-encompassing judeoplutocratic conspiracy' (György Péteri, personal conversation. See also: Arato 1994: 106; Szalai 1994).

Csurka used to be a prominent member of the *Magyar Demokratikus Forum* (Democratic Forum of Hungary), which in the early postcommunist years was the leading non-socialist party attracting various groupings from the decent traditional Conservative Right to some extreme rightist positions. He was expelled from this party in 1993 for his radical rightism and anti-Semitism, which shows that his politics of fear and hatred is far from acceptable to all Hungarians. His fascist party does, however, have seats in parliament, and there is a danger that it will improve its position in the coming elections.

The idea that Gypsies 'don't work' and are 'unproductive parasites' has been widespread in different historical periods. It has been a factor in stirring up anti-Gypsy feelings during the interwar period and under state socialism, and has evoked similar emotions during the past twelve postsocialist years. Confronted with increasing economic insecurity and the hard rules of capitalism, many poor Hungarians have blamed the Gypsies. As Michael Stewart stated:

> Those rare individual Gypsies who have succeeded in manipulating the new possibilities have brought down the wrath of their non-Gypsy neighbours. Often the success of these Gypsies is interpreted as the result of a cunning, simultaneous manipulation of both the market and the state benefit system – just as in the past the Gypsies were thought to benefit both from the state handouts and from the semilegal trade sector … . It is, then, at the rich Gypsies, as much as at the half-starved Gypsy pickpockets and thieves, that the ethnic cleansers now direct their fury. (Stewart 1997: 7–8)

Alaina Lemon (2000) has argued that Russians have long pictured 'commerce' as a non-Russian ('Gypsy' or 'Jewish') suspicious activity. Although 'network-based strategies of attaining goods and priviledges' were widespread amongst Russians and non-Russians in the Soviet period, and both Russians and non-Russians have been involved in postsocialist trade, racial discourse has been used to brand Roma and other

Hi Darragh,

Since you're interested in politics (and maybe anthropology) you might find this book interesting (or very dull...). Keep it if you like it. If you want to talk [...] come for dinner in Bangor with your mum!

96 Seacliffe road
BT20 5EZ

You can reach us at
m.svasek@qub.ac.uk

No offence if you don't

untrustworthy aliens as the new market enemies who are unreliable and threaten the impoverished Russians (ibid.: 66).

In his study of Serbs and Gypsies in Novi Sad, Mattijs van de Port (1998) has claimed that Gypsies evoked strong feelings of contempt among the majority of Serbs. Interestingly, however, whereas the Serbs considered Gypsy speech acts to be an endless stream of lies and cheats, they regarded Gypsy music, in all its tragic sentimentality, to be the most truthful rendering of Serbian life experiences. In Serbia, the idea that the emotions are the realm of the 'really real', the domain where non-negotiable truths can be found, has a very strong appeal. It is an idea that became particularly attractive during the recent war when people felt the pain of losing relatives, friends, the homestead, communal life, and feelings of hatred towards those who inflicted these wounds. These feelings were hard to translate into words, and Serbs admired Gypsy musicians for their ability to express them in music.

As in the other postsocialist countries, in the Czech Republic, too, discrimination against Romanies has worsened since November 1989. In a study by Renata Weinerová (1994), Romany respondents gave several reasons why life had been better before the introduction of political 'freedom'. Economically, they had been better off because of the lower costs of living, the right to employment and better housing policies.[10] Socially, they had been in a better position because people had been more willing to help each other, they had felt safer, and there had been 'criminal proceedings against the expression of personal views disloyal to the regime', which had meant that people were not allowed to form fascist groups, and had feared to express racist views in public (ibid.: 25). After the 1989 Velvet Revolution, groups of skinheads were openly violent against Romanies. In 1993, a seventeen-year-old Czech girl who participated in a televised beauty contest stated in an interview that she wanted to become 'a public prosecutor' because it would enable her to 'clean our town of its dark-skinned inhabitants' (Stewart 1997: 2)

Politics and Emotions in the Post-Cold War Context

The various contributions to this book demonstrate that after the end of the Cold War, as a result of the globalising forces of capitalism, migration, forced migration, and the creation of transnational forms of political and military cooperation, the emotional experiences and discourses in and of the regions have been influenced by a variety of local and extra-local factors.

While the end of state-socialism allowed for a strongly increased but still selective transit of people, goods, information and capital from the capitalist West to the former East bloc and vice versa, it also created immense socioeconomic differences within the postsocialist countries, and 'gave an enormous boost to new transnational coalitions, linking East European to other Eurasian elites' (Kalb 2002: 318).

Transnational emotional politics have both united and divided social groups and individual actors. The ongoing enlargement of the European Union has shaped the political debates in various postsocialist countries, and has generated emotional exchanges between the proponents and antagonists of future membership, as is clear in Golanska-Ryan's analysis in Chapter 7 of the Polish campaigns against EU membership. The enlargement has also created tensions between those countries that have been accepted in the first round and those that have not. In addition, the existence of transnational, European political and legal bodies such as the European Parliament, the European Commission and the European Court of Justice has transnationalised local and national legal discourses. Numerous local actors and interest groups in different countries have addressed these European bodies to protest against particular national policies and attempt to gain certain rights. European institutes are being used strategically by local interest groups as transnational political platforms in an attempt to influence national and European politics. In Chapter 3, Zerilli describes how thousands of Romanian former house owners sent complaints to the European Court of Justice in Strasbourg in an attempt to force the Romanian government to change ownership and restitution laws.

Transnational discourses and practices may be used strategically, but the models used are not 'automatically' applied to local conditions. Even though various postsocialist countries have chosen to introduce Western-style democratic systems, and to adopt a Western-style market economy, they have not simply 'reprogrammed' themselves according to a unitary Western model. Ethnographic studies have shown that democracy and privatisation have many different faces in Central and Eastern Europe, and that postsocialist transformations can bring about unexpected outcomes. In a Transylvanian village undergoing decollectivisation, the villagers revalorised certain forms of collectivism, and resisted the transition from public to private ownership (cf. Verdery 1999a). In another cultural setting, Bulgarian villagers who had been critical of Communist Party policy, began to give their support to the Socialist Party as a form of protest against the postsocialist economic reforms (cf. Creed 1999). In other words, local processes counteracted transnational neoliberalism.

Throughout postsocialist Europe, local actors have, willingly or less consciously, resisted or failed to apply 'ideal' democratic standards, propagated by Western democracies. This is clearly illustrated by Müller's analysis of local politics in a Czech village in Chapter 8, which explores reactions to the Mayor's plan to invite a German investor to establish a large cement factory near the village. Despite the official democratisation of Czech society, the political debate that followed did not in any way mirror 'Western-style' democratic culture. Instead, the debate turned into slanderous attacks and the writing of unpleasant anonymous poems that were basically personal accusations on the basis of old enmities. The poems did not reflect the ideological differences between the two main political factions in the village – the communists and the ecologists – but instead served to fuel personal battles and to express and generate negative emotions. In Müller's view, the mutual attacks fundamentally differed from the political controversies in which representatives of various political convictions may passionately discuss standpoints about society in public 'without fear of personal reprisal be it from public authorities or fellow villagers'.

Yet, despite local idiosyncrasies and resistance to 'Western' influence, the postsocialist states are undoubtedly affected by the global forces of transnationalism. The 'international community', for example, has actively interferred in war-torn Yugoslavia (basing its policies on its own diverse experiences of war and trauma, cf. Fierke 2002), and has continued to play a role in the newly established post-Yugoslav nation-states. This was clearly demonstrated by the fact that the International Yugoslav Tribunal in The Hague successfully demanded the extradition of Miloševic and other politicians whom they regard as responsible for crimes against humanity. Obviously, due to increasing interaction in the post-Cold War era, politics and emotions in Western and postsocialist parts of Europe are *mutually* intertwined, which is well-illustrated by the following.

One of the issues about which Miloševic is being questioned is his involvement in the massacre at Srebrenica, a dreadful event in which the Dutch military force played what is regarded by many as a doubtful role. In July 1995, the Bosnian Serb army occupied the enclave, an area that had been designated a 'safe haven' for Bosnian Muslims in 1993. *Dutchbat*, the Dutch UNPROFOR battalion of peacekeepers that protected Srebrenica, made the questionable decision to cooperate with the occupying army, and after their withdrawal, thousands of Muslims were massacred by the Serbs. As a result of emotional outcries in the Dutch media, which sharply criticised the politicians responsible for the mission, the Dutch government commissioned the Dutch Institute for War Documentation to investigate the Dutch role in Srebrenica. The report was published in April 2002 (Nederlands Instituut voor Oorlogs Documentatie 2002), and a few days later, the Dutch government decided to accept its responsibility by stepping down.

The Srebrenica case once again reinforces the main argument of this book, namely that the study of political dynamics *needs* a focus on emotions to be able to unravel the complexities of political interaction in local, national and global settings. Such a perspective has become even more urgent after the proclaimed 'War on Terror' in the aftermath of 9/11, the attack on the Twin Towers in the USA. Consequently, the chapters that follow propagate a research agenda that puts 'emotions' at the very centre of the study of politics.

Acknowledgements

I would like to thank György Péteri for his thoughts on the development of neo-fascism in Hungary, and Zlatko Skrbiš, Birgit Müller and Carolin Leutloff-Grandits for their comments on an earlier version of this introduction. I am also grateful to Berghahn's anonymous reviewer for his/her helpful suggestions.

Notes

1. Aristotle explored people's different emotive states of mind, the social context in which they felt specific emotions, and the reasons for their emotivity. In the case of anger, he posed the questions: 'What is the state of mind of angry people?', 'With whom do they usually get angry?', and 'On what grounds do they get angry'? (Lyons 1980: 34). The cultivation of rhetoric, 'the art of using language so as to persuade or influence others', became an important field of study in medieval universities (cf. Blackburn 1994: 330).
2. One of the key issues of economic change in postsocialist Europe is the privatisation and restitution of former state-owned property. Several anthropologists, who all regard ownership as a multidimensional sociocultural phenomenon, have explored this process (see, for example, Abrahams 1996; Hann 1998; Verdery 2003). Chris Hann (1998: 34) noted that: 'A concern with property relations requires investigations into the total distributions of rights and entitlements within society, of material things and of knowledge and symbols. It requires examination of practical outcomes as well as ideals and moral discourses, and an appreciation of historical processes, both short-term and long-term.' Verdery (1998: 161) similarly claimed that property 'is best analysed in terms of the whole system of social, cultural, and political relations, rather than through more narrowly legalistic notions such as "rights" and "claims"'.

3. Not all psychologists and anthropologists differ as fundamentally in their approaches as Ekman and Rosaldo. Numerous scholars in the disciplines of anthropology and psychology have also influenced each other. Various clinical psychologists have developed a sensitivity to the cultural dimensions of emotional discourse and display. Due to large-scale migration, therapists all over the world have been confronted with a variety of patients from different cultural backgrounds. This has led to debates about the culturally specific nature of certain behavioural problems, and to the development of specific therapies that take cultural dimensions into account. Such therapies agree with Obeyeskere's view that universalistic approaches to diseases such as depression 'impose medico-centric interpretations on decontextualised observations' (Lutz and White 1986: 414). In recent years, a number of anthropologists have been inspired by the work of innovative psychologists such as Damascio (cf. Kay Milton 2001). The anthropologist Harvey Whitehouse (2000) has developed theories of emotions, ritual and religion in response to the work of cognitive scientists.

4. Attacking the notion of universalist core emotions, Anna Wierzbicka (2004: 82) argued that the English understanding of 'grief' connotes the culturally specific experience of 'an acute but short-term emotion following an exceptional event (death)'. This particular understanding of confrontation with loss does not exist, she claimed, in Polish or French culture, nor did it occur in premodern England, when the word 'grief' existed but referred to 'a combination of misfortune and suffering seen as common in life' (ibid.: 82).

5. Anthropologists have conducted research in a large number of different cultural settings, and dealt with topics as varied as, for example, emotion and feeling in Sinhalese healing rites (Kapferer 1979), headhunting and emotional dynamics in the Philippines (Rosaldo 1980, 1983, 1984), anger and shame in Papua New Guinea (Schieffelin 1983), emotions and conviviality in native Amazonia (Overing and Passess 2000), love for nature in the British environmentalist movement (Milton 2002), love and grief for kin amongst Spanish Gypsies (Gay-y-Blasco 2005), and emotional intersubjectivity during fieldwork (Tonkin 2005).

6. Various anthropologists have analysed the politics of emotion in non-European communities. In 1980 Michelle Rosaldo examined the importance of headhunting in political processes among the Ilongots in the Philippines, and found that indigenous notions of 'passion' and 'knowledge' were crucial to Ilongot political behaviour. Another well-known example is Lila Abu-Lughod's study of the oral lyric poetry through which women and young men in a Bedouin community in Egypt express personal feelings that violate the moral code underlying the political system (1986). Other anthropologists have – albeit more indirectly – dealt with the political aspects of emotional discourse and display in places such as Papua New Guinea (Schieffelin 1983), the Solomon Islands (White 1985), and India (Seymour 1983). Several anthropologists have also examined emotional dynamics in the context of violence and repressive state policies, exploring the effects of political intimidation and murder (see, for example Suárez-Orozco 1992). Years after their escape, traumatised refugees and migrants who have been part of these 'cultures of terror' (Taussig 1987) are still afflicted by syndromes of terror and guilt over selective survival. For the survivors of war and atrocities, one of the ways of dealing with traumatic experiences is by expressing one's thoughts and feelings in words.

The reconstruction of the trauma story can be an essential stage in the recovery process during which traumatised selves are reconstituted and order is imposed on disorder (Lewis Herman 1992; Stein 1993; but see Leys 2000: xx). In the context of this book, it is important to note that trauma narratives can also be *politically* highly significant (Svašek 2005b; Volkan 1999). They can be constructed and played out in the public domain, and have radical political consequences.

7. Obviously, the label 'positive' is somewhat problematic because people often have mixed emotions, and to isolate 'positive' feelings from 'negative' ones can hide complexities and mystify experiental reality. Furthermore, what is experienced as a positive emotional interaction by one person can have a depressing impact on somebody else.

8. The notion of 'emotional empowerment' may wrongly create the impression of humans as passive individuals, steered and overwhelmed by their passions. Even though at the other extreme – the image of people fully in control of their feelings – is equally unrealistic, people do actively manage their emotional life, and induce or suppress particular feelings through what Arlie Russell Hochschild has called 'emotional labour' (1983: 7). Politicians are involved in such 'labour' when they strategically evoke or strengthen people's sentiments or when they justify ideas and policies through moral arguments that appeal to commonly shared feelings and emotions. Angry and disappointed citizens manage and perform their emotions in acts of public protest.

9. The role concept has also been incorporated into various psychological and sociological theories of emotion. Hochschild (1983) argued that institutional roles and cultural scripts influence the ways in which emotions are expressed and felt, and Averill (1980) and Sarbin (1986) claimed that the enactment of emotions is influenced by the cultural content of emotional meaning. These insights support the view that emotional dynamics are intrinsic to cultural and political processes.

10. Romanies were also the victims of discrimination in the job market. Private employers took advantage of their difficult situation, and often employed them without any form of legal recognition, health insurance or rights. According to Renata Weinerová (1994), the increased internal economic differences within the Romany communities in Prague between a small minority of prosperous Romany entrepeneurs and the majority of the poor unemployed, have increased feelings of inferiority and helplessness among the latter.

Bibliography

Abrahams, R. ed. 1996. *After Socialism. Land Reform and Social Change in Eastern Europe*. Oxford: Berghahn.

Abu-Lughod, L. 1986. *Veiled Sentiments. Honour and Poetry in a Bedouin Society*. Berkeley: University of California Press.

Abu-Lughod, L. and Lutz, C.A. 1990. 'Introduction: Emotion, Discourse, and the Politics of Everyday Life', in *Language and the Politics of Emotion*, ed. C.A. Lutz and L. Abu-Lughod. Cambridge: Cambridge University Press and Paris: Editions de la Maison des Sciences de l'Homme, pp. 1–23.

Appadurai, A. 1990. 'Topographies of the Self. Praise and Emotion in Hindu India', in *Language and the Politics of Emotion*, ed. C.A. Lutz and L. Abu-Lughod. Cambridge: Cambridge University Press and Paris: Editions de la Maison des Sciences de l'Homme, pp. 92–112.

Arato, A. 1994. 'Revolution and Restoration. On the Origins of Right-wing Radical Ideology in Hungary', in *The New Great Transformation? Change and Continuity in East-Central Europe*, ed. C.G.A. Bryant and E. Mokrzycki. London: Routledge, pp. 99–119.

Aretxaga, B. 1995. 'Dirty Protest. Symbolic Overdetermination and Gender in Northern Ireland Ethnic Violence', *Ethos* 23(2): 123–48.

Aristotle. 1941. *Rhetoric*, Bk.II.

Ash, T.G. 1990. *We the People. The Revolution of 89 Witnessed in Warsaw, Budapest, Berlin and Prague*. London: Granta Books.

Averill, J.A. 1980. 'Emotion and Anxiety. Sociocultural, Biological, and Psychological Determinants', in *Explaining Emotions*, ed. A. Oksenberg. Berkeley: University of California Press, pp. 37–72.

Bailey, F.G. 1983. *The Tactical Uses of Passion. An Essay on Power, Reason, and Reality*. Ithaca and London: Cornell University Press.

Bauman, Z. 1994. 'After the Patronage State. A Model in Search of Class Interests', in *The New Great Transformation? Change and Continuity in East-Central Europe*, ed. C.G.A. Bryant and E. Mokrzycki. London: Routledge, pp. 14–35.

Berdahl, D. 2000. 'Introduction: an Anthropology of Postsocialism', in *Altering States. Ethnographies of Transition in Eastern Europe and the Former Soviet Union*, ed. D. Berdahl, M. Bunzl and M. Lampland. Ann Arbor: University of Michigan Press, pp. 1–13.

Binga, T. 1995. *Being a Muslim the Bosnian Way. Identity and Community in a Central Bosnian Village*. Princeton: Princeton University Press.

Blackburn, S. 1994. *The Oxford Dictionary of Philosophy*. Oxford: Oxford University Press.

Borneman, J. 1991. *After the Wall. East Meets West in the New Berlin*. New York: Basic Books.

———— 1997. *Settling Accounts. Violence, Justice, and Accountability in Postsocialist Europe*. Princeton: Princeton University Press.

Bourdieu, P. 1977. *Outline of a Theory of Practice*. Cambridge: Cambridge University Press.

Bowman, G. 1994. 'Xenophobia, Fantasy and the Nation. The Logic of Ethnic Violence in Former Yugoslavia', *Balkan Forum* 2(2): 135–64.

Bryant, C.G.A. and Mokrzycki, E. 1994. *The New Great Transformation? Change and Continuity in East-Central Europe*. London: Routledge.

Buroway, M. and Verdery, K., eds. 1999. *Uncertain Transition. Ethnographies of Change in the Postsocialist World*. Lanham, MD: Rowman and Littlefield.

Casey, E.S. 1987. *Remembering. A Phenomenological Study*. Bloomington: Indiana University Press.

Cirtautas, A.M. 1994. 'In Pursuit of the Democratic Interest. The Institutionalization of Parties and Interests in Eastern Europe', in *The New Great*

Transformation? Change and Continuity in East-Central Europe, ed. C.G.A. Bryant and E. Mokrzycki. London: Routledge, pp. 36–57.

Cohen, A.P. 1994. Self Consciousness. An Alternative Anthropology of Identity. Oxford: Routledge.

Creed, G.W. 1999. 'Deconstructing Socialism in Bulgaria', in Uncertain Transition. Ethnographies of Change in the Postsocialist World, ed. M. Buroway and K. Verdery. Lanham, MD: Rowman and Littlefield, pp. 223–43.

————— 2002. 'Economic Crisis and Ritual Decline in Eastern Europe', in Postsocialism. Ideals, Ideologies and Practices in Eurasia, ed. C.M. Hann. Routledge: London, pp. 57–73.

Csordas, T.J. 1990. 'Embodiment as a Paradigm for Anthropology', Ethos 18(1): 5–47.

—————, ed. 1994. Embodiment and Experience. The Existential Ground of Culture and Self. Cambridge: Cambridge University Press.

Čtvrtek, K. 1992. 'Stanou se z Československa Euroregiony?', Haló noviny, 23 May.

Deacon, B. et al. 1992. The New Eastern Europe. Social Policy: Past, Present, and Future. London: Sage.

Denich, B. 1994. 'Dismembering Yugoslavia: Nationalist Ideologies and the Symbolic Revival of Genocide', American Ethnologist 21(2): 367–90.

De Soto, H.G. and Dudwick, N. 1999. Fieldwork Dilemmas. Anthropologists in Postsocialist States. Madison: University of Wisconsin Press.

Duijzings, G. 2000. Religion and the Politics of Identity in Kosovo. London: Hurst and Company.

Ekman, P. 1980. 'Biological and Cultural Contributions to Body and Facial Movement in the Expression of Emotions', in Explaining Emotions, ed. A. Rorty. Berkeley: University of California Press, pp. 73–101.

Fierke, K. 2002. 'The Liberation of Kosovo. Emotion and the Ritual Reenactment of War', Focaal. European Journal of Anthropology 39: 93–113.

Foucault, M. 1979. Discipline and Punish. Harmondsworth: Penguin.

————— 1980. The History of Sexuality. Volume 1: An Introduction. Harmondsworth: Penguin.

Gay-y-Blasco, P. 2005. 'Love, Suffering and Grief among Spanish Gitanos', in Mixed Emotions. Anthropological Studies of Feeling, ed. K. Milton and M. Svašek. Oxford: Berg, pp. 163–77.

Giordano, C. and Kostova, D. 2002. 'The Social Production of Mistrust', in Postsocialism. Ideals, Ideologies and Practices in Eurasia, ed. C.M. Hann. Routledge: London, pp. 57–73.

Goffman, E. 1967. Interaction Ritual. New York: Doubleday Anchor.

Graziano, F. 1992. Divine Violence. Spectacle, Psychosexuality, and Radical Christianity in the Argentine Dirty War. Boulder, Co: Westview Press.

Haney, L. 1999. '"But We are Still Mothers". Gender, the State, and the Construction of Need in Postsocialist Hungary', in Uncertain Transition. Ethnographies of Change in the Postsocialist World, ed. M. Buroway and K. Verdery. Lanham, MD: Rowman and Littlefield, pp. 151–87.

Hann, C.M. ed. 1998. *Property Relations. Renewing the Anthropological Tradition.* Cambridge: Cambridge University Press.

Harré, R. and Parrott, G.W. eds. 1996. *The Emotions. Social, Cultural and Biological Dimensions.* London: Sage.

Hayden, R.M. 1994. 'Recounting the Dead. The Rediscovery and Redefinition of Wartime Massacres in Late and Post-communist Yugoslavia', in *Memory, History, and Opposition under State Socialism*, ed. R.S. Watson. Santa Fe: School of American Research Press.

Heatherington, T. 2005. '"As if Someone Dear to Me Had Died". Intimate Landscapes, Political Subjectivity, and the Problem of a Park in Sardinia', in *Mixed Emotions. Anthropological Studies of Feeling*, ed. K. Milton and M. Svašek. Oxford: Berg, pp. 145–62.

Hochschild, A.R. 1983. *The Managed Heart. Commercialization of Human Feeling.* Berkeley: University of California Press.

Honig, J. and Both, N. 1996. *Srebrenica. Record of a War Crime.* London: Penguin.

Humphrey, C. 1997. 'The Villas of the "New Russians". A Sketch of Consumption and Cultural Identity in Post-Soviet Landscapes', *Focaal. European Journal of Anthropology* 30–1: 85–106.

Jansen, S. 1996. 'Homeless at Home: Narrations of Post-Yugoslav Identites', in *Migrants of Identity. Perceptions of Home in a World of Movement*, ed. N. Rapport and A. Dawson. Oxford: Berg, pp. 19–28.

————— 2002. 'The Violence of Memories. Local Narratives of the Past after Ethnic Cleansing in Croatia', *Rethinking History* 6(1): 77–93.

————— 2004. 'The (Dis)comfort of Conformism. Post-war Nationalism and Coping with Powerlessness in Croation Villages', in *Warfare and Society in Archaeological and Social Anthropological Perspective*, ed. H. Vankilde, T. Otto and M. Throne. Aarhus: Aarhus University Press.

Josephides, L. 2005. 'Resentment as a Sense of Self', in *Mixed Emotions. Anthropological Studies of Feeling*, ed. K. Milton and M. Svašek. Oxford: Berg, pp. 71–90.

Kalb, D. 2002. 'Afterword. Globalism and Postsocialist Prospects', in *Postsocialism. Ideals, Ideologies and Practices in Eurasia*, ed. C.M. Hann. Routledge: London, pp. 317–34.

Kalb, D., Svašek M. and Tak, H. 1999. 'Approaching the 'New' Past in East-Central Europe', *Focaal. European Journal of Anthropology* 33: 9–23.

Kapferer, B. 1979. 'Emotion and Healing in Sinhalese Healing Rites', *Social Analysis* 1: 153–76.

Kideckel, D.A, ed. 1995. *East European Communities. The Struggle for Balance in Turbulant Times.* Boulder, Co: Westview Press.

Kocik, L. 1996. 'The Privatisation and Market Transformation of Polish Agriculture. New Conflicts and Divisions', in *After Socialism. Land Reform and Social Change in Eastern Europe*, ed. R. Abrahams. Oxford: Berghahn, pp. 115–32.

Lampland, M. 2002. 'The Advantages of Being Collectivized. Cooperative Farm Managers in the Postsocialist Economy', in *Postsocialism. Ideals, Ideologies and Practices in Eurasia*, ed. C.M. Hann. Routledge: London, pp. 31–56.

Leavitt, J. 1996. 'Meaning and Feeling in the Anthropology of Emotions', *American Ethnologist* 23(3): 514–39.

Lemon, A. 2000. *Between Two Fires. Gypsy Performance and Romani Memory From Pushkin to Post-Socialism*. Durham, NC and London: Duke University Press.

Lewis Herman, J. 1992. *Trauma and Recovery*. New York: Pandora.

Leys, R. 2000. *Trauma: A Genealogy*. Chicago: University of Chicago Press.

Lutz, C.A. 1988. *Unnatural Emotions: Everyday Sentiments on a Micronesian Atoll and Their Challenge to Western Theory*. Chicago: University of Chicago Press.

Lutz, C.A. and Abu-Lughod, L., eds. 1990. *Language and the Politics of Emotion*. Cambridge: Cambridge University Press and Paris: Editions de la Maison des Sciences de l'Homme.

Lutz, C.A. and White, G.M. 1986. 'The Anthropology of Emotions', *Annual Review of Anthropology* 15: 405–36.

Lyon, M.L. 1995. 'Missing Emotion: the Limitations of Cultural Constructionism in the Study of Emotion', *Cultural Anthropology* 10(2): 244–63.

Lyon, M.L. and Barbalet, J.M. 1994. 'Society's Body. Emotion and the "Somatisation" of Social Theory', in *Embodiment and Experience. The Existential Ground of Culture and Self*, ed. T.J. Csordas. Cambridge University Press, pp. 248–68.

Lyons, W. 1980. *Emotion*. Cambridge: Cambridge University Press.

Lysaght, K. 2005. 'Catholics, Protestants, and Office Workers from the Town. The Experience and Negotiation of Fear on the Streets of Belfast', in *Mixed Emotions. Anthropological Studies of Feeling*, ed. K. Milton and M. Svašek. Oxford: Berg, pp. 127–43.

Merleau-Ponty, M. 1962. *Phenomenology of Perception*. Trans. James Edie. Evanston, IL: Northwestern University Press.

Mertus, J. et al. 1997. *The Suitcase. Refugee Voices from Bosnia and Croatia*. Berkeley: University of California Press.

Milton, K. 2002. *Loving Nature. Towards an Ecology of Emotion*. London and New York: Routledge.

———— 2005. 'Meanings, Feelings and Human Ecology', in *Mixed Emotions. Anthropological Studies of Feeling*, ed. K. Milton and M. Svašek. Oxford: Berg, pp. 25–41.

Milton, K. and Svašek, M., eds. 2005. *Mixed Emotions. Anthropological Studies of Feeling*. Oxford: Berg.

Mitszal, B.A. 1996. *Trust in Modern Societies*. Cambridge: Polity.

Mocek, M. 2002. Verheugen: Dekrety jsou minulost. *Mladá fronta dnes*, 10 April, pp. 1, 9.

Nederlands Instituut voor Oorlogsdocumentatie. 2002. *Srebrenica*. Amsterdam: Boom.

Obeyesekere, G. 1992. *The Apotheosis of Captain Cook. European Myth Making in the Pacific*. Princeton: Princeton University Press.

O'Nell, T.D. 2000. '"Coming Home" among Northern Plains Vietnam Veterans. Psychological Transformations in Pragmatic Perspective', *Ethos* 27(4): 441–65.

Overing, J. and Passes, A., eds. 2000. *The Anthropology of Love and Anger. The Aesthetics of Conviviality in Native Amazonia*. London and New York: Routledge.

Parkinson, B. 1995. *Ideas and Realities of Emotion*. Routledge: London and New York.

Pine, F. 2002. 'Dimensions of Inequality. Gender, Class and "Underclass"', in *Postsocialism. Ideals, Ideologies and Practices in Eurasia*, ed. C.M. Hann. Routledge: London, pp. 95–113.

Plutchik, R. and Kellerman, H., eds. 1980. *Theories of Emotion*. New York: Academic Press.

Polanyi, K. 1944. *The Great Transformation. The Political and Economic Origins of Our Time*. Boston: Beacon.

van de Port, M. 1998. *Gypsies, Wars, and Other Instances of the Wild. Civilization and Its Discontents in a Serbian Town*. Amsterdam: Amsterdam University Press.

Poulton, H. 1995. *Who are the Macedonians?* London: Hurst and Company.

Reinerová, R. 1994. *Romanies – in Search of Lost Security? An Ethnological Probe in Prague 5*. Prague: Prague Occasional Papers in Ethnology.

Rieff, D. 1995. *Slaughterhouse. Bosnia and the Failure of the West*. New York: Simon and Schuster.

Rosaldo, I.R. 1984. 'Grief and a Headhunter's Rage. On the Cultural Force of Emotions', in *Text, Play, and Story. The Construction and Reconstruction of Self and Society*, ed. E.M. Bruner. Illinois: Waveland Press, pp. 178–95.

Rosaldo, M.Z. 1980. *Knowledge and Passion. Ilongot Notions of Self and Social Life*. Cambridge: Cambridge University Press.

——— 1983. 'The Shame of Headhunters and the Autonomy of Self', *Ethos* 11(3): 135–51.

Sarbin, T.R. 1986. 'Emotion and Act. Roles and Rhetoric', in *The Social Construction of Emotions*, ed. R. Harré. Oxford: Blackwell, pp. 83–97.

Scheper-Hughes, N. 1985. 'Culture, Scarcity, and Maternal Thinking. Maternal Detachment and Infant Survival in a Brazilian Shantytown', *Ethos* 13(4): 291–317.

Scheper-Hughes, N. 1990. 'Mother Love and Child Death in Northeast Brazil', in *Cultural Psychology. Essays on Comparative Human Development*, ed. J.W. Stigler et al. Cambridge: Cambridge Univerity Press.

Scheper-Hughes, N. and Lock, M. 1987. 'The Mindful Body: A Prolegomenon to Future Work in Medical Anthropology', *Medical Quarterly* 1: 6–41.

Schieffelin, E.L. 1983. 'Anger and Shame in the Tropical Forest. On Affect as a Cultural System in Papua New Guinea', *Ethos* 11(3): 181–209.

Seymour, S. 1983. 'Household Structure and Status and Expressions of Affect in India. *Ethos* 11(4): 263–77.

Simmel, G. 1950. *The Sociology of Georg Simmel*. Trans. and ed. K.H. Wolff. New York: Free Press.

Stark, D. 1992. 'Path Dependence and Privatisation. Strategies in East Central Europe', *East European Politics and Societies* 6: 17–54.

Stein, H.F. 1993. 'The Holocaust, the Self, and the Question of Wholeness: A Response to Lewin', *Ethos* 21(4): 485–512.

Stewart, M. 1997. *The Time of the Gypsies*. Oxford: Westview Press.

Suárez-Orozco, M. 1990. 'Speaking of the Unspeakable. Toward a Psychosocial Understanding of Responses to Terror', *Ethos* 17(3): 353–83.

Svašek, M. 1997. 'Gossip and Power Struggle in the Post-communist Czech Art World. *Focaal. European Journal of Anthropology* 29: 101–22.

———— 1999. 'History, Identity, and Territoriality. Redefining Czech-German Relations in the Post-Cold War Era', *Focaal. European Journal of Anthropology* 33: 37–58.

———— 2000. 'Borders and Emotions. Hope and Fear in the Bohemian-Bavarian Frontier Zone', *Ethnologia Europeae* 30(2): 111–26.

———— 2002. 'Contacts: Social Dynamics in the Czechoslovak State-Socialist Art World', *Contemporary European History* 11(1): 67–86.

———— 2003. 'Narratives of Home and Homeland. The Symbolic Construction and Appropriation of the Sudeten German "Heimat"', *Identities. Global Studies in Culture and Power* 9: 495–518.

———— 2005a. 'Introduction. Emotions in Anthropology', in *Mixed Emotions. Anthropological Studies of Feeling*, ed. K. Milton and M. Svašek. Oxford: Berg, pp. 1–23.

———— 2005b. 'The Politics of Chosen Trauma. Expellee Memories, Emotions and Identities', in *Mixed Emotions. Anthropological Studies of Feeling*, ed. K. Milton and M. Svašek. Oxford: Berg, pp. 195–214.

Szalai, E. 1994. 'The Power Structure in Hungary after the Political Transition', in *The New Great Transformation? Change and Continuity in East-Central Europe* eds C.G.A. Bryant and E. Mokrzycki. London: Routledge, pp. 120–43.

Taussig, M. 1987. *Shamanism, Colonialism, and the Wild Man. A Study in Terror and Healing*. Chicago: University of Chicago Press.

Tonkin, E. 2005. 'Being There: Emotion and Imagination in Anthropologists' Encounters', in *Mixed Emotions. Anthropological Studies of Feeling*, ed. K. Milton and M. Svašek. Oxford: Berg, pp. 55–69.

Veblen, T. 1953. *The Theory of the Leisure Class. An Economic Study of Institutions*. New York: New American Library.

Veenis, M. 1999. 'Consumption in East Germany: The Seduction and Betrayal of Things', *Journal of Material Culture* 4(1): 79–112.

Verdery, K. 1996. *What Was Socialism and What Comes Next?* Princeton: Princeton University Press.

———— 1998. 'Property and Power in Transylvania's Decollectivization', in *Property Relations. Renewing the Anthropological Tradition*, ed. C.M. Hann. Cambridge: Cambridge University Press, pp. 160–80.

———— 1999a. 'Fuzzy Property. Rights, Power, and Identity in Transylvania's Decollectivization', in *Uncertain Transition. Ethnographies of Change in the Postsocialist World*, ed. M. Burawoy and K. Verdery. Lanham, MD: Rowman and Littlefield, pp. 53–82.

———— 1999b. *The Political Lives of Dead Bodies. Reburial and Postsocialist Change*. New York: Columbia University Press.

———— 2003. *The Vanishing Hectare. Property and Value in Postsocialist Transylvania*. Ithaca, NY: Cornell University Press.

Visser, O. 2003. 'Property and Post-communist Poverty: Can the Mystery of Capital Be Exported to the Former Soviet Countryside?', *Focaal. European Journal of Anthropology* 41: 197–201.

Volkan, V. 1999. *Bloodlines. From Ethnic Pride to Ethnic Terrorism*. Boulder, Co: Westview Press.

Weinerová, R. 1994. *Romanies – in Search of Lost Security? An Ethnological Probe in Prague 5*. Prague: Institute of Ethnology.

White, G.M. 1985. 'Premises and Purposes in Solomon Islands Ethnopsychology', in *Person, Self, and Experience. Exploring Pacific Ethnopsychologies*, ed. G.M. White and J. Kirkpatrick. Berkeley: University of California Press, pp. 328–66.

———— 1990. 'Moral Discourse and the Rhetoric of Emotions', in *Language and the Politics of Emotion*, ed. C.A. Lutz and L. Abu-Lughod. Cambridge: Cambridge University Press and Paris: Editions de la Maison des Sciences de l'Homme, pp. 46–68.

———— 2000. 'Emotional Remembering. The Pragmatics of National Memory', *Ethos* 27(4): 505–29.

Whitehouse, H. 2002. 'Conjectures, Refutations, and Verification: Towards a Testable Theory of Modes of Religiosity', *Journal of Ritual Studies* 16(2): 44–59.

Wierzbicka, A. 2004. 'Emotion and Culture: Arguing with Martha Nussbaum', Ethos 31(4): 577–600.

Zbierski-Salamek, S. 1999. 'Polish Peasants in the "Valley of Transition", Responses to Postsocialist Reforms', in *Uncertain Transition. Ethnographies of Change in the Postsocialist World*, ed. M. Burawoy and K. Verdery, Lanham, MD: Rowman and Littlefield, pp. 189–222.

Chapter 1

Nostalgia and the Emotional Economy: a Comparative Look at Rural Russia

Patrick Heady and Liesl L. Gambold Miller

An emotion that emerges again and again in accounts of the postsocialist world is nostalgia. In many countries large parts of the population are prone to claim, with obvious feeling, that this or that aspect of life was better before the collapse of the communist regimes. A full understanding of the specific characteristics of postsocialist emotional life requires, therefore, a conception of the sources and functions of nostalgia. Anthropologists are well placed to investigate this question, since ethnographic techniques of in-depth interviewing and participant observation are ideally suited to gather both the content of memories and the variety of ways they are deployed in contemporary social life.

However, the exercise of collecting and interpreting these data highlights a radical difference between the ways in which nostalgic memories are understood in the local society, and the ways in which they are commonly analysed by anthropologists. For local people one of the key points about nostalgic memories is that they are true, or at least an aspect of the truth. Anthropologists, on the other hand, often consider the truth or otherwise of these memories as a secondary matter, preferring to focus on the way they are deployed in the contemporary context. In a sense anthropologists treat memories as Malinowski treated myths, as charters for contemporary claims (Malinowski 1978 [1935]: 341–51). For instance, they can be seen as a source of 'emotional capital', drawing on the analogy with Bourdieu's

(1977, 1984) concepts of 'symbolic' and 'social' capital, but stressing the extra impact that emotional discourse can give to such claims (Skrbiš 2002).

We do not want to dispute the validity of these analyses, but we do want to dispute their completeness. Our arguments centre round the question of the truth of nostalgic memories. An individual who is playing on nostalgic sentiments to advance a claim may not be particularly concerned with whether his nostalgic claims are true or not. Nevertheless, it is important even to him that his audience should believe in their essential truth – since the emotional effect he is trying to evoke depends on the mutual acceptance of the authenticity of shared memories. Memory can be seen as 'individual knowledge of the past, as distinct from institutionalised memories, or history', which gives it a living quality (Wanner 1998: 37). Shared memories represent the cognitive maps that communities have and validate those personal memories informing daily decisions.

In connection with this we want to make two points. The first of these is comparatively simple: that the relatively impersonal claims in people's nostalgic accounts are often true, and easily shown to be so. The second is rather more complex and relates to the frequent nostalgic assertions that personal relationships were better in the past, that people were more spontaneously friendly and also more practically helpful. These claims are not only almost impossible to verify directly, they often seem inherently improbable or even contradictory. Nevertheless, we want to argue that claims about worsening personal relationships may often be true to people's actual experience.

The factual basis of our argument will be set out below, but the underlying theoretical point can be stated here. This is that participation in economic activity requires not merely mental and physical effort and a rational expectation of gain, but also an appropriate emotional orientation towards the work and towards those with whom one is cooperating or competing. If the organisation of economic activity changes rapidly it disrupts this pattern of emotionally meaningful practical relationships, leading to a sense of violated expectations and emotional loss.

The assertion that emotions are central to the everyday functioning of economic life runs counter to the dominant academic tradition. This tradition, embodied in formal economics, has emphasised rational choice alone. Starting from the work of Adam Smith, the approach has been to assume instrumentally rational actors operating under objective constraints, and to try and deduce from this assumption both explanations of observed behaviour and recommendations as to the set of policies (on tax, tariffs, regulation, property etc.) that would maximise the welfare of particular groups or of society as a whole. This framework is common to classical economics (Ricardo, Marx), the marginalist revolution of neoclassical economics (Jevons, Marshall), the work of Keynes, and most contemporary economic theory[1]. Most relevantly in the present context, it includes the deductive use of games theory to attack the idea of collective property (Hardin 1968).

However, side by side with formal economics there has been another tradition, not so dominant but refusing to disappear entirely, which encases instrumental rationality within a larger frame of less calculating motives. This tradition stretches from Hume, who derived property institutions from rational self-interest but emphasised the importance of mutual sympathy in maintaining support for them (Hume 1978 [1739–40]: 526, 575–78, 618–19), to the recent boom in experimental game theoretic studies in which hypotheses of self-centred rationality are tested (and usually rejected) rather than simply assumed (Henrich et al. 2001), to Putnam's (1994) version of social capital theory.[2]

Some of the most stimulating contributions to this tradition have come from social and cultural anthropologists, or from sociologists who have drawn on and influenced anthropological work. Weber argued that any project of rationalisation must rest on irrational premises. He suggested that there were 'elective affinities' between specific kinds of economic activity and particular religious views, as a result of which work becomes a way of meeting emotional needs generated by a particular religious view, and vice versa (Weber 1991 [1915], especially pp. 282–84). Durkheim and Mauss were preoccupied with the ways in which individualistic motives could be reconciled with collective solidarity (both in the sense of cooperation and in the sense of emotional commitment to the group). Their related, but distinct, approaches were exemplified in Durkheim's (1984 [1893]) study of the division of labour in society in which he posited alternative patterns of solidary relationships, and in Mauss's studies of seasonal variations of the Eskimo (Mauss and Beuchat 1979 [1905]) and the gift (Mauss 2002 [1923]), which offered rather more subtle explorations of the interaction between individualistic, competitive and solidary motives.

Anthropology needs to develop a fuller account of the relationship between emotions, social life and economic organisation, and we believe that the outline of such an account already exists in this tradition of sociological and anthropological analysis. However, for present purposes we simply wish to draw on this tradition in a rather simple way. A key idea that we take from all these contributions is that people have to manage both their emotions and their practical lives. The way they manage the one interacts with the way they handle the other. In both cases the experience concerned (practical reality or emotion) is partly subject to, and partly outside, their conscious control. Among the emotions intrinsic to economic life are both individualistic ones of ambition and self-interest, and also the more social emotions of shared experience and fellow feeling. The particular way these motives are balanced and contrasted will differ according to the kind of economic organisation. We will argue that a key to understanding the emotional effect of the transition from a collective to a more individualistic pattern of economic organisation is the role played by emotions of mutual sympathy, and the contexts in which people feel able to act on them.

We use the expression 'emotional economy' to refer to these systems of economically significant emotional relationships, and will return to this topic later on in the paper. But first we will expose the reader to a blast of nostalgia, followed by an analysis of how much of it corresponds with ascertainable facts.

In this article, we will draw on the following fieldwork experience. Liesl Gambold Miller worked in Moshkino, a village in Nizhegorodskaya Oblast, to the east of Moscow, for a year in 1997–98, returning for a five-week visit in the summer of 2002. Patrick Heady has carried out four months of fieldwork in Russia. In 2002 he spent ten weeks, split between early spring and late summer, in the village of Listnoe,[3] in Lipetsk Oblast, about 400 kilometres south of Moscow.

Nostalgia for the Past in a Village in North-central Russia

Sasha stands in a blue-and-white striped tank top and black sweatpants weeding and picking the 'Colorado' bugs from around the strawberries. He's gained a little weight around the middle in the four years since we last met. His beard is bright red and stands out against his dark hair. He shuffles away on his bad leg, stiff and awkward, washes his hands and sits on a bench in the shade near the house. I sit with him and his elderly aunt with whom he now lives and they quickly fill me in on how life has been in the village over the past few years. Nadia describes her failing health and the exodus of young people from the village, then shrugs in exasperation, 'Things were so much better, and stronger before. If the *kolkhoz* were back it would be so much better. We could even earn some money!' When asked what she misses most about the Soviet Union, she wrings her hands and says, 'I miss everything from before, when the USSR was together. It was all much better. We in the countryside were stronger. Now we are all weak.

We went from being a strong farm to being no farm. Everything suddenly disappeared, and now we have only each other.'

Nadia's lament was not surprising or new. Her sentiments were echoed by many of the villagers of Moshkino when Liesl Gambold Miller (LGM) lived and worked there from 1997 to 1998. At that time, however, many were still holding on to optimism about the prospects for independent farming and the potential their former collective farm had in the privatised agricultural economy. The pensioners were most critical early on, for they recognised their own limited opportunities in the free market system. But now, four years later, it seemed that the spirit in the village had not risen, but had soured. Everywhere villagers were toiling away in their gardens – not because they took great pride in their large harvests of vegetables and fruits, to be stored in the root cellar, canned or pickled – but because they were now almost entirely dependent on their gardens for subsistence.

Valya oversees the storage and distribution of grain on the Moshkinskoe farm, and monitors the petrol used by the tractor drivers. For her work she receives a small wage on top of her pension.[4] She also sells milk regularly in Gorodets, the town fifteen kilometres away. Valya was disappointed by the way the farm was struggling. She had felt proud of the collective throughout her life and now wondered how they could continue. She said, 'It used to be a really good *kolkhoz*, Maxim Gorky. We were very strong. My uncle used to be the head of the *kolkhoz* and he was a good, strong leader. I thought we would have such a strong farm again. As it turned out, we aren't so great.' Valya's concerns aren't only with the farming operations. She, and others, feel that people in the village have become more selfish. Valya said that everything during communist times was better, '… the economy was better and people were more friendly. Now people are angry at one another. People used to help one another and now people are like beasts [*kak zveri*]!' Dmitri is fifty-three years old and works in a timber factory but lives in Moshkino. He worked for the collective until 1994 when he was let go because of the restructuring process. He has no particular skills or training in agriculture and couldn't find a position on the newly reorganised farm. He said, 'People have changed. They think differently now. We see each other rarely so we don't help each other as much as we used to. If I need to borrow money, like 1000 roubles, I can ask everyone and no one will give me the money. People aren't as friendly as they used to be. They don't feel sympathy [*nye simpatichen*] for one another.'

These sentiments about people being less friendly, more calculating, and less sympathetic are echoed throughout Moshkino. Villagers of all ages claim that the general feeling in the community is more isolating (*chuvstvo izolyatsii*) and suspicious (*podozritelny*) than it was before (see also Mihaylova, Chapter 2, for a case study of increasing isolation and marginalisation in Bulgaria). People reminisce about how they used to visit one another and drink together. Asked why they don't visit one another as much any more, one thirty-four-year-old woman said, 'Everyone is too busy trying to survive. We have to work all the time now.'

Despite this, the villagers do not assert that all personal relationships at present are unsatisfactory. All of the twenty-three households interviewed by LGM in 2002 said that their neighbours were very helpful and 'good people'. Nor do they claim that everything in the past organisation of collective farms was wonderful. Many admit that their past was not without struggles and hardships, placed on them by the Soviet government. Dmitri talked about being a child on the collective farm. He was not full of praise for the *kolkhoz* but couldn't completely disregard its allure either.

Dmitri's mother had six children and woke at 4 a.m. each day to prepare breakfast, tend to the domestic animals and prepare for work on the *kolkhoz*. Dmitri said that he remembers the head of the collective coming to their house to find out why his mother was late for work. She explained that she had to finish cooking. The chairman then grabbed a pan of water and threw it onto her fire, saying 'I guess you're done cooking now – come to work!' But even Dmitri says that, 'Everything is relative. We used to have a different system and I can't say everything was great but I can't say that about these times either. I think something is wrong now too. Really wrong. If I need help I only have God and myself'.

The positive evaluation of collective, as opposed to individualistic, activity colours perceptions of the opportunities opened by the recent reforms, even in the case of people who were initially willing to give the reforms a chance. Sasha, whom we met at the start of this section, typifies this attitude. In 1997 he had said, 'I'm just a horse worker. I don't know what they are going to do in there [gesturing toward the farm offices]. But I think that now we really have a chance to do well. Maybe we can grow and be an even stronger farm. Everyone would do better. That would be ok with me!' Five years later Sasha was not at all optimistic. 'I'm done. I can't work anymore, and even if I could it wouldn't matter. The farm doesn't work, everyone is suffering and we don't even know what will happen. Thank God we have our garden and I have my pension and I can still walk.' Interestingly, Sasha's optimistic feelings about the potential for private farming in Russia were never about his own possible gains. In many conversations he referred to the farm growing, strengthening or enlarging, but never himself becoming a private farmer or becoming wealthy.

The emotional ties to collective property in Moshkino were all the stronger because collective organisation was still perceived as economically essential. In the late 1990s, the villagers were less concerned with who actually 'owned' the land than with how work was organised and decisions were made in the village. In fact, questions of 'ownership' were often viewed as inconsequential since very few villagers actually felt as though they were 'owners' of anything other than their house and their personal gardens (for a discussion of changing notions of ownership in Czech village contexts, see Müller, Chapter 8 and Svašek, Chapter 4). When asked about the certificates of ownership distributed during the farm restructuring, people laughed and said they had no idea where their certificate was. '[That certificate] doesn't mean anything! I don't own anything, it's the *kolkhoz* land, not mine. I can't work [that land], I don't have a tractor,' said Pasha, a Moshkino resident.

The emotional content of the villagers' discussions increased when talking about the *kolkhoz* as a unifying source of labour with definite social and economic implications. Lena, a thirty-eight-year-old accountant in the Moshkino farm office, spoke for many in the village when she said that farming should remain collective in Russia because 'it's been that way for so long and we are a farm together, not separately'. This coincides with the pervasive sentiment of allegiance felt towards the farm as opposed to the village. Seventy-nine percent of villagers surveyed in Moshkino expressed a greater sense of remorse over the decline of the Sixty Years October *kolkhoz* than of the general state of affairs in Moshkino.[5] One woman, when asked to whom or what she felt an allegiance, replied, 'If I live here, then I have to give my support to the farm.'

Nostalgia and the Factual Record

References to the integrity of the farm in the past are a reflection of the relative strength of the Moshkinskoe farm prior to reorganisation. In March 1994 the collective farm 'Sixty Years October' was divided as part of the collective farm restructuring process. At the auction most of the collective's 3,109 hectares were divided among three newly created farms – Mir, Kolos and Moshkinskoe. Up until this time Moshkino and most of the other twenty-four villages in its administrative area were collectively organised in the Sixty Years October collective farm, which by local standards was a strong farm, enjoying a reputation as one of the leaders in the region.

The Sixty Years October collective was founded during an official farm-consolidation drive – in one of the Soviet government's many attempts to increase productivity at a national level. Before that, the Moshkino area had been united in the Maxim Gorky collective farm, named after the local son and famous writer. The other collective in the area was called Kirov. Many of the older Moshkino residents remembered their years in the Maxim Gorky *kolkhoz* quite favourably, which correlates with some of the broader changes going on in collective farming across the Soviet Union. In the late 1950s Khrushchev began to send specialists to state and collective farms in an attempt to raise the overall level of productivity. Many Soviet farms soon found themselves with livestock experts and subsequent increases in output. In addition, the persistent inequality between state and collective farm wages – state farm workers often being paid double to that paid to collective farm workers for performing the same work – began decreasing as Khrushchev and later Brezhnev increased wage rates on collective farms. For many Moshkino residents those years as the Maxim Gorky collective were their most favourable memories. Local records indicate that the collective was a relatively strong one and the workers also reaped the benefits of government policies that directly improved their quality of life. In 1977, however, the Maxim Gorky collective was forcibly united with the Kirov collective to form the Sixty Years October *kolkhoz*. Many villagers were unhappy about the loss of their collective, but as Sixty Years October prospered villagers were convinced that they would once again be part of a successful collective farm.

When reorganisation occurred in 1994 there were some residents in Moshkino who felt that they should not decollectivise the Sixty Years October farm because it was such a strong farm. Even some local administrators wondered if it was a wise move, but the push from the local and federal governments to create private farms and to break up the large collective and state farms prevailed. In order to be eligible for funds from the British Know How Fund or World Bank, who were organising the farm restructuring process in the Nizhegorodskaya Oblast, and to comply with Yeltsin's decree that all farms must reregister as independent businesses, the Sixty Years October farm was broken up. Following the break-up, Moshkinskoe registered as a Joint Stock Company and received 1,477 hectares of land, becoming the largest of the three successor farms.

The collective farm in Moshkino has not ceased to function, but has changed its organisational form and radically reduced its labour force as a result of the economic reforms. In Moshkino, as in much of Russia, these reforms have resulted not in the expansion of private, individual farming, but in the creation of a new form of farming – the private collective farm. Moshkinskoe's director, Ekaterina Nikolaevna, now employs roughly forty full-time workers, almost all former *kolkhoz* employees, though this number is far fewer than in the *kolkhoz* days. They work some 900 hectares of land, most of it land 'shares' distributed in the reorganisation process to villagers who then gave them to Ekaterina, hoping the success of the farm would result in dividend payments.[6] No one has ever received a dividend payment and most of the farm workers rarely receive a full salary payment. Payments in kind account for almost half of the average worker's monthly pay. Thus, the cash economy of the village is weak.

Households have responded to the strained economic conditions in several ways. First, most have attempted to increase their personal farming output from their *ogorody*, or vegetable gardens, in order to be able to feed themselves for most of the year. The main items regularly purchased from the village store are bread, sweets, cigarettes and vodka. Second, many now rely more heavily on neighbours and kin for assistance in planting or harvesting and the sharing of some food items such as meat or milk.[7]

So the nostalgic laments about material impoverishment and the decline of support from the local collective farm have a definite basis in fact. In this Moshkino is typical of Russia as a whole. During the 1990s, the level of output in the former collective farms (including those that had formally become private corporations) went into steep decline. The 1999 figure for total output in former collective farms was only 40 percent of the level that had been attained in 1991, the last year before the reforms.

People's reluctance to take their own land shares out of the collective farms is also characteristic of Russia in general. When families were given their certificates of ownership, legal provision was made for them to farm this land themselves, and also to rent further land so as to set up commercial family farms on quite a large scale. However, since the start of the reforms this category of farmers – known in Russia as *fermery* – has never amounted to more than 2 or 3 percent of the labour force in Russian agriculture. The number of *fermery* has actually declined slightly since 1996, after special subsidies were discontinued (Stroev 2001: 601). Whether this reluctance to set up as largish-scale commercial farmers is a product of objective constraints, a preference for collective over individual enterprise, or a mixture of the two, is subject to debate (O'Brien and Wegren 2002).

However, one of the claims made by LGM's informants can be verified. When Lena said that farming should remain collectivised because it had been that way for so long, she may well have been thinking of the time since collectivisation in the early 1930s. But most of Russia peasant farmland had in fact been owned and regulated by the community as a whole for about two centuries before that. In a series of scattered developments between the seventeenth and nineteenth centuries, the peasant commune, or *mir*, took on the role of distributing land between peasant families. This was partly a movement from above, promoted by landowners and state officials concerned to ensure that all peasants had enough land to meet their tax, rent and service obligations, and partly a movement of the peasants themselves aimed at ensuring that all had the means to survive in the face of intensifying official and aristocratic exactions (Blum 1961: 508–27; Dunn and Dunn 1988: 8–11; Shanin 1986: 76).

So the situation in the prerevolutionary years was that peasant land was owned by the *mir* and distributed to families on the basis of need. It was farmed by the individual families, subject to some coordination by the *mir*. This can be seen as an example of what Scott (1976) refers to as the moral economy of the peasant: a tendency to prioritise security in a difficult environment by emphasising solidarity and mutual aid. An officially sponsored drive towards land privatisation in the final decade of tsarism was reversed by the peasants themselves during the years of revolution. The collectivisation drive of the early 1930s imposed a strict form of state direction on a system of ownership and organisation which already had very strong collective elements. It was not, by and large, a matter of expropriating private family landholdings, because the peasants themselves believed that the land they farmed belonged to the community as a whole.

Nostalgia and the Emotional Economy

This leaves the most characteristically nostalgic claim of all: that people used to be more caring and helpful in the past. As we noted at the start of this paper, claims of this kind are virtually impossible to assess directly. In the present instance, the claim is made particularly implausible by a contradiction in the descriptions people give of present-day relationships and motives. Speaking on their own behalf, they express themselves in ways that suggest a strong sense of commitment to the collective well-being of the community and the collective farm, and they also acknowledge that their neighbours are good people. Other people in the village, however, are described as selfishly irresponsible individualists, possibly little better than wild beasts. Since statements of these kinds are made by most people, we would have to conclude, if we took them literally, that most people were *both* good people concerned with the welfare of their neighbours and the community as a whole *and* antisocial cynics reckless of the welfare of others. We seem to have a clear contradiction in people's depiction of contemporary life, which leaves us with little grounds for faith in what they say about the past.

Despite this, it may in fact be possible to say something about the changes in interpersonal relationships in Moshkino over the past decade. Admittedly, this is not something that we can assess directly since, even if we were to carry out a survey of the present-day extent of mutual aid between individuals and families in Moshkino, we do not have a pre-reform survey with which to compare the results. However, we do have data on one aspect of mutual aid and its connection with emotional togetherness. This is the work of the collective farm itself. During LGM's fieldwork in 1997–98 the collective was still the site for regular celebrations of togetherness and mutual solidarity. There were many occasions for mid-afternoon parties, including the first anniversary of a wedding, one of the milkmaids obtaining eighth place in a regional milking contest, a visit by a committee from the district administration to check the crops, or any day before a state holiday. At these times, the farm workers gathered to drink, eat and relax for a few minutes. What was striking was the genuine closeness displayed by many of the people. One could not help feeling they were 'one big family'. The workers themselves often describe the collective as a family and contrast it with other collectives where things might have changed.

In this connection, it is worth noting that Moshkino is not a big family in the literal sense. Like many rural communities in northern Russia, it has been created rather recently, as part of the reorganisation of collective farms in the second half of the twentieth century. Among twenty-three households surveyed in 2002, only six out of forty-seven adults had been born and raised in Moshkino. There would thus have been no time for the development of really extensive kinship ties among the village families. So, despite strong ties amongst those kin present, and generally good relations between neighbours, the only context in which truly village-wide solidarity could develop was the collective farm itself. As the farm has declined, employing fewer and fewer villagers, the range of people included in its regular celebrations of togetherness must also have decreased. Because of this, it does seem likely that the experience of solidarity outside the immediate circle of kin and neighbours has declined.

This interpretation is consistent with some of the specific memories of local people. In Moshkino, villagers' memories of Soviet times often centre on collective rituals such as harvest festivals and youth celebrations. For Olga, an accountant for the collective, her memories of being in the Young Pioneers were most vivid. She said, 'We were so enthusiastic. But I'm not sure if it was about the real message of the *pioniri* or just having all of the children together to celebrate. We felt happy about our future and our farm. We ate and sang songs. We really believed that we were the best country in the world.' When asked if the Young Pioneers could be replaced today by something like Girl Scouts or Brownies, she wasn't so sure. 'The thing with Young Pioneers was that everyone *had* to participate and it was about more than just you. It was about the group [*o grupe*] and I don't know about these 'Brownies' or if they think like we did.'

Moshkino residents complained that the village as a whole used to gather together more often. Because the village and the collective were rather synonymous, harvest celebrations were affairs that involved almost all villagers. Today only some of the farm workers (usually those in the administration) gather to celebrate together (for workers' accomplishments etc.) and there are very few collective rituals. Even occasional dances or films at the Club are no longer attended by anyone other than teenagers looking for a place to gather and drink. The decreased opportunity for collective celebrations was seen as both a symptom of what is wrong in the village today and a cause for the further damage being done to their collective identity.

The sentiments expressed relative to these shifts mark more than mere individual emotional states, for the perceived changes are occurring on multiple levels. It might be argued that for some, like collective farmers, work exists as more than a rational choice regarding livelihood and the domestic economy. Certainly the former Soviet Union provides a justifiable site where work was indeed argued to be about precisely what the Moshkino villagers have expressed – camaraderie, cooperation, social cohesion and collectivity. Needless to say, many Soviet workers were not at all enchanted with their work, but for some, work might have been felt as an expression of emotion connected to both cultural meaning and bodily feelings. The expression of these feelings can often be incongruent with what a rational critique might make of them, but therein lie some of the problems with the way emotions have been figured into the equation – as something insubordinate, disparaging and easily dismissed (Campbell 1994). The research findings here suggest that the emotional quality of work extended far beyond the economic realm in rural Russia and that the yearnings of the villagers amount to more than irrational nostalgia for retracted state support. The legitimacy of this interpretation comes in understanding the very lack of rationality – on the ground level – in the agricultural privatisation process and the suggestion that 'what is not within my power to affect may not provide a rational ground for my actions or responses (Cambell 1994: 52).

The analysis in the last few paragraphs suggests a different interpretation of the apparently contradictory image of social relations in present-day

Moshkino that we discussed at the beginning of this section. Suppose that people *wish* to behave generously to each other, and so derive both the practical and emotional benefits of mutual comradeship, but only feel able to do so when they are sure that their behaviour will be reciprocated rather than being exploited. A key point here, as a number of game theorists have emphasised, is the ability to monitor each other's behaviour. It is generally safe to behave generously to another person if one has good information about his behaviour and can stop one's own generosity if there are any signs that he might not reciprocate (Axelrod 1984). For this reason the existence of a stable structure within which behaviour can be mutually monitored provides the basis for the trust that is needed if people are to put generous motives into practice. This may explain why neighbours, who are in a constant relationship in which they can monitor each other's behaviour, generally do manage to set up relationships of mutually beneficial cooperation. Similarly, those people who have a continuing close involvement with the *kolkhoz* are in a set of close relationships, in which messages about good or antisocial behaviour will travel fast.

However, once someone has dropped out from this set of regular interactions – as a result perhaps of the decline of employment in the *kolkhoz* and the need to seek work and income elsewhere – then the network of communications connecting him with the community at large becomes rather attenuated, and the regular evidence needed for mutual trust is no longer there. Thus any two members of the community who are not united by ties of neighbourhood, kinship or regular *kolkhoz* participation may both want to behave generously to each other, but not feel the level of trust that would enable them to behave as they might wish. Each of them feels that his own motives are good, but judges the other by his behaviour. From his point of view it is easy to assume that the other person is a selfish individual who has gone bad as part of the general moral decline of the village.

Though this argument is somewhat hypothetical, and also slightly starry-eyed in its working assumption that people would be nice to each other if they could (since after all conflict and ill will are also parts of social reality), we nevertheless think it fits the evidence we have presented at least as well as the assumption that people simply invent a nostalgic image of the past for rhetorical purposes. However, the argument would be strengthened if we could point to an instance in which the supposed interaction between emotions, interactions and the need for practical security explained the existence of a currently viable system of friendly cooperation – and not merely the disappearance of a system of cooperative relationships that may have existed in the past. This is the theme of the next section of this paper.

Degrees of Nostalgia and the Differential Impact of Social and Economic Change

Although most of the Russian countryside has suffered a severe economic decline, the severity of the decline has varied between regions, with the most extreme instances of poverty and social disintegration being reported in the northwest (Visser 2003) while in the extreme south of European Russia farming is actually booming (Nikulin 2003). If we are correct in claiming that nostalgia reflects actual changes in economic and social circumstances, then expressions of nostalgia should be less in places where economic and social life has been less severely disrupted. Although neither of us has worked in the areas of most extreme poverty or prosperity, we are able to test this prediction, because one of us has worked in an area whose general situation is a good deal more favourable than that of Moshkino.

Working in Listnoe, situated about 400 kilometres south of Moscow, just inside the northern edge of the fertile black-earth country, Patrick Heady (PH) did not hear as many intensely nostalgic reminiscences as LGM. Although both collective farms in this large and long-established village (of about 4,000 inhabitants) were in decline, and many families no longer saw them as their main source of income, the impact on living standards seems to have been less severe than in Moshkino. A major reason for this was that the fertile soil, and the proximity of Moscow, made it possible for families to feed themselves and in addition earn a substantial cash income from the produce of their household plots and of limited amounts of land rented from the village administration or a collective farm. Another reason was that over the previous two decades most village households had received piped gas and water for the first time. Indeed, when PH asked about recent changes in material living standards he was as likely to be told that they had improved as that they had declined: the advent of piped gas and water being cited as the reason.

Although one family did complain to PH that people were less helpful than in the past, far more talked about mutual aid as a present-day reality, and something without which living in the countryside would be virtually impossible. Some said that they helped each other out of mutual sympathy (literally 'from the soul', *ot dushi*), but others explained that they took care that the amount of help that they offered to and received from each person with whom they worked remained in balance. This corresponded with the fact that a good deal of mutual aid actually took place, drawing on the extensive networks of kin that existed in this long-established community. PH was in Listnoe during the season of the potato harvest in 2002, and observed how families helped each other during this period. Potatoes were grown by private families, for their own consumption and for sale, on their household plots and on small additional plots of rented land, but it was rather rare for a household to harvest its potatoes without outside help. PH recorded the composition of twenty-four groups of potato harvesters, ranging in size from two to nineteen, with a median size of eight people. In all but one case the majority of the harvesters were relatives of the householder. No payment was made to the helpers (except for payments to a horse or tractor owner for ploughing the land to extract the potatoes), but the work generally ended with a celebratory lunch or picnic for the workers involved.

Liesl Gambold Miller did not observe inter-household cooperation on anything like this scale in Moshkino, but the continuing viability of cooperation in Listnoe can be explained on exactly the same principles which we used to account for the supposed decline in mutual helpfulness in Moskino – namely the importance of a set of continuing close relationships within which cooperative behaviour can be monitored and trust can be sustained. The key factor that is present in Listnoe, but absent in Moshkino, is a set of dense and active kinship networks which provide a continuing framework for this combination of generosity, fellowship, and mutual performance monitoring.

There are other reasons as well for Listnoe's comparative freedom from the sense of social collapse that is such a feature of life in Moshkino. The two major collective farms had never been the sole focus of collective identity in Listnoe. Middle-aged and elderly informants told PH of the lively rivalry that used to exist between the two church parishes into which the village had once been divided, even after the disappearance of the actual churches. Other focuses of social life include a new church (recently built with the help of public subscription and voluntary labour, as well as the financial help of a villager who has moved to a local city and done well in commerce); two discos (a public disco for teenagers in the dilapidated house of culture, and a private one for slightly older people in a building nearby), and various celebrations organised by the local council and the village schools.

All this is not to say that there is no nostalgia in Listnoe. People regret that the business of earning a living is now more complex than it used to be when collective farm salaries provided adequate incomes, and there are also regrets for the decline of the sense of security and order since the break-up of the Soviet Union. Nevertheless it seems reasonable to say that there is less nostalgia, either economic or social, in Listnoe than in Moshkino, because there is less objective occasion for it. Material living standards

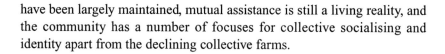

have been largely maintained, mutual assistance is still a living reality, and the community has a number of focuses for collective socialising and identity apart from the declining collective farms.

Conclusion

We have tried to show that what seems to be no more than nostalgic rhetoric may rest, more often than we as anthropologists sometimes suppose, on shared memories of real changes in both objective circumstances and real, though less easily measured, patterns of emotionally significant behaviour. By implication our argument lends support to the school of thought that sees economic activity not merely as a matter of rational self-interest, but also as the expression of emotional attitudes and commitments. We would like, in conclusion, to comment further on the implications of this idea, in general terms and in the Russian context.

The basic argument is that, interwoven with the practical relationships of economic life, there is also an *emotional economy*: a pattern of emotional commitments and rivalries in which people's practical activities also make sense as expressions of their sense of personal identity and community. Some activities are primarily motivated by self-interested rationality, while others may be mostly motivated by the emotional structure of economic relationships – but the activities which will be pursued most vigorously are those which make sense in both rational and emotional terms.

There will always be situations, in any society, in which emotion and rational self-interest pull in different directions. However, in ideal circumstances the practical and emotional sides of economic life would evolve together, and there would be time for them to adapt to each other – so that, by and large, what was economically rational would also be experienced as emotionally appropriate. But in times of economic or political upheaval (which are far from rare in the history of both capitalism and socialism) situations are often likely to arise in which rational self-interest conflicts with established emotional commitments. The question this raises is what happens when a particular kind of activity only makes sense in one of these two possible ways.

In this article we have focused on what happens to an emotional commitment to mutual assistance when it no longer makes sense in terms of individual self-interest. The conclusion was that, although people still felt the sense of commitment, they would not act on that commitment unless they were also reasonably sure that they would not lose out as a result. Where the new economic arrangements meant that mutual aid had become more risky for the potential helper, rational prudence took precedence over emotional generosity.

But what about the opposite situation, in which the new economic arrangements provided people with practical opportunities which made little sense in terms of their existing emotional commitments? Do people's dismissive attitudes to their new certificates of land-share-holding, and their declared preference for collective working styles, help to explain the very low Russian response to the opportunities to set up commercial family farms? There seems no reason to dismiss what people say, given that their statements are consistent with the economic actions they take (or rather don't take). This conclusion is reinforced by some limited anecdotal evidence from our field sites which suggests that those few ordinary (non-elite) Russian country dwellers who do try to make it as *fermery* face emotional difficulties in pursuing their unusual course (Miller and Heady 2003).

These findings tend to confirm our hypothesis that when the courses of action suggested by rational self-interest and by existing emotional commitments are in conflict, neither emotional commitments nor rational opportunities will be properly acted on. They also suggest that further theoretical and research work on the interplay of rationality and emotion in economic life might bring major benefits – improving our ability both to predict the practical success of alternative economic policies, and to assess their potential impact on psychological well-being and social order.

Acknowledgements

Liesl L. Gambold Miller's research in Russia in 1997–98 was funded by the University of California at Los Angeles' International Studies and Overseas Program and the Department of Anthropology, and in 2002 by the Max Planck Institute for Social Anthropology, Halle, Germany. I would also like to thank the people of Moshkino who continue to be exceedingly generous and helpful in my fieldwork, and Masha, my friend and assistant.

Patrick Heady's fieldwork in Russia was carried out during a research fellowship at the Max Plank Institute for Social Anthropology, Halle, Germany. I am also very grateful to colleagues at the State University of St Petersburg and the Moscow Higher School for Social and Economic Sciences for their support during my initial fieldwork in Russia, and during my time in Listnoe, respectively. Finally, I would like to thank the very hospitable family with whom I stayed in Listnoe, and the people who generously gave up their time to answer my questions.

Notes

1. Introductory accounts of the work of these authors and of their place in the main tradition of academic economics are given in Pressman (1999: 20–26, 35–40, 48–53, 57–60, 64–68, 99–105).
2. A case could be made for adding Marx's name to this list, since his critique of capitalism includes its impact on working relationships and the meaning of work (denying workers autonomy and the possibility of creative self-expression). However, for Marx, the potential emotional significance of work is destroyed by capitalism, rather than forming an intrinsic part of the economic system. His analysis of how capitalism operates focuses on the objective relationships of production and exchange, and in that sense belongs in the main economic tradition of analysing rational choice under constraint (Fine and Saad-Filho 2004; Pressman 1999: 48–53).
3. Not its real name.
4. Her pension is 1,100 roubles a month and her wage 700 roubles a month. This is roughly US $60 at the 2002 exchange rate.
5. Of sixty-five adults surveyed.
6. Because in the early 1990s Russians were given land but had no right to sell it, many had no choice but to 'give' their shares back to the new director. In addition, this was considered by many to be the 'right' thing to do in order to keep the collective land together.
7. See Miller and Heady (2003).

Bibliography

Axelrod, R. 1984. *The Evolution of Cooperation*. New York: Basic Books.

Blum, J. 1961. *Lord and Peasant in Russia from the Ninth to the Nineteenth Century*. Princeton: Princeton University Press.

Bourdieu, P. 1977. *Outline of a Theory of Practice*. Cambridge: Cambridge University Press.

———— 1984. *Distinction: a Social Critique of the Judgement of Taste*. London: Routledge and Kegan Paul.

Campbell, S. 1994. 'Being Dismissed. The Politics of Emotional Expression', *Hypatia* 9(3): 46–65.

Dunn, S. and Dunn, E. 1988. *The Peasants of Central Russia*. Prospect Heights, IL: Waveland Press.

Durkheim, E. 1984 [1893]. *The Division of Labour in Society*. Basingstoke: Macmillan.

Fine, B. and Saad-Filho, A. 2004. *Marx's Capital* (fourth edition). London: Pluto Press.

Hardin, G. 1968. 'The Tragedy of the Commons', *Science* 162(3859) (13 December 1968): 1243–48.

Henrich, J., Boyd R., Bowles, S., Camerer, C., Fehr, E., Gintis, H., McElreath, R. 2001. 'In Search of Homo Economicus: Behavioural Experiments in 15

Small-scale Societies', *American Economic Review* (Papers and Proceedings), 91(2): 73–78.

Hume, D. 1978 [1939–40]. *A Treatise of Human Nature*, ed. L.A. Selby-Bigge and P.H. Nidditch. Oxford: Oxford University Press.

Malinowski, B. 1978 [1935]. *Coral Gardens and Their Magic*. New York: Dover Publications.

Mauss, M. 2002 [1923]. *The Gift: the Form and Reason for Exchange in Archaic Societies*. London: Routledge.

Mauss, M. and Beuchat, H. 1979 [1905]. *Seasonal Variations of the Eskimo: a Study in Social Morphology*. London: Routledge and Kegan Paul.

Miller, L. and Heady, P. 2003. 'Cooperation, Power, and Community: Economy and Ideology in the Russian Countryside', in *The Postsocialist Agrarian Question: Property Relations and the Rural Condition*, ed. C. Hann. Münster: LIT.

Nikulin, A. 2003. 'Kuban *Kolkhoz* between a Holding and a Hacienda: Contradictions of Post-Soviet Rural Development', *Focaal. European Journal of Anthropology* 41: 137–52.

O'Brien, D. and Wegren, S., eds. 2002. *Rural Reform in Post-soviet Russia*. Baltimore and London: The Johns Hopkins University Press.

Pressman, S. 1999. *Fifty Major Economists*. London and New York: Routledge.

Putnam, R. 1994. *Making Democracy Work*. Princeton: Princeton University Press.

Scott, J.C. 1976. *The Moral Economy of the Peasant*. New Haven: Yale University Press.

Shanin, T. 1986. *Russia as a 'Developing Society'*. Vol. 1 of *The Roots of Otherness: Russia's Turn of the Century*. New Haven and London: Yale University Press.

Skrbiš, Z. 2002. 'The Emotional Historiography of Venetologists. Slovene Diaspora, Memory and Nationalism', *Focaal. European Journal of Anthropology* 39: 41–56.

Stroev, E.S. 2001. *Mnogoukladnaya agrarnaya ekonomika i rossiskaya derevniya*. Moscow: Kolos.

Visser, O. 2003. 'Property and Post-communist Poverty: Can the Mystery of Capital be Exported to the Former Soviet Countryside', *Focaal. European Journal of Anthropology* 41: 197–202.

Wanner, C. 1998. *Burden of Dreams*. Pennsylvania: Pennsylvania State University Press.

Weber, M. 1991 [1915]. 'The Social Psychology of the World Religions', in *From Max Weber: Essays in Sociology*, eds. H.H. Gerth and C. Wright Mills. London: Routledge, pp. 267–301.

Chapter 2

Social Suffering and Political Protest: Mapping Emotions and Power among Pomaks in Postsocialist Bulgaria

Dimitrina Mihaylova

What have we not suffered! We are in the end here, far from God and Government! And now, we are again left to deal alone, where is the state? It is in Sofia, it does not give us money any more, it does not want us, it wants us to leave, but we have no other state to go to, we are like the Palestinians!

Pomaks from the village of Dren.

Introduction

The Bulgarian mountainous borderlands along the state border with Greece underwent significant socioeconomic and political transformations during the socialist period. The socialist state had transformed the isolated and infertile mountain borderlands of southeastern rural Bulgaria into a symbolic 'head' of national territory because it was the land along the state Cold War frontier with Greece. The region was viewed and treated as a national economic treasure because of the production and export of tobacco, the main source of hard currency at the time. Special economic incentives such as tax reduction, special border overhead payment, higher salaries and free utilities, were provided. This was adjoined by the introduction (at times forceful) of practices associated locally with 'modernity', 'urban culture' and 'civilisation': depeasantisation, modern infrastructure (roads, hospitals, electricity, machines), secularism, modern dress, civil customs and education.

Since socialism's demise, the state has stripped this border region of its national symbolism and importance. It discontinued its economic privileges and restituted the scattered and unwanted land in the midst of growing socioeconomic and political crises and a decline in tobacco prices. These crises have resulted in significant transformations of local social and political relations, and mostly in the repeasantisation, remarginalisation and outmigration of Pomaks[1] who inhabit the borderland between Bulgaria and Greece (see, for an analysis of the emotional dimensions of economic marginalisation in rural Russia, Chapter 2, this volume). These developments have been especially felt after the reopening of state borders and their loss of ideological dress at the end of the Cold War. New socioeconomic divides on both sides of the border have become more visible with the European Union (EU) formation: Greece has become a member of the EU while Bulgaria has remained an ascending country. Today's abrupt abjunction from the nation-state and its previous 'modernity', the rapid decline of living standards, growing poverty and increased perception of powerlessness have all been experienced and expressed locally as an extreme form of social suffering and a 'return to the past', to pre-socialist 'backwardness', insecurity and misery.

In these circumstances Pomaks have created an elaborate rhetoric of poverty, loneliness and devastation that is expressed and lived as poetics of suffering (Herzfeld 1985). This rhetoric is an expression of the tension between conflicting social categories arising from the loss of the domesticated socialist system (Creed 1998). But it is also an expression of dissatisfaction with the state which, by withdrawing abruptly from this region, has transformed it into an impoverished periphery. The dominating emotional landscape is also fuelled by an acute anxiety in the process of local redefinition of ethnic and national belonging stemming from the community deepening marginalisation. Locally, this is interpreted as a form of ethnic discrimination against a Muslim minority. Narratives and performances of social suffering do indeed dominate everyday practice in the area and, as such, became not only a background tune of my research, but also have become the very subject of it, like the experience described by Ferguson (1999: 18). I follow Bourdieu (1999: 64) in his definitions of 'social suffering' as 'the destiny effect from belonging to a stigmatised group' in the 'abandoned sites that are fundamentally defined by an *absence* – basically, that of the state and of everything that comes with it ...' (ibid.: 123, author's emphasis), 'characterised by a lack of power over the present', 'absolute uncertainty about the future' , 'the feeling of being tied to a degrading ("rotten") place' (ibid.: 185), which puts you in an 'inferior, obscure position in a prestigious and privileged universe' (ibid.: 4).

This chapter examines one case of how borderlanders' 'suffering' (*stradane, maka, bolka*) of disconnection, humiliation and socioeconomic and political disadvantage (Bourdieu 1999, Ferguson 1999), was transformed into emotional capital (Skrbiš 2002). The latter was, in turn, employed in a political protest: in a strike addressing the government about the low tobacco prices. Through the combined perspective of emotions as strategic narrative performance and embodied experience, I study how people used their emotions to overcome fear of protest, and to empower and protect themselves in a political action (Svašek 2002: 18). Thus, the chapter engages current anthropological debates about the significance of emotions to political, economic and social life in postsocialist societies, which demonstrate 'how people use emotional dynamics to actively respond to and generate a wide variety of changes', whereby they should be considered as 'active players in a complex field of interconnected local, national and transnational political and therefore emotional settings' (ibid., 21).

In the first part of the chapter I show the major ways in which social suffering (*narodno stradanie*, people's suffering) is experienced and expressed in the Pomak village of Dren and its surrounding area – not only as a local sentiment of disconnection and powerlessness but also as a strategy to preserve dignity and pride. The second part describes the main stages in the preparation and performance of the village protest and strike (*stachka*) and demonstrates how these were set in the emotional style of 'social suffering' for particular strategic reasons, not only because they dominate everyday life in the area. The villagers used emotional arguments to justify moral accusation of the government, to put the politicians 'to shame' and to reclaim their lost rights in the name of socioeconomic justice. My main focus is on the political significance of emotional discourses and I aim to provide an insight into the dialectics of politics and emotions (ibid., 12) through depicting how an emotion such as suffering is transformed from a signification of powerlessness into political capital that in its turn transforms the everyday experience of 'pain'.

The ethnography of decline in the postsocialist transition cannot be understood simply in the examination of stages of development before and after socialism or of how people adapt to the transition. Instead, I examine a range of reactions and strategies that shift over time in ways that do not sustain a simple linear narration (see also Ferguson 1999: 20). Although changes during socialism were significant, it is impossible to classify them as completed acts of 'modernisation'. This was a modernisation 'through the looking glass' that is today 'the object of a nostalgic reverie' while 'backwardness' is 'the anticipated (or dreaded) future' (Ferguson 1999: 13).

The myth of the 'modernisation' of life, as imposed by the socialist state, has provided a set of categories that continue to shape people's experiences and interpretations (Creed 1998: 273; Ferguson 1999: 14). Thus, the cultural style[2] of socialism, one that is locally defined as 'urban', 'civilised' and 'Bulgarian' went together with a rapid improvement in living standards that are now irretrievably lost. This cultural style, designating a certain social category, that of the peasant who does not perceive him/herself as 'a wild and uncultured Pomak peasant' but as a 'modern, secular and cultured Bulgarian citizen', is now inhibited by socioeconomic and political developments, peripheralisation and marginalisation. The current social categories' reclassification is thus experienced as a return (or a threat to return) to what is locally seen as the 'premodern past': that of wilderness, misery, disconnection, peasant unculturedness, subsistence agriculture, and Islamic religious practice.[3]

It is the very tension between socialist and postsocialist cultural styles (believed by the Pomaks to be opposite experiences) that generates feelings of misery and despair among the Pomaks. In this particular sociohistorical and geographic context, postsocialist suffering signifies (the real or perceived) differences and tensions between rural and urban communities. Inherent to this process is the production and reinforcement of images of 'civilised versus uncivilised', 'cultured versus wild and uncultured', 'Bulgarian versus non-Bulgarian', 'moral versus immoral', 'Christian versus Muslim' and 'secular versus religious'. Furthermore, the suffering of the victims of transition is opposed to the happiness of their perceived victimisers, namely, the politicians and the government, seen locally as 'the state'. The expression of suffering also entails a performative competence and requires not just a situational motive but also a whole set of internalised capabilities acquired overtime (Ferguson 1999: 96).

Social Suffering and the Experience of 'Absence'

Dren (a pseudonym) is an entirely Pomak village[4] in the border municipality of Birgrad (also a pseudonym). The population of the municipality is mixed and comprised of Turks (a majority), Pomaks, Bulgarians of Christian origin (a minority) and some Roma. The town of Birgrad is the only town in this border municipality. The borderline follows the watershed of the mountain and the highest peaks. The strip of land along the border, the highest part of the mountain, is also known locally as 'Dren and the region', and includes all Pomak villages along the border on the tarmac road passing through the main village of Dren (of about 450 people).

The municipality of Birgrad (about 20,000 people) is in a rural mountainous area, dominated by tobacco cultivation and primary processing. Pomaks live in small and scattered villages (ranging between five and 1,200 people). Pomak settlements are along the border, in the highest parts of the mountain, while Turks and Roma live in the lower parts of the mountain and around the town, where most Bulgarians of Christian origin are to be found. Although the border is only about 30 kilometres from the town and between two and ten kilometres from the Pomak villages, there is no legal border crossing in this area and the nearest one (of two for the whole border) is about 120 kilometres east of Birgrad. This area is indeed remote and very few visitors are ever to be seen. As middle-aged Pomaks often say: 'it is a dead place [*martvilo*], no one comes here, there is no one to break your silence [*Da ti narushava tishinata*]'.

This lack of noise is associated with 'lack of life' (*nyama zivot*), and this refers to both demographic and economic stagnation: the lack of young people and the rapid depopulation of the whole mountain. 'Dead silence' (*martvilo*), standing for loneliness, poverty and decline, is experienced as one of the major fuels of suffering. It refers to a comparison with the late socialist period where: 'there was a lot of noise, a lot of life'. Locals describe in detail how one could hear a rich variety of sounds and the following is the summary of their descriptions in a number of local narratives. Prominent noises of socialism, for example, came from the machines in the fields (symbols of depeasantisation, industrialisation and mechanisation of the cooperatives), from the school over crowded with children, or from the singing of the village folk group that used to travel to many national and international folk festivals (but does not exist anymore). The frequent references to suffering as an absence of sound and bodily movement suggests that suffering is experienced bodily, and should thus not be analysed as a purely mental or discursive practice. Instead, the experience of suffering is embodied, and on an analytical level, thus bridges the domains of body and mind (Leavitt 1996; see also Svašek, Chapter 4).

Socialist modernisation had, indeed, transformed local cultural style by bringing big two-or three-storey houses, more high school and university graduates, modern schools, surfaced roads, new cars, constant electricity (and the TV, radio and gramophone), modern water systems, huge savings and pensions. This is remembered today with the constant national music, news or instructions from the village sound system that included the village in the wider national collective through uniform style. Exuberant joy and laughter, buzzing life and the large number of parties where people used to sing and dance dominate the memories of socialism. The most popular type of party was the so-called *cheverme*, called after the way meat is prepared: the whole lamb is barbequed in the open air by turning it slowly over fire. In those days, families and friends would often retreat to selected nature spots with cold water and deep shade to have *cheverme* but today, hardly anyone organises it. In other words, the postsocialist experience of silence is interpreted as a signifier of disconnection and marginalisation (Creed 2002). As one middle-aged woman put it: 'I sometimes feel like shouting from this dead silence (*martvilo*), there is no more life here anymore.'

Then, most people had full-time 'state' jobs as factory workers, tractor drivers and mechanics, whilst others were teachers or administrators in the TKZS (the cooperative farm Trudovo Koopertivno Zemedelsko Stopanstvo). More importantly, very few had full-time occupation as farmers. Tobacco was only grown for the state during weekends, holidays and before or after work. Tobacco was also considered a second category and a 'woman's job'. Today, in contrast, subsistence agriculture has expanded owning to the scarcity of money to buy food, and tobacco growing has remained the only reliable occupation for both men and women.

Socialist Myths of Modernisation and the 'Civilisation' of Pomaks

Even though, initially, socialist rule had imposed a particular cultural style by force, this style became gradually less conflicting and even desired by many. This can partly be explained by the fact that Pomaks perceived it as a possibility given by the state to escape from the stereotype of 'backwardness'. This was achieved predominantly through disassociation from peasant identities (Creed 1998: 273) that, in the case of Pomaks, had a specific ethnic flavour, as described elsewhere (Mihaylova 2003). Pomaks adopted and displayed the 'modern', 'socialist' and 'civilised' cultural style, dropped their Muslim names and Islamic practice, and embraced the names and the civil rituals enforced by the state.

Pomaks have inhabited the Balkan Mountain Ranges from the Eastern Rodhopi to the North Albanian Mountains for centuries. They have been predominantly pastoralists and farmers (Georgieva 1998). The rest of their history is highly controversial, and has sat uneasily within the antagonistic Balkan nationalisms, which sought to achieve a 'pure nation' without minorities and within the widest borders possible, based on medieval legacies and notions of an 'ethnic' homeland. Following this model of the 'nation', the assimilation of smaller religious and ethnic groups had become a preoccupation of the Balkan states (ibid.: 291–92).

National ideologues have considered Pomaks to be incomplete Bulgarians for two main reasons (Alexiev 1998; Mancheva 2001; Mihaylova 2003). Firstly, one of the Ottoman legacies is the association of 'Muslim' with 'Turkish' identity, irrespective of whether the Muslim is Bulgarian, Gypsy or Turk. The nation was defined according to common language, territory, history and culture, including religion (Christian Orthodoxy), whereby Pomaks were not 'true' Bulgarians. Every effort was directed towards distancing Pomaks from any type of pro-Turkish or pro-Islamic influence and restoring their 'Bulgarian roots'. Even a slight relation to anything Turkish was claimed to be a further betrayal of the Bulgarian nation in post-Ottoman times. Secondly, Pomaks were seen to be more religious and less cultured than other Bulgarians and this resulted in their being thought of as backward (Alexiev 1998).

The central state engineered various operations to remove the signs of Muslim identity from the Pomaks such as their names, clothing, religious rituals and traditions and mosques. The last and most thorough action ('Revival Process') was in the 1960s–1970s when all Pomak names were Slavicised (e.g. Ibrahim became Ivan), modern dress replaced traditional one, religious practice was completely forbidden and mosques destroyed. Most Pomaks in Dren today do not want to see themselves being divided in any way from Bulgarians in public discourse or treated as 'the other', especially when the old pejorative connotations of 'Pomak' as 'uncultured peasants' are invoked in opposition to the 'civilised Bulgarians'. After 1989, only about thirty elderly men and women have returned to using their Muslim names in their documents (passports, identity cards, etc.); the rest of Dreniots have kept their 'Bulgarian' names, use them in everyday life and continue to give such names to the newborn. Children born today do not tend to have Muslim names given even symbolically.

The Postsocialist 'Civilisational' and 'Moral' Decay

Today, with freedom of religious practice and ethnic self-identification, the ambiguous position of Pomaks in the Bulgarian nation has reappeared with full force in both national and local discourses about origin and belonging. The only new noise in the village today is the singing of the *imam* in the newly built mosque[5] in the village on Fridays. The majority of young and middle-aged people who grew up during or after socialism perceive this as a return to 'backwardness' and to 'the past before socialism' that is remembered as 'misery' and 'wilderness/unculturedness' (*mizeria i prostotia*). Several villagers mobilised themselves and organised the building of a Christian Orthodox chapel in the village to balance what they call 're-Islamisation of naïve people' and reclaim the thinning links to what they define as 'modernity' and, today, even as 'Europeanness'.

Regardless of whether they belonged to the pro-Islamic or the pro-Christian group in the village, Pomaks became increasingly sensitive to public debates about their 'ethnic' origin and have recently begun to question previously accepted answers. The tensions between self-understanding, self-presentation and categorisation have re-emerged in the process of postsocialist restructuring. The resulting ambiguity of their socioeconomic positions has become another source of tension in village life and breeds a significant amount of suffering as a result of becoming 'the other' not only among Bulgarians but also among co-villagers (as a result of rapid social diversification). Being a peasant and remaining in the village leads not only to a cycle of poverty but places one in a marginal ethnic and religious minority. The ideal today is to migrate to the towns. Such migrations of individual families usually involve hiding of the Pomak (Islamic) origin and self-presentation as Bulgarians. Pomak origin is not disclosed at any price when Pomaks establish in towns unless they live surrounded by other Pomaks.

Most, however, cannot afford to establish themselves in the towns and have engaged in international labour migration (usually illegal) to gather funds (Mihaylova 2002). Most young and middle-aged men work abroad, and, in the last few years, the number of women is increasing too. Older people say: 'Our children are all leaving, and when they are away or when they suffer [*machat*] here in poverty, it hurts us, we miss them painfully [*detsata bolyat*]', or 'We, the old, have to stay in the village to feed the young ones that go to the town, but while people in the West look forward to getting old, we fear it: if we get ill, there is not money for treatment, no one to help, and our children are dispersed [*detsata se razprasnaha*]: women on one side, men on the other, their children on third, everyone in a different country trying to earn money, everyone is a labour migrant [*gurbetchia*]'. Thus, the increased migration and separation of families is painfully experienced every day, especially by the older generation. The inability to look after the children and the aged (that is, to educate children to the highest level possible and help them financially; and to remain close to one's parents to care for them when they age) is considered locally as immoral and shameful. Thus, the inability to provide care for the youth and the aged has become another source of suffering.

Repeasantisation and Tobacco Production

These multiple sources of suffering have recently become channelled though the way people feel about tobacco and its central role in their life. Pomaks' livelihoods depend solely[6] on tobacco production, a 'state' culture. Introduced by the state in the 1950s, and soon afterwards made obligatory, it became the state's 'gold' – one of the best sources of hard currency during socialism. However, tobacco production was mechanised and often just a supplement to another job of a higher status in the cooperative farm or elsewhere. It was well-paid.

Ever since the arrival of tobacco in Dren (and up to 2004), the central state owned and fully regulated the tobacco business, including the ownership and management of the tobacco industry and market. Recently, parts of this sector have been privatised and some private companies appeared in the buyer's market. Despite variation in prices, state regulation persists and most importantly, the central state allocates special premiums (price-top up per kilogram of tobacco) for both tobacco companies and tobacco producers. For the Pomaks, tobacco embodies their relationship with the state, and it is the very last link that people perceive to be alive today.[7]

People often contrast growing tobacco today to growing other cultures in the valleys around the bigger towns in Bulgaria. As it was put by a middle-aged couple from Dren: 'The villagers in the valley say they planted some pumpkins so they now claim they are *Fermeri* ['farmers', that is, 'businessmen' or 'modern capitalists' as sometimes the locals define it], while we plant tobacco and we can only be *tutunjii* [people who grow tobacco], that is, *prost narod* [uncultured/wild people], even here in the village people say that they have planted tobacco and a few private things which means that we also do not see tobacco as a private job, it is all for the state, it is a state job, but before the state used to pay state jobs well.'

The relationship between Pomaks and the state, based on tobacco, is a relationship of power imbalance and is very negatively perceived. Tobacco growing today is seen to be a dirty and demeaning job (once reserved mainly for women), paid rather poorly for what it entails, as local define it: 'dirt and heavy work, being bent, all year round'. It is often repeated in conversations that 'the state has enslaved us: one family (parents and two children) can hardly cover its annual expenses with the maximum of tobacco they can physically plant and sell in one season' (for an analysis of negative perceptions of 'the state' in Poland, see Kalb and Tak, Chapter 9, this volume).

Further complicating this relationship is the fact that tobacco farmers tend to be ethnic and religious minorities, mainly Turks and Pomaks, who happen to inhabit the most suitable terrains for it. For this reason, *tutunjii* (people who grow tobacco) has acquired a negative connotation as reference to a minority, 'an other' of an inferior status. As this is a mostly rural and mountainous population who also practise Islam, this negative stereotype also has connotations of backwardness, religious fanaticism and unculturedness. Thus, *tutunjii* (like 'Pomaks') is a pejorative and demeaning term in every sense of the word. Even during socialism, when it used to be highly paid and mechanised, tobacco farming was the alternative civilisational choice to the prestigious state administrative and industrial jobs. It was mainly the least well educated and those who only wanted to supplement their income that grew tobacco. Nowadays, any villager in the locality having to become *tutunjia* again therefore becomes a 'Pomak' and by extension, a 'non-Bulgarian', a second-class citizen.

The conditions of work in the tobacco fields today strengthen the perception of a return to the 'precivilised era'. As one villager observed: 'We used to have tractors to plough the land, there was no need to dig, now it is all work by hand, we spend the summers bended over; now you see people ploughing with their donkeys and cows, some women or men strand themselves as animals to be able to plough their own land, I feel like crying when I see this, this is how our ancestors used to live in the past of misery, primitivism and backwardness.' This hatred is also directed to the land: 'We now hate the land, our ancestors used to love it and look after it as they would look after a child, now, you can see it is full of stones, no one clears it, no one protects it from erosion. We use it as an instrument for money and would use all the shortcuts to get paid without much care for the land itself, land is a burden, everyone dreams of leaving it and its dirty tobacco.'

The way local people indeed perceive this situation today is one of 'enslavement' by the state. Tobacco is 'dehumanising' and 'primitive' yet it is their only option for survival. Its negative perceptions have been made more acute since locals were able to meet their Pomak relatives and neighbours from the Greek side of the border where tobacco is much better paid owing to European Union subsidies. Even though Pomaks in Bulgaria think of them as people in a lower civilisational category (for being very Islamic, speaking Turkish, and preserving patriarchal traditions), they find themselves socioeconomically inferior. Pomak women from Dren and its region often work illegally or semi-legally for cash for Greek Pomaks but complain about their 'backwardness'. They say, 'we have to work for them, while we have better education and we are more "civilised" or "European" than them: we wear European clothes and are equal with men, they have to stay at home all day and never go out with their husbands'. While the official national discourses all expressed pride in the former socialist border as 'the beginning and the end of the motherland', it is now an embarrassment and a humiliation. The opening of the socialist border has exposed socioeconomic barriers and divisions. The deepening economic and sociopolitical crisis has thus resulted in a perceived return to 'a primitive past', in repeasantisation, remarginalisation and outmigration.

Narratives of Suffering as Social Instruments

With time, I came to realise that the constant repeat and exchange of an endless variation of one and the same narrative about suffering had deeper importance than the mere informative function about what was going on. It created a comforting reassurance between people about their similar situation. This is how it masked the rapidly increasing new social divisions (within a community valuing egalitarianism), based on growing gaps between people in poverty and the few who were getting richer. More importantly, it appeared that this was a way to demonstrate competence of what they knew they deserved: in this way, one's poverty was not one's immoral quality – it was inflicted on them, who were being trapped and victimised by the state (cf. Boltanski 1993; Iliev 2003). It was also a specific form of protest free from fear of political persecution or of the social stigma of being a 'protester'.

The rhetoric of suffering was not exclusive to the borderlands. Even people in the capital feel similarly disconnected and 'betrayed' by a state which is undergoing all sorts of crisis and perpetually restructuring (Mihaylova 2003). But Pomaks on the border believe this to be specific to their situation alone, or at least that they are in the worst situation. Conflict between fantasies, practices and experiences, with the state surrounding simultaneously social categorisation, politics, marginalisation, ethnicity, border, tobacco and land have charged tension and suffering in the process of coining self-understanding and aspirations. This is how a group of informal village leaders decided to break the silence of suffering. They were determined to communicate their pain to the politicians, express clearly how they felt and address them with a specific demand to relieve their situation: the increase of tobacco prices.

The Strike: Social Suffering as Emotional Capital

This section describes some of the main elements of the protest meeting (called locally and further below *stachka*) in order to demonstrate how emotions were employed as a political weapon in the claims for social justice (see, for an analysis of the emotional dimensions of political protest in Poland, Golanska-Ryan, Chapter 7, this volume). It is beyond the scope of this paper to provide a full situational analysis of the strike and here I only illustrate the main arguments of this chapter with the ways suffering was staged and expressed during the actual protest. Individual and community social suffering was used by the organisers to demonstrate, firstly, the moral legitimacy of their claims and, secondly, to mask the political meaning of their act because of the fear caused by threats they had received from local authorities and tobacco companies (if they proceeded with the protest). The suffering was also used to put government and politicians 'to shame'. It was an instrument of accusation and a threat too: they demonstrated inability to continue to contain these strong emotions of pain and their transformation into anger. This anger was shown as capable of becoming a motor of justified breaching of legal regulations: the threat that the whole village would cross the border and move to Greece without seeking permission; people would sell their tobacco in Greece instead – at higher prices; that they would burn this year's crop and would not produce tobacco the following year (which villagers believed to be a really serious threat, as it would diminish the state quotas of tobacco in the negotiations for joining the EU).

Thus, the protesters declared that no one would sell their tobacco until prices were corrected. A further list of demands prepared by the organisers, all based on legal regulations, was also declared. However, these were only read at the end of the public meeting. The preceding two stages of the the *stachka* included two very important elements: the first one was a presentation of the general circumstances of life causing the suffering of the people and the major injustice caused by the politicians. The second element was a series of individual presentations of 'pain' on the stage.

The *stachka* was organised on an autumn morning in October 2000 after tobacco had been gathered from the fields and was being prepared for sale. At around that time, the central government was expected to announce the prices at which tobacco would be bought that season starting from November. The preparatory phase of the strike included searching for supporters in the village, informing neighbouring villages and other tobacco-producing regions, securing the arrival of media reporters and informing the municipality (according to the legal requirements for announcing an organised protest). Most of these actions were executed through personal contacts of the organisers. They called their relatives, friends and contacts. For example, they telephoned mayors from further-away regions whom the mayor of Dren knew, they called the cleaner at a big international news agency in Sofia to ask her to tell the people there to report the strike; and they went around neighbours and relatives in the village to make sure these would turn up on the square the morning of the strike. At the same time, the organisers watched the TV news and picked up the telephone numbers after the program; then called and announced the strike and asked for cameras and reporters. Most central and local newspapers and radio stations were also informed either through personal contacts or formal telephone calls.

The night before the strike there was a village meeting, where the order of activities during the protest was defined and tasks were delegated to different people outside the strike committee. The demands to the government were read out aloud and a few comments were incorporated. Slogans and posters were prepared, shouting in groups was practised. The mechanisms of strike preparation were spontaneously based on an idea of what a strike should be like. As the organisers explained: 'You go about preparing the strike as you do anything else in the village: you see what your neighbour does and you do the same. We saw from the TV and from the newspapers how other people do their strikes and we do the same.'

The strike committee consisted of several informal leaders from the village of Dren and three couples in their late thirties or early fourties (including the mayor of Dren and his wife). However, the strike became known locally as a 'women's affair' as the men stayed in the background of all preparations and execution for fear of being fired or sanctioned in some other way. All those men had state jobs and were reluctant to protest against the government but they provided a safety shield: they were ready for negotiations and compromise and to declare the strike a 'silly women's enterprise', in case the tobacco companies refused to buy the tobacco or prolonged its buying until spring (when it would be mouldy and would lose its price). The latter was a sanction that everyone knew the companies had applied in another region that had organised an unsuccessful strike a few years ago. In that case people had been forced to sell their tobacco at very low prices. Although Dreniots threatened that they would not sell their tobacco, it was clear to everyone that they had no other choice to provide income for the coming year. This position of powerlessness was covered up during the strike with the threats that they would go and work abroad, or sell the tobacco in Greece, or just eat the food they produced in their own fields.

On the morning of the strike, Dreniots gathered in the village square, waited for some supporters from neighbouring villages and for journalists to arrive. Then, the prepared performance of suffering began. It was meant to address the government and all Bulgarian politicians through the camera lenses, radio broadcasts and newspaper articles. In the first part of the strike, the wife of the mayor spoke about the general consequences of low tobacco prices. She explained how the legally provided state premium (of one Lev per kilogram, that is about US$ 0.50 per kg) for stimulation of tobacco production and manipulation had not reached the producers but remained instead in the pockets of the companies that bought tobacco. This was caused by lack of governmental control over how the state premium is distributed and used. It was a clear breach of agreement with the tobacco producers, who were supposed to receive their share.

The villages in this municipality that were mentioned as participating in the strike were only the Pomak ones. Later on, during the *stachka*, they read a support letter from a neighbouring, mainly Pomak, tobacco-producing municipality, which claimed to be ready to join (this was assured through a personal contact). Although locally the ethnic character of the strike was obvious (Turks, Roma or Bulgarian Christians from neighbouring areas of the same municipality were not directly involved), everyone knew that in the national public space it would have been hard to tell it by just hearing names of villages that meant nothing to outsiders of the local ethnic geography. The subtlety in this formulation came from the fact that *tutunji* (tobacco producers) is indeed associated with 'Muslim minorities'. Thus, the 'Pomak' character of the strike was implied without being officially stated.

The organisers played the 'ethnic card' of protest in the subtlest way possible. This diplomatically addressed also The Movement for Rights and Freedoms (called locally the 'Turkish Party' for being dominated by ethnic Turks), who were a major political force in the region[8] and in the national tobacco affairs (and a coalition partner in the government at that time). This party was seeking the region's Pomak votes, without much prior success.

More importantly, as they explained to me later on, in order to demonstrate their loyalty to the state, Dreniots never mentioned anything about their ethnic or minority status. This deliberate silence on the ethnic theme was also dictated by fear of further sanctions. Thus, the central part of their suffering, caused by their belief that they are discriminated against on ethnic grounds, remained unvoiced. The protest was instead based on legitimate (cf. Boltanski 1993) common sensibilities, 'nation wide popular' language expressions and well-known themes from the national TV and press: the future of children, the situation of pensioners, the unfulfilled promises of the government, the return to a higher living standard from the years of misery before socialism.

The first part continued with the speech of a woman from a neighbouring village who was summoned in order to widen the participation of the population. An ex-socialist activist and a member of the Bulgarian Socialist Party (BSP), she spoke at length about injustice and misery. This woman was skilled in socialist phraseology and presentations on the 'needs of the people'. She was also occasionally interrupted by the audience, who were shouting the prepared and exercised slogans written on posters: 'It is enough – we are people and not voters'; 'We do not want crumbs for our gold'; 'We do not want crumbles, we want money'; 'We want bread and a future for our children'; 'Why do you force us to become *gurbetchii* [migrants]?'

The speakers illustrated their arguments with some examples of how much a family earns and spends from tobacco: a family of four could produce on average about 850 kg, which the preceding year would have been valued at about Lev 2,500 (about US$ 1,000), of which about Lev 1,500 would be used to post-pay the production expenses. The remaining 1,000 would be divided by twelve months: about eighty Lev per month, which is then divided among four members of the family and the result is about twenty Lev per person monthly income. The speakers cited a press publication stating that people living with under two US dollars a day should be considered on the border of poverty, then they shouted together with the crowd: 'At which border are we then with sometimes less than two Lev per week?'. Then the organisers invited people from the audience (as if spontaneously, but this had also been prepared at the meeting preceding the protest): 'Please now, those who are not ashamed to express their pain, come on the stage and tell us how you feel, everyone should feel free to express their pain.'

This opened up the second part of the strike: a number of prearranged speeches and some spontaneous ones. All of them were expressions of individual or family suffering and most provoked tears and crying among both men and women in the audience. The older women in the audience cried intermittently most of the time but particularly when the subject of children was discussed.

Three main categories of people spoke (most of whom were women), and these were clearly roles chosen by the organisers from the current national discourses of 'people's suffering' (*narodno stradanie*): the suffering mother who cannot feed and educate her children; the young people who suffer because they cannot continue to study and who feel pressurised to emigrate; and the pensioners who suffer seeing that their children are dependent on their pensions or who live alone as their children had to leave the area in search of a better life. Only three men spoke – two pensioners and one student.

The speakers were presented as the morally elevated, deserving and loyal people who sacrificed themselves for the state but had in the end become its victims – a local tragedy that has to be read as an indivisible part of the national one. They re-invoked the socialist discourse that was well internalised among the local strike organisers and often used in national media discourses to address the Pomak situation (e.g. the Pomaks as victims of various policies, see also Mihaylova 2000).

Each of the three main categories of people who spoke (mothers, youth and pensioners) presented one major aspect of community-wide suffering. These included the inability of parents to provide for their children, the lack of access to education or the job market of young people and the loneliness of the elderly. All of these presented a different version of the narrative of return to 'precivilised times' and most gave examples of how people worked the fields by hand, with donkeys and cows, and using a wooden plough instead of machines. This was seen as a sign of return to premodern and precivilised times. All of these sources of suffering were meant to put the government 'to shame' for allowing it all to happen: 'We should express our pain without shame because those politicians in Sofia should see it as it is so that they finally look at us as what we are: human beings. They live on our work, they are stealing from us, from our people, but it is high time they must start appreciating our work accordingly!' Other villagers noted: 'We suffer a lot, our children cry every day, and we cry with them, let them see how we really live and be ashamed!', or 'We are ashamed to be living in Bulgaria.' This is how, through simultaneously challenging the unjust policies of the state while adhering to the legitimate and formal nation-state discourses, fantasies and experiences of suffering, Dreniots deconstructed one face of the nation-state while they constructed another (cf. Navaro-Yashin 2003).

The strike was shown briefly on national television and was initially unsuccessful. However, a few weeks later, it was repeated by the same organisers in the town of Birgrad, the centre of the local municipality. Eventually, the government did not, as the protesters had wanted, change the tobacco prices but instead enforced the payment of the premium of 1 Lev per kilo of tobacco made to the companies *and* the producers. This policy change was not so much a direct consequence of the strike itself but rather resulted from political competition, as some of the political players involved decided to defend their own interests while arguing that they represented this popular unrest. Regardless of its initial failure, the strike had significant indirect effects. It did open a new chapter in the negotiation between the state and the tobacco producers. This triggered a significant chain of events that redefined the relationships between people and state and increased the scope of citizens' civic participation because of – and despite – the wrapping of this political process in emotional practices.

Conclusion

Pomak social suffering was born with the loss of the previously higher living standard, and the loss of their elevated status as a borderland population. As victims of the transition, the Pomaks have been forced to leave the state as migrants, cross the border illegally, or break legal contracts with tobacco producers. Furthermore, they are no longer perceived as 'true Bulgarians' and are turned into the postsocialist ethnic 'other'. Their current situation seems to be marked by humiliation and desperation.

Yet the Pomak complaints do not only express feelings of hopelessness and despondency. Performed in the context of public protest, they actively demand moral justice and true citizen rights from the Bulgarian state. All performances during the strike stressed the unjust division of Bulgarians into 'suffering' and 'non-suffering' citizens, and by extension into 'powerless' and 'powerful' subjects. On the basis of these perceived oppositions, a politics of pity (Boltanski 1993) was demanded from the state. The emotional cry for help, however, also carried the threat that the Pomak feelings of suffering could transform into anger, trigger accusations of injustice, and generate more strikes that would potentially affect the wider society.

Performances of individual suffering were used as a political tool to achieve the wider public's compassion, as well as demand policy change. This form of political activism was part of the nationwide public discourse about justice for all citizens, in particular for the most disadvantaged (Leutloff 2002: 59). The villagers also successfully contributed to nation wide debates about the more widespread economic problems inherent in the transition process. They almost literally reflected the main outlines of numerous TV and newspaper reports on women with many children, poor pensioners and young people's problems. By incorporating local experiences into a much more widespread discourse of 'small versus big', the Pomak demand for justice was rendered publicly legitimate. Another strategy the protesters used was to confront their public with highly personalised portrayals of human suffering in an attempt to reach audiences that were distanced from their locality (Boltanski 1993: 55–56).

Suffering in the Pomak border area was not only strategic narrative performance. It was a daily reality that was experienced both mentally and physically. The tough and depressing bodily experiences of absence and tobacco labour were part and parcel of this process. Suffering was the embodied experience of what many locals perceived as postsocialist state 'enslavement'. In addition, as an emotional style, suffering signified the tension between previously perceived or constructed social categories, and new categories that had been formed under the pressure of postsocialist change. Rapid impoverishment and the creation of a seemingly irreversible disconnection from 'modernity', 'culturedness', 'civilisation', the 'nation' and the 'state' characterised this style.

Notes

1. In this article, I use 'Bulgarian' to denote Bulgarians of Christian origin and 'Pomak' to denote people who understand themselves as 'Pomaks', as well as those whose origins are understood locally as 'Pomak' even when they may self-identify as 'Bulgarians' or as 'Turks'. In my fieldwork location, Pomaks did not identify as 'Turks' and they identified as 'Bulgarians' only in front of outsiders or when they meant Bulgarian citizens. In some other instances they identified themselves as 'ethnic' Bulgarians, but of Muslim origin. Most scholars refer to the Pomaks (they were Islamised during the Ottoman times) as 'Muslim Bulgarians' or 'Bulgarian Muslims', stressing the fact that they speak Bulgarian but are of Muslim origin (see Kaneff 1998; Konstantinov 1992 and 1997; Krasteva 1996 and 1998; Tsibouridou 2000). Scholars have already described most debates surrounding the category 'Pomak' (see Brunnbauer 2001; Georgieva and Zhelyazkova 1994; Mancheva 2001; Todorova 1994; Tsibiridou 2000).

2. Here 'style' is defined after Ferguson (1999: 95): 'The concept of style can serve as a general analytic tool by being extended to include all modes of action through which people place themselves and are placed into societal categories.' Cultural style refers to practices that signify differences between social categories; it is not a total behaviour but poles of signification cross-cut by other poles (Ferguson 1999: 95).

3. The revival of some Islamic practices has been seen (especially by the younger generation) as a return to the past.

4. Until the 1960s and 1970s there were almost as many Bulgarians of Christian origin in the village but they gradually outmigrated and the last ones died or left at the end of the 1980s.

5. The old mosque was destroyed in the 1970s.

6. Dreniots have recently begun experiments with other cultures such as herbs and mushrooms. They are also increasingly involved in international labour migration. However, tobacco remains their major source of income.

7. While during the 1950s tobacco meant 'advancement' and enrichment, and in the 1980s it was a symbol of socialist cooperative mechanisation, today its meaning is inverted. When it was first introduced by the state, it was a reliable source of cash in a subsistence economy, and opened possibilities; then, in late socialism, it was worked with machines and was heavily subsidised by the state, and overpaid; today, its only association is poverty.

8. The municipality was run by the Movement for Rights and Freedom (the so-called 'Turkish Party' for being demographically almost exclusively Turkish), who won the local government elections because of being a demographic majority in this municipality.

Bibliography

Abu-Lughod, L. and Lutz, C.A. 1990. 'Introduction: Emotion, Discourse and the Politics of Everyday Life', in *Language and the Politics of Emotion*, ed. C.A. Lutz and L. Abu-Lughod. Cambridge and Paris: Cambridge University Press and Editions de la Maison des Sciences de l'Homme, pp. 1–23.

Alexiev, B. 1998. 'The Population of Rhodopes in the Bulgarian Historiography', in *The Muslim Communities in the Balkans and in Bulgaria*, ed. Antonina Zhalyazkova. Sofia: IMIR.

Boltanski, L. 1990. *L'amour et la justice comme competence. Trois essays de sociologies de l'action*. Paris: Metailie.

———— 1993. *La souffrance a distance: morales humanitaire, media et politique*. Paris: Metailie.

Bourdieu, P. 1999. *The Weight of the World. Social Suffering in Contemporary Society*. Cambridge: Polity Press. (First published in France as *La misere du monde*, Editions du Seuil, 1993, English translation by Priscilla Parkhurst Ferguson et al.)

Brunnbauer, U. 2001. 'The Perceptions of Muslim Communities in Bulgaria and Greece: Between "Self" and "Other"', *Journal of Muslim Minority Affairs* 21(1): 39–61.

Creed, G. 1998. *Domesticating Revolution. From Socialist Reform to Ambivalent Transition in a Bulgarian Village*. Pennsylvania: Pennsylvania State University Press.

———— 2002. 'Economic Crises and Ritual Decline in Eastern Europe', in *Postsocialism. Ideals, Ideologies and Practices in Eurasia*, ed. C. Hann. London: Routledge, pp. 57–73.

Ferguson, J. 1999. *Expectations of Modernity. Myths and Meanings of Urban Life on the Zambian Copperbelt*. Berkeley: University of California Press.

Georgieva, Ts. 1998. 'Pomaci – Balgari Musulmani' [Pomaks – Bulgarian Muslims] in *Obshnosti i identichnosti v Balgaria* [Communities and Identities in Bulgaria], ed. A. Krasteva. Sofia: Petexton, pp. 121–48

Georgieva, Ts. and A. Zhelyazkova 1994. 'L'Identite en Periode de Changement (Observation sur Certaines Tendances du Monde Mixte des Rhodopes)', *Cahiers internationnnaux de Sociologie* XCVI: 125–43.

Herzfeld, M. 1985. *The Poetics of Manhood: Conflict and Identity in a Cretan Mountain Village*. Princeton: Princeton University Press.

Iliev, I. 2003. 'Normal Life and Food Consumption Practices in Contemporary Bulgaria, conference presentation, 2nd IASEA conference, 20–23 February, Graz, Austria.

Kaneff, D. 1998. 'When "Land" Becomes "Territory": Land Privatisation and Ethnicity in Rural Bulgaria', in *Surviving Post-Socialism: Gender, Ethnicity and Underclass in Eastern Europe and the Former USSR*, ed. S. Bridger and F. Pine. London: Routledge.

Konstantinov, Y. 1992. '"Nation-state" and "Minority" Types of Discourse – Problems of Communication Between the Majority and the Islamic Minorities in Contemporary Bulgaria', *Innovation* 5(3).

———— 1997. 'Patterns of Re-interpretation: Trader-tourism in the Balkans (Bulgaria) as a Picaresque Metaphorical Enactment of Post-totalitarianism', *American Ethnologist* 23(4): 762–82.

———— 1998. 'Strategies for Sustaining a Vulnerable Identity: the Case of the Bulgarian Pomaks', in *Muslim Identity and the Balkan State*, ed. H. Poulton and S. Taji-Farouki. London: Hurst and Company, pp. 33–54.

Krasteva, A. 1996. 'Glasat na Maltsinstvata v Post-Komunisticheskoto Publichno Prostranstvo', in *Post-Socialisticheskia Prehod*, ed. Jean Pierre Guerrie. Sofia, pp. 145–69.

———— ed. 1998. *Obshnosti i identichnosti v Balgaria* [*Communities and Identities in Bulgaria*]. Sofia: Petexton.

Leavitt, J. 1996. 'Meaning and Feeling in the Anthropology of Emotions', *American Ethnologist* 23(3): 514–39.

Leutloff, C. 2002. 'Claiming Ownership in Post-war Croatia: the Emotional Dynamics of Possession and Repossession in Knin', *Focaal. European Journal of Anthropology* 39: 73–92.

Lutz, C. and White, G.M. 1986. 'The Anthropology of Emotions', *Annual Review of Anthropology* 15: 405–36.

Mancheva, M. 2001. 'Image and Policy: the Case of Turks and Pomaks in Inter-War Bulgaria, 1918–44', *Islam and Christian-Muslim Relations* 12(3): 355–74.

Mihaylova, D. 2000. 'Burn, Burn Little Flame: Media Representations of Pomaks in Post-Communist Bulgaria', *The Linacre Journal* 4: 99–122.

———— 2002. 'Nesting Transnationalism and Migration: How Pomaks from South Eastern Bulgaria Cross Borders', unpublished conference paper, Erfurt University, Germany, 7–9 November 2002.

———— 2003. 'Between a Rock and the Hard Place', *Focaal. European Journal of Anthropology* 41: 45–58.

Navaro-Yashin, Y. 2003. *Faces of the State. Secularism and Public Life in Turkey*. Princeton: Princeton University Press.

Reddy, W. 1997. 'Against Constructionism: the Historical Ethnography of Emotions', *Current Anthropology* 38(3): 327–51.

Skrbiš, Z. 2003. 'The Emotional Historiography of Venetologists. Slovene Diaspora, Memory, and Nationalism', *Focaal. European Journal of Anthropology* 39: 41–56.

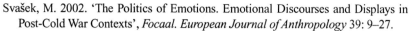

Svašek, M. 2002. 'The Politics of Emotions. Emotional Discourses and Displays in Post-Cold War Contexts', *Focaal. European Journal of Anthropology* 39: 9–27.

Todorova, M. 1994. 'Identity (Trans)formation among Bulgarian Muslims', in *Redefining Global Security*, University of California at Berkeley, Center for German and European Studies, Working Paper 6.5.

Tsibiridou, F. 2000. *Les Pomaks dans la Thrace Grecque: Discours ethnique et pratiques socioculturelles.* Paris: L'Harmattan.

Chapter 3

Sentiments and/as Property Rights: Restitution and Conflict in Postsocialist Romania

Filippo M. Zerilli

The indications that Mr. Dumas and I gave for tears are valid for many other expression of sentiments. It is not only the weeping, but all kinds of oral expression of sentiments that are not exclusively psychological or physiological, but essentially social phenomena, marked by the sign of non-spontaneity and by the most perfect obligation.

Mauss 1969 [1921]: 269, my translation.

Ethnographic Prelude: Dying of Eviction

While doing fieldwork in Bucharest in the torrid August of 1999, I participated in a protest meeting in Revolution Square, organised by Associaţia Chiriaşilor (a national association of tenants living in nationalised houses). I was recording the event with a videotape and suddenly a woman came to me and indicated what would have been most relevant to any film: just around the corner an old tenant lying on the pavement had just had a heart attack and was obviously suffering. Around him a group of people was evidently worried; some were screaming, a woman was weeping. I decided not to film the scene. In fact, I felt emotionally disturbed by the scene and considered it inappropriate to film what seemed to me a private and delicate sphere of pain and emotion. Moreover, I suspected that this was a mere 'accident' that was not necessarily connected to the problem of housing restitution I was investigating.[1]

It would have been sufficient to examine the August issue of the association's newspaper, a monthly called *Radical*, distributed on that same occasion, in order to understand that those 'emotions' (of pain and suffering?) which I had witnessed in Revolution Square were not at all external to my research agenda. The third page contained the obituary of nine persons accompanied by the following note: 'tenants deceased as a consequence of court rulings in favor of restitution'. In other words, the obituary of *Radical* stated that one can die of eviction from one's house in today's Romania. This was what I indeed observed with my own eyes and what I was explicitly asked to film. In that context, was my 'sentiment of prudery' to be considered appropriate or inappropriate? Was I carefully managing local (or 'universal'?) sentiments or was I introducing an emotional meaning external to my informant's purposes and desires?

While as an anthropologist I can easily acknowledge that notions we bring into and find in the field are not neutral and need to be refined through communication and negotiation, both within scientific communities and at a local level (Palumbo 1991), I had never thought of emotions (mine or others') and the role these could play in a study concerning property and privatisation.[2] When I developed the research project of which the present paper is a part, I assumed that the privatisation process in the Eastern European countries of the former Soviet bloc did not only imply specific problems when compared to the privatizations that take place in Western countries (Kideckel 1995: 47–48), but also represented a vantage point for seeing cultural changes as they are experienced by 'real people doing real things' (Ortner 1984: 144). In other words, I was looking at the recent transformations in Romanian society by starting from the everyday life experience of certain groups and individuals who, far from being passive onlookers, can and should be considered both the agents and the beneficiaries of this process of transformation.

Property and Sentimental Dramas

As demonstrated by the anthropological tradition itself (Hann 1998: 23–34), property relationships are not limited to defining relations between persons and 'things', but also express and help define social relations. The transfer into private property of assets that formerly belonged to the state represents a central dimension of the social restructuring currently experienced by the former socialist countries. The controversial (re)privatisation of real estate, and especially the issue of restitution of nationalised houses, is therefore only one component of a much wider process intimately affecting these societies, not only from a political and economic point of view, but also from the point of view of the dynamics of social relations (see also Svašek, Chapter 4, this volume) The buildings used for habitation are only one specific element of this complex (which also includes buildings with other functions), an element that may help us to understand the reciprocal relationship between the 'private sphere' and the 'public sphere' or, to return to the title of this paper, between sentiments and property rights.

By focusing especially on discourses, practices and strategies of the protagonists in the process of (re)appropriation of controversial real estate, the former owners and the tenants living presently in the houses that were nationalised during socialism, I will try to challenge the point of view that sees strong human sentiments and such apparently technical things as property rights as belonging to different spheres of social life. The hypothesis I propose is that between sentiments, or more precisely sentimental dramas, and various legal acts and discourses we do not actually find the discrepancy that is often assumed to be there: on the one hand, the private, subjective realm of emotions or feelings; on the other hand, the public field of property rights, encoded in legal norms. They are not separated but intimately linked. And such links are often produced in intermediate social fields, such as the judiciary and contending civic groups, in concrete interactions of manoeuvre and discourse, all shaping the arena in which sentiments and property rights confront, comfort, overlap and sometimes defy each other.

As Hann has pointed out for land assets in postsocialist Hungary, sentimental attachment to property is subject to different interpretation even within the same family unit, in relation to age, gender, and more generally to individual interests and life projects (Hann 1993a: 310). Similar considerations could be taken into account concerning real estate property. Nevertheless, if property is socially and historically constructed, as is widely recognised by the juridical tradition itself (Rodotà 1981), it could be argued that ownership rights of particular 'objects' are often peculiar and ambiguous interpretations of what property is. In this respect, sentimental attachment to the object 'home' introduces a wide range of different conceptualisations of the notion of property.

Based on fieldwork in urban contexts (mainly in Bucharest) in different periods between 1996 and 2000, this chapter discusses two apparently different concepts of property, referring to two different sentimental dramas, both originating from a profound loss (*pierdere* in Romanian). The loss of the 'family house', a loss situated in the past and evoked through memories and family stories; and the loss of one's actual living space, often inhabited and maintained for years. In some, not uncommon, cases the object of attachment is literally the same.[3] Again, this implies that different social actors in the same social context establish a particular kind of relationship with the same 'objects' which they perceive as theirs, this perception being legally recognised or not.

By using the expression 'sentimental dramas', I am trying first of all to avoid the risk of 'imputing emotions to others' (Leavitt 1996: 514). Even if I personally witnessed symptoms of highly personal emotional states, in this chapter I prefer to treat them as discursive performances that are acted out in particular social and political contexts, and that are part of a multivocal public discourse about justice and property. I am not saying that sentiments are fake. Most of them certainly are genuine, but they are also collectively encoded in given social and political contexts. To quote Marcel Mauss, they are 'essentially social phenomena, marked by the sign of non-spontaneity and by the most perfect obligation' (Mauss 1969: 269, my translation). Hence, my concern here is not with defining what sentiments or emotions are. Rather, I will try to highlight how different emotional dynamics represented by various local terms such as *frică* (fear), *durere* (pain), *suferinţă* (sufference), *furiă* (anger), *indignaţie* (indignation), *disperare* (despair), and notably *pierdere* (loss) are primarily enacted, strategically used, and possibly manipulated in order to support moral and judicial claims.[4] In this perspective, I find it useful to refer to the theatrical metaphor of drama for a range of related reasons. First, it helps to emphasise that emotions are not simply private or individual states; rather, they are social actions brought into play, in other words they have a performative and collective dimension. Second, using drama I make explicit reference to their narrative and fictional – though not false – character. In fact, even though they are unquestionably lived and felt, from an ethnographic stance emotions are firstly socially communicated, namely told to others (including anthropologists) by various means and with different purposes. While apparently universal, love or hate, for instance, could be hardly defined by their supposed intrinsic emotional content; in fact, they rather work to relationally orchestrate collectivities, that is 'to align some subjects with others and against other others' (Ahmed 2004: 25). Unsurprisingly, the sentimental dramas I will discuss below are themselves part of larger contested narratives (i.e. life before and during socialism, postsocialist transition, EU enlargement process etc.) that give shape to and are shaped by the content of different emotional dynamics. Finally, the notion of drama, like that of 'embodiment' (Csordas 1990; see also Svašek's introduction, this volume) permits the bridging of action and narrative, undermining the separation between what is (physically) felt and what is (mentally) thought or narrated. I consider the drama metaphor especially useful to appreciate how emotional 'experience' (physical *and* mental in concert) can be politically articulated by social actors, according to the way they situate themselves to past, present, and prospective events and projects in given temporalities (see Throop 2003). From this standpoint, the notion of drama clearly includes the historical processes in which emotions are settled, lived and played out. In this manner, it also makes less ambiguous (and hence tolerable) the inevitable objectifying outcome of any imaginative attempt to speak and write about 'others' and their emotional predicaments.

In the next section, I will clarify why the sentimental dramas I discuss below, cannot be fully understood unless we make reference not only to the uncertain national Romanian legal context, but also to the transnational context, and particularly to European Union legal institutions.

In Revolution Square: Sentiments and/or Human Rights

During the public meeting convened by the tenants' association in Bucharest's Revolution Square,[5] from a dais set on the platform of an old truck that had just been used to transport several dozen protest banners distributed to the hundreds of participants gathered in the square, a dark-haired man in his forties was fervently urging the audience to join him and shout together: '*Jos cu ei, jos cu ei*' (down with them), '*mafioşii*' (mobsters), '*jos bandiţii*' (down with the bandits), '*hoţii, hoţii, hoţii*' (thieves).

Should anyone have had any doubt as to who the mobsters, the thieves and the bandits, were, these doubts would have disappeared moments later when one of the organiszers of the meeting started reading a letter that had just been sent by the association to the Hague Tribunal, requesting the pro-secution of certain Romanian political leaders accused of having committed 'crimes against humanity'. The defendants were clearly addressed: Valeriu Stoica (Minister of Justice), Nicolae Noica (Minister for Public Works and for the Territory), Victor Babiuc (Minister of the Interior), Radu Vasile (Prime Minister) and Emil Constantinescu (President of the Republic).[6] They were allegedly guilty of having promoted the 'deportation' of hundreds of Romanian citizens. After reading the letter, the man addressed the audience with the following words:

Do not accept the deportation from your houses, for we are not in the times of slavery; those of you who have invested in the houses you have been occupying for decades are now co-owners by virtue of the repairs that you have made and by prescription of titles; the civil code gives you this right; the magistrates who ignore this right of yours are infamous bastards.

Even though I had been concerned for some time with the debate on the restitution of nationalised houses – and was therefore familiar with the strong language used by the tenants' association – I was nonetheless struck by phrases like 'crimes against humanity', 'deportation' and 'slavery'. I still had my doubts as to whether the tenants had been really subject to or threatened with anything similar, and wondered about the reasons for the radicalisation of the protest.

Significantly, only five days before, 25 August, the House of Representatives, after a long and tortuous parliamentary debate, had passed a new bill based on the principle of full 'restitution in kind' (*restituţio in integrum*), of the nationalised buildings to their former owners. The reference made to deportation was related to the second chapter of the Government Ordinance no. 40 issued in April 1999. This regulation, under the heading 'mandatory exchange of dwellings' (*schimbul obligatoriu de locuinţă*) gave the former owners the right to take possession of an item of real estate if a court of law had restored their respective ownership right, provided that they were able to provide a new dwelling for the tenant who was currently occupying it. If these two new regulations – one already in force and another under discussion in the Senate, that is right in the building in front of which the meeting was taking place – were at the origin of the protest, the symbolism of its staging and the choice of a privileged institutional interlocutor (the Hague Tribunal) can only be understood if considered in relation to the discourses and strategies adopted by the other main interest group involved in this matter, namely that of the former owners.

At the beginning of 1990 many of these former owners began to organise themselves, in groups or individually, and began to demand by means of letters, memorandums, petitions and the like the assistance and attention of various, mainly European, institutions. They complained about the non-observance in Romania of property rights, acknowledged as one of the fundamental rights of the Universal Declaration of Human Rights. The tenants' association rapidly identified the reference to the principles of democratic liberalism as a major obstacle for the recognition of their own rights. The president of the tenants' association, in the summer of 1997, openly revealed to me the reason why he was so eager to talk, saying that:

I need people who would support our cause in the light of human rights; they [the former owners] speak of human rights when it comes to property, but I have no access to human rights; are there no human rights for me too? Am I not a part of this world? What is the difference? I live in this country, I worked in this country...

The tenants' association recognised that the defenders of property restitution must be countered with legal arguments derived from the same hegemonic transnational liberal discourse, in particular as enshrined in the bodies of the European Union.

The plea for the recognition of fundamental human rights addressed to the European Union institutions responsible for the defence of these rights has become a major topic in the property restitution debate ever since Romania was included in the Council of Europe in 1993. From that moment on, representatives of the European institutions began monitoring the country, providing precise indications that were to be followed in various fields, including that of property, such as the report issued by the Commission for Judicial Matters and Human Rights (known as the Jansson Report), which required that Romania, among other things, modify current legislation regarding property restitution (Jansson 1997: 4). The requirement for a solution to the issue of property restitution was explicitly stated as a condition for accession by the European Union during the Helsinki summit of December 1999, when Romania became an official candidate member of the Union, an event of great symbolic value, hailed by certain national newspapers as 'the end of transition'.

In this framework, the street protests of the tenants become comprehensible. Interestingly, their claims were not presented as an alternative to the principle of property restitution, which was acknowledged by the tenants themselves but mainly in the form of financial compensation.[7] By means of the public display of feelings such as deprivation, uncertainty, and especially anger, driven by the very real fear of being thrown out of what they perceive as 'their' homes without any notice whatsoever, and by stating that their very lives were in danger, the tenants resorted to the fundamental rights consecrated by the European Convention on Human Rights of 1953 (signed by Romania in 1993). This document largely inspired the Romanian Constitution of 1991 (Focşeneanu 1998), referring to the right to life, the inviolability of one's home, social protection, and the right to privacy (see Romanian Constitution, Chapter II, Art. 22–27).

The emotions of the tenants living in nationalised houses were therefore recognised and rendered legitimate by legal stipulations that seemed to be just as noble and undeniable as the ones invoked by former owners. In that context, the European legal framework can be considered as a sphere where emotions are settled and made socially meaningful. Weeping, suffering or even death are made into symbols that help the tenants to attempt to construct and communicate their ideas on justice and property. This is not simply because someone else (the political parties that were against the new bill) were manipulating people's sentiments, as is easily intimated in postsocialist contexts. In spite of their differing personal situation (one is awaiting a sentence of eviction, another has just bought an apartment from the state, etc.) the tenants themselves are involved in a battle in which sentiments may play a crucial role to the extent to which they can obtain judicial legitimacy. In this respect, one can see these emotions or sentimental dramas as attempts at challenging the political elite, and as a fertile ground for collective organisational activity. Interestingly, both the former owners and tenants explicitly appeal to supranational entities (the Strasbourg Law Court or the Hague Tribunal), thus showing the actual cogency of the transnational legal context in understanding local claims and rights (Merry 1992).

At the end of the protest organised in Revolution Square, the tenants gathered round a folk singer who was also a member of their association and who, after speaking about the misfortunes he had experienced with his dwelling, invited all those present to sing together: 'we are Romanian, we are Romanian'. In the given context, the recourse to feelings of national identity took on a rather peculiar function: that of raising or legitimating the doubt that expatriate Romanians should be granted the right to reclaim assets that were confiscated from them by socialist governments.[8]

The Sentimental Drama of the Former Owners

The plight of the former owners is probably better known in Western Europe than in Romania, as it enjoyed little public visibility in Romania before 2000. This is partly due to the fact that the group under discussion is numerically less significant than that of the tenants, but also because of the choice of a different strategy for the public communication of their drama. Rather than gathering in the city square, the former owners, since the creation in 1990 of their association by the former owners themselves, have generally preferred to convene periodic private meetings in a place of highly symbolic value: the halls of the Bucharest University Law School.[9] It is here that they discuss the issue of restitution with the representatives of various political forces, promoting legal action in favour of their interests.

The tragedy of the former owners is known: they, or rather, some members of their families, who are now deceased, have been subject to confiscation of assets and in certain cases to imprisonment, persecution and deportation. The narrative of their life histories is often marked by the sudden introduction of a new order that came to radically change what had seemed to be the natural flow of events. An elderly retired person living in Bucharest, owner of two buildings in the Prahova region, told me:

> I come from a respectable family. My father was a merchant, my grandfather was a merchant; just like my great-grandfather before him, I was to be the fourth generation to become a merchant; but then came the communists and everything …, the houses were confiscated. (Dumitrescu, a former owner)

If, after 1945, life in Romania changed for many if not for everyone, owner or not, the housing policy, implemented by socialist governments, which was meant to assist in rendering more homogeneous the various social categories of the country, caused numerous former owners to reduce their own dwelling space in favour of the new tenants 'distributed' by the state according to specific criteria (officially, by the job they held, but in fact by the closeness and fealty to the political power).[10] This is why it became customary to see, especially in urban contexts, a system of cohabitation between the former owners and the tenants, a system that is often presented as the cause of much suffering in the complaints of the former owners. The son of a lawyer, who was imprisoned for some time, remembers the consequences after the nationalisation of the family mansion in the centre of Bucharest:

> It was terrible, it was terrible, let me tell you why: first of all, the house had only one bathroom, for it was a family house, and when we came to have 28 tenants (one family per room), the contract gave everybody access rights to the bathroom, anyone could disturb you, even in the middle of the night, to go to the bathroom, take a bath or whatever. (Caliga, a former owner)

The same informant, apart from the hardships caused by the forced sharing of private quarters, also speaks of the demeaning status and of the threats he was constantly subjected to in those peculiar living conditions, dominated by suspicion and conspiracy (on which see Liiceanu and Sélim 1999). Under these circumstances, characterised by the ideology of 'class struggle', often evoked in these very words by the former owners themselves, being an owner was perceived as something to be afraid and ashamed of. A woman who was the heir to a luxurious Bucharest building that used to belong to her paternal grandfather (today hostsing one of the most prestigious hotels of the city), remembers that, as a child, whenever she and her aunts passed by this building, they maintained a distance, because they felt guilty and afraid of being recognised as representing the class of the exploiters. For this lady, recalling this fear is another way of struggling against the state and redefining her social identity as a Romanian expatriate.

What does the reappropriation of their former houses by themselves or by members of their families mean for these men and women? Naturally, no one ignores the economic value of these assets, which often justifies the considerable investment required by lawsuits that can last between three and ten years, if not longer. Moreover, beyond the desire to see that 'justice is done', there is the need to symbolically end a tragedy of the past (see Borneman 1997; see also Müller, Chapter 8, this volume). This is quite clear in the plans made for the future of the almost recovered houses: one person wants to create a museum in memory of a family member who was the victim of injustice and humiliation; another intends to donate the building to the village school; and yet another wishes that his ageing mother, at least once, before she passes away, be able to walk barefoot in the garden of the house which she never got to inhabit. These sentimental reasons, so to speak, strive to be included in the existing legislation – for instance, in the very law at the time under discussion in the Senate – and seek full recognition in a court of law or, as a last resort, at the Strasbourg European Court of Human Rights.[11]

Beyond its economic component, which plays an absolutely essential part as the driving force behind the ongoing expensive litigation, restitution is basically perceived as the payment of a moral debt incurred by the state. This is what causes the indignation of the former owners with regard to the postrevolutionary governments that have been dragging their feet in the search for a solution that would satisfy everybody. For the same reason, the choice of the owners clearly favours the restitution 'in kind' of their estates: for them justice will be done only when everything that was confiscated is returned, and not simply its equivalent (money, assets, stocks or other values mentioned in the new bill). Consequently, even if the state were today capable of offering financial compensation for the nationalised assets at their current market value, many of the former owners would declare themselves sentimentally (or morally) dissatisfied.

The Sentimental Drama of the Tenants

On what grounds are the tenants challenging the demands presented by the former owners? If the protest from Revolution Square has indeed anticipated certain elements, the dwelling problems of various individuals bring forth others.

All the tenants living in nationalised houses whom I had the chance to talk to, agree that the former owners must receive compensation. In other words, they recognise and sometimes share the drama of the former owners and of their families. Many of the tenants even agree with the idea of restitution in kind.[12] Nevertheless, when one comes to the individual cases the matter becomes complicated, and the tenants come up with a recurring series of objections against the principle of restitution. These arguments are in fact the solid basis on which they build their drama of despair. The most frequent ones regard the restructuring and the changes made by the tenants to the houses that, for this reason, they perceive as being their own. One tenant said:

> I have a lot of respect for property rights; by this I mean that if you erected a house at which you worked, and strove hard to see it built, you have my full respect. But when a representative of I don't know what generation comes and claims a house for which he has done nothing at all, then I think that I should have priority, for I lived in that house and took care of it. (Ariton, a tenant)

For this woman the right to property is directly related to the labour invested in the creation of the respective asset, be it directly, in its construction, or indirectly, in securing the funds for its purchase. Labour, as the intellectual philosophical tradition which could be traced back to John Locke's reflections on property holds, becomes thus a precondition of property rights. When, during the same conversation, I simply asked her what she understood by property, she answered: 'property means that which you own and which you yourself made. That's what property means. Most certainly'.

But in order to be a respectable owner, say the tenants, it is not enough to have built your own house: you must also know how to take care of it as time goes by. In the words of Filipescu, another tenant: 'when you have a piece of property you take care of it, you don't go away, you don't leave it in the hands of the state, you must preserve it, that's what property rights are all about'. This perception underlies a strategy for the appropriation of assets which, in the context of the relationship between past and present, can, on the one hand, be related to the status of 'almost-property' (see also Smidova 1997) enjoyed by tenants during socialism, and, on the other, serves the idea of a financial compensation that the parties would have to agree upon, should the court rule in favour of eviction.

Another argument frequently used to oppose the principle of restitution in kind is that of time, as allegedly too long a time has passed for a claim to be made for a piece of property that is no longer what it used to be. It is worth quoting here the extraordinary question put to me by a tenant who was showing himself as morally devastated by the fact that he was forced to give back the house left to him by a colleague and friend who emigrated to Germany more than twenty years ago, and who had now decided to come back and settle in Bucharest:

> You know Naples, don't you? Have you seen the Vesuvius? Who owns that place covered by sand and ashes? There must have been owners there. Now don't tell me that the grandson of Titus Livy, and so on, owns it. You see, such rights disappear in the course of time. There is no such thing as eternal property and eternal property rights. (Filipescu, a tenant)

The time factor plays a role also in the issue of the restitution of property to Romanian citizens currently living abroad. The same tenant pointed out that his friend had voluntarily left the country, as shown by the papers he had signed before leaving. Arguably, things may have actually been somewhat different, but the fact remains that once the legitimate owner had moved somewhere else, he was no longer capable of taking direct care of his assets. To paraphrase a group of tenants who were very insistent upon this aspect, we could say that the feeling of moral indignation expressed by them sprang from the following question:

> How is it that we who have worked hard, paid taxes and thus contributed to the creation of the total real estate of the country are now denied the right to own a house, whereas those who left the country and led a cozy life someplace else are now getting back their houses, not in order to live there, but in order to sell them and transfer the money abroad? Should we endorse this, then the present property bill is anti-national. (Popescu, a tenant)

The fear of losing their homes expressed by the tenants legitimates these and other arguments stressed more or less firmly, depending on the temperament of the claimant, or rather of reclaimant, as they are often considered to be: should he or she be a third-generation heir, the genealogical distance is too great and makes his or her rights questionable. In a similar vein, if the claimant left the country a long time ago, his/her morality as a citizen (and as a taxpayer) becomes dubious, because of the fact that he/she failed to take care of these assets.

Nevertheless, the tenants' anger is not directed against the former owners, whose presence appears as the opponent in litigation for eviction and not for restitution (see Zerilli 2003: 290–91). It is rather the state that is called into question. Moreover, it should be clear that the drama of the tenants is not simply that of becoming evicted. That possibility could be

seen as merely a consequence of a faulty legislation failing to secure their
rights as tenants. What the tenants perceive and represent as their drama is
the loss of something they consider as belonging to them. Obviously the risk
of eviction, according to them, means the dissolution of neighbourly and
friendship relationships, the loss of contact with a particular neighbourhood,
with a certain urban and social landscape. The real drama thus concerns
losing the house where they have lived for years, where they may have
grown up, in which they have invested labour and money and in so doing
made financial and moral sacrifices. These houses are obviously part of
their social and personal identities. From this perspective, if losing the
house should have direct consequences in the present, and affect the tenant's
everyday life in the future, fighting against this possibility must bring into
question their life histories along with an (auto)evaluation of their past as
Romanian citizens. In so doing, they elaborate a rhetoric of guiltlessness
based on a peculiar elaboration of the meaning of property under socialism.
As one of the tenants, a sixty-year-old retired rural sociologist, said:
'because of socialism we renounced, against our will, becoming owners
ourselves'. That statement is in fact a mystification since a different type of
private real estate was allowed and even promoted under socialism,
especially from the late 1970s on. What he does express is a conviction that
to accept living under socialism (and being a member of the Communist
Party) did not necessarily mean sharing collectivist principles. The quoted
statement also reinforces the widespread idea that it is up to the new
democratic state to repair the injustice suffered by the tenants by finally
allowing them to become owners.

Collective versus Private Property?

Apparently, we could identify an opposition between two distinct concepts
of property: that of the former owners, who stress its transmissibility, its
'perennial validity', and often its 'sacred nature', and that of the tenants,
who, quite the contrary, see property as an asset that is acquired through
labour and use, a right that is subject to changes and even cancellation in the
course of time.[13] These two concepts might be reduced to the dichotomy
capitalism/market economy versus socialism/planned economy (Câmpeanu
1993). I do not think, however, that what is presented as a conflict between
former owners and tenants can be related to an opposition between two
radically opposed political or economic cultural ideologies. Nor do I think
that we should see them as an expression of two radically different social
categories: on the one hand, the former owners and the heirs of the very few

wealthy owners of buildings, land, factories and other means of production that existed before 1945, and on the other, the tenants along with the rest of the country (numerous agricultural labourers, craftsmen, workers, professionals, etc.)[14] The confiscation of assets undertaken by the state during socialism affected sectors of the Romanian population that were considerably larger and socially more heterogeneous than those defined in the nationalisation decrees issued after 1947, decrees under which, to put it bluntly, the state did not – with minor exceptions – take away a lot from a few but a little from many.[15] Even in Bucharest, relatively modest pieces of property were requisitioned, while others, of far greater importance, were spared. It would therefore be misleading and historically debatable to maintain that the present conflict was generated by or can be understood in the light of the social relations preceding 1945 (on which see Popescu 1998). Instead, it seems necessary to investigate in depth the mechanisms and processes of social recomposition that occurred because of and during the socialist era, a work already initiated in post-1989 anthropological studies in Romania (Kideckel 1993b; Verdery 1996). Moreover, we should observe how people strategically give sense to and make use of their social identities in the present in order to obtain advantages for the future (Moore 1987, 1994).

Fieldwork I conducted in Bucharest suggests that manifestations of protest, representations of past and present misfortunes, and different moral claims regarding restitution all collocate in a fluctuating perimeter defined by the current uncertain legislation, be it in defiance or in support of its principles. While the protest staged by the tenants in Revolution Square finds legitimacy in a peculiar interpretation of the European human rights legislation, the recurrent elements of the sentimental drama of both tenants and former owners confront each other within a recent and extremely complex legal framework, at once raising the question of the continuity between the present constitutional state order and that of the socialist regime (on which see Focşeneanu 1998).

Because of limited space I will not delve into the question of the continuous changing legal regulations concerning property restitution or discuss their relevant and highly technical interpretations provided by lawyers and legal scholars (e.g. Adam 2001; Cosma 1995). Suffice it to maintain that both sentimental dramas here discussed are not at all external to political and legal debates. Instead, they are inscribed and creatively reproduced in those debates. As many social actors and civic groups did not fail to understand, the capacity to organise and give adequate political expression to such emotional predicaments represents an effective weapon in securing electoral consensus (see also Golanska-Ryan, Chapter 7, this volume) and, what's more, in influencing the process of definition and redistribution of property rights.[16] The controversial discussion on property restitution shows, in fact, that just as the legal discourse circulates feelings and, at the same time, draws from them support and legitimacy, the feelings themselves are or can be used in securing the recognition of certain rights. In this respect we can observe the existence of a dual discourse in the representations given by tenants and former owners to the issue of housing restitution: if it can be argued that they advocate a different concept of property, in fact both parties refer to a specific sentimental drama and adopt strategies of (re)appropriation based on the recognition of rights within an objective, albeit highly uncertain, legal framework.

If we consider law from an anthropological perspective, that is, 'law as process' (Moore 1978) or 'law in action' (Moore 2001), we must discard the alleged autonomy of the legal thought and procedure that represent the foundation of the 'force of law' (Bourdieu 1987). We should admit that law reflects the need to legitimate political goals, and therefore we might wonder what mechanisms govern the control over social production and reproduction: basically who controls whom and what, with what methods, and to what ends (Sims 1995). From this point of view, the discourse on property voiced by the Romanian tenants and former owners is doubly connected to the processes and the conflicts related to the use of political and economic capital, directly or indirectly accumulated by representatives of the socialist nomenklatura.[17] This does not mean an intended reconstitution of a collectivist model of state ownership in today's Romania. The ethnographic material considered does not suggest the presence of social practices that would promote an alternative to the principle of 'exclusive possession' ascribed by the liberal tradition to private property rights, as pointed out by ethnographic research of land restitution conducted in postsocialist Hungary (Hann 1993b) and Romania (Kideckel 1993a; Verdery 1996: 133–67, 1999). In those cases a more 'inclusive' system of collective land management seems to prevail over (or rather coexist with) 'exclusive' property rights conceptions. The dramatic representations of the issues related to house restitution conform instead to the liberal ideology of ownership, even if the tenants resort to discursive strategies that sometimes seem to challenge some of its principles (mainly transmissibility over time of the respective assets). What we witness is a dramatic – and factual – representation of citizens' interests and desires, inspired and supported by the binding legislation (e.g. Law 112/1995), a representation that fuels those interests and desires.

Obviously, socialism has produced particular cultural behaviours and expectations. However, I would not argue that present popular moral claims, such as those put forward by the Romanian tenants' association, should be seen as evidence of a persisting 'collectivist mentality' inspired by socialism. Nor do I believe that socialist historical experience itself suffices to explain the wide range of different conceptualisations of property rights, as shown in the conflicts surrounding the housing restitution. An actor-centred ethnographic approach to the present can help us to see the historical experience of socialism as an 'order of discourse' (Foucault 1971) to which different groups and individuals refer in order to differentiate their different (life) histories within a collective narrative. Within this perspective, specific 'meanings and feelings' (Leavitt 1996) associated with property rights and assets are essentially produced in the present struggles for the interpretation of the socialist and presocialist past. Remembering life before and during socialism is in fact the common basis from which both tenants and former owners derive their sentimental dramas in order to substantiate their claims concerning property and justice in the present. Interestingly, both groups create images of the past which do not necessarily conflict with each other. Tenants and former owners are well aware that they actually fight for their interests and compete for the future shape of the Romanian state and its legal system. As I hope to have shown in this chapter, this engagement with the state involves not only pure legal-contractual relations but intense moral and emotional stakes as well. Therefore, discourses and actions of despair and contestation gain much of their resonance from the positing of 'justice' and 'property' as strongly sentimental and ethical problems.

Acknowledgements

A slightly different version of this paper has previously appeared in *Focaal. Journal of Anthropology* 39(2002): 57–71. I am grateful to Maruška Svašek, Julie Trappe, and a *Focaal* anonymous reviewer for comments on earlier drafts.

Notes

1. Concerning the interest of 'events' that are not apparently central to previously established research plans, I would like to recall the 'processual approach' as theorised by Sally Moore, a scholar to whom my ethnographic practice in/of the present conducted in Bucharest during the late 1990s owes a great deal (Moore 1987, 1994; see also Sanjek 1991).

2. In spite of some brilliant intuitions (e.g. Henry 1936; Mauss 1969) and even if the psychology/anthropology debate dates back at least to the 'culture and personality' school, emotion is a relatively unexplored field of anthropological investigation. Since the 1980s, and especially after Lutz and White's review article (1986), emotions gained new attention within anthropology (see at least Lutz and Abu-Lughod 1990, and the special issue of the French journal *Terrain* devoted to emotions [*Les émotions*, Vol. 22, March 1994] which also includes a bibliographic selection of US titles on this topic, see p. 118). Nevertheless, the specific subject I discuss in this chapter (the relationship between sentiments and property or legal, and more widely, political order) represents a far less considered aspect of the growing literature (see, however, Humphrey 2001; Reddy 1999; Svašek 2000, Svašek, Chapter 4, this volume; Yanagisako 2000).

3. During my fieldwork in Bucharest it was not uncommon to discover that the very same nationalised house or apartment could legally belong contemporaneously: (a) to a former owner whose respective ownership rights have been restored by a court of law judgement; (b) to a tenant actually living it, who legally bought it from the City Hall, following Law 112/1995 regulations; (c) to the state itself, at least to a certain extent. In this context it would be worthwhile to distinguish between 'possession', 'disposal', and 'use', as a number of Western legal traditions actually do in conceptualising property.

4. Interestingly, in Romanian the verb 'to weep' (*a plânge*) also means 'to complain' (*a (se) plânge*) and 'to claim' in its judicial meaning. Accordingly, the Romanian expression *a depune o plângere impotriva cuiva* is commonly used in judicial jargon for the English 'to bring an action against somebody'.

5. Bucharest's Revolution Square is a place intimately linked to Romanian current and past political life: it hosts, right in front of the Royal Palace (now the National Museum of Art), the buildings that used to symbolise communist power and conspiracy (the Central Committee of the Communist Party and the secret police, a.k.a. *Securitate*) and which, after the revolutionary events of 1989 (part of which took place right in this square), became the centre of postsocialist democracy, hosting today the Senate of the Romanian Parliament.

6. Here and in what follows I refer to institutional roles held by political actors during my investigations (in that case, August 1999).

7. Quite the contrary, private property has become for the tenants themselves something that has to be defended, to the extent enabled by the legislation of 1995 which gave them the right to buy the houses they had previously rented from the state and thus acquire the status of 'new owners' (see Law 112/1995, Art. 7–11, reproduced in Cojocaru 1997: 116–18).

8. On the contradictory forces shaping identity and national(ist) sentiment in Romania (during and after socialism) see Verdery's brilliant analysis (1996: chapters 4 and 5).

9. Nevertheless, a few days after the street meeting of the tenants, the owners' association also decided to take to the streets (in front of the government building, in Victory Square) and protest against the same bill, declaring that the criteria for restitution and the forms of compensation it stipulated were insufficient.

10. On the 'repartition' regulations and the typology of Romanian dwellings during socialism see the civil law handbook by Stătescu (1970).

11. More than a hundred similar claims have been addressed from Romanian citizens to the Strasbourg Court since 1993 (see *Adevărul*, 25 September 2003). For an ethnographic analysis of some property restitution lawcases in Romania, see Zerilli (2003: 285–92).

12. An opinion poll conducted on this issue during the summer of 1999 revealed that more than 80 percent of the Romanian population approved of a complete restitution of all nationalised assets (see *România liberă*, 28 August 1999).

13. The Romanian Civil Code, whose conception is largely indebted to the Napoleonic one, recognises the 'usufruct right' (*drept de uzufruct*) (see Book II, Title III, Art. 517–575). Also, the same Civil Code, which has never been cancelled under socialist rule, contains an entire section on 'prescription' (*prescripție*) (see Book III, Title XX, Art. 1837–1911). It is worth noting that some of those articles are currently invoked by lawyers to sustain property restitution in judicial litigation contexts (see Adam 2001: 82–83).

14. According to recent estimates, between the First and Second World War the great Romanian owners of land, industries and real estate property amounted to no more than 2 percent of the total active population (Popescu 1998: 128). Substantial ethnographic data regarding communal ownership and the use of property typical of rural Romania between the two world wars can be found in the monumental study of Dimitrie Gusti's pupil Henri H. Stahl (1982).

15. This is especially the case of Decree no. 92 of 19 April 1950 (regulating real estate nationalisation), the juridical interpretation of which is actually crucial in the ongoing litigation concerning restitution processes (see Adam 2001).

16. Not surprisingly, following his tenacious engagement in defence of tenants' rights, the president of the tenants' association has been elected deputy in the November 2000 national elections (within the Greater Romania Party [*România mare*], conducted by the ultranationalist Corneliu Vadim Tudor).

17. That is obviously a major aspect of the rehierarchisation process affecting contemporary Romanian society, which unfortunately, as Althabe argued (Althabe and Bazin 1999), remains a rather neglected field of ethnographic research (see, however, Sampson 2002).

Bibliography

Adam, I. 2001. *Legea nr. 10/2001. Regimul juridic aplicabil imobilelor preluate abuziv*. București: All Beck.

Ahmed, S. 2004. 'Collective Feelings. Or, the Impressions Left by Others', *Theory, Culture & Society* 21(2): 25–42.

Althabe, G. and Laurent, B. 1999. 'Entretien avec Gérard Althabe. Un paysage social incertain. La Roumanie post-communiste', *Journal des Anthropologues* 77–78: 35–51.

Borneman, J. 1997. *Settling Accounts. Violence, Justice, and Accountability in Postsocialist Europe*. Princeton: Princeton University Press.

Bourdieu, P. 1987. 'The Force of Law: Towards a Sociology of the Juridical Field', *Hastings Law Journal* 38: 814–53.

Câmpeanu, P. 1993. 'Europe: l'Est n'est pas au Sud. Considérations sociologiques sur la démocratisation en tant que dé-stalinisation', in *L'état des lieux en sciences sociales*, ed. A. Duțu and N. Dodille. Paris: L'Harmattan, pp. 129–38.

Cojocaru, O. 1997. *Legea caselor naționalizate. Explicații teoretice, întrebări și răspunsuri.* București: Numina Lex.

Cosma, D. 1995. 'Hotărârea nr. 1/1995 a secților unite ale curții supreme de justiție: o analiză critică', *Revista Româna de Drepturile Omului* 8: 8–32.

Csordas, T.J. 1990. 'Embodiment as a Paradigm for Anthropology', *Ethos. Journal of the Society for Psychological Anthropology* 18(1): 5–47.

Focșeneanu, E. 1998. *Istoria constituțională a României (1859–1991).* București: Humanitas.

Foucault, M. 1971. *L'ordre du discours.* Paris: Gallimard.

Hann, C.M. 1993a. 'From Production to Property: Decollectivization and the Family-land Relationship in Contemporary Hungary', *Man* 28(2): 299–320.

———— 1993b. 'Property Relations in the New Eastern Europe: the Case of Specialist Cooperatives in Hungary', in *The Curtain Rises. Rethinking Culture, Ideology, and the State in Eastern Europe.* ed. H.G. DeSoto and D.G. Anderson Atlantic Highlands: Humanity Press, pp. 99–119.

———— ed., 1998. *Property Relations. Renewing the Anthropological Tradition.* Cambridge: Cambridge University Press.

Henry, J. 1936. 'The Linguistic Expression of Emotion', *American Anthropologist* n.s., 38.

Humphrey, C. 2001. 'Inequality and Exclusion: a Russian Case Study of Emotions in Politics', *Anthropological Theory* 1(3): 331–53.

Jansson, G. 1997. *Rapport sur le respect des obligations et engagements contractés par la Roumanie.* Bruxelles: Conseil de l'Europe.

Kideckel, D.A. 1993a. 'Once Again the Land: Decollectivization and Social Conflict in Rural Romania', in *The Curtain Rises. Rethinking Culture, Ideology and the State in Eastern Europe.* ed. H. DeSoto and D. Anderson. Atlantic Highlands: Humanities Press, pp. 88–106.

———— 1993b. *The Solitude of Collectivism. Romanian Villagers to the Revolution and Beyond.* Ithaca: Cornell University Press.

———— 1995. 'Two Incidents on the Plain in Southern Transylvania: Pitfalls of Privatization in a Romanian Community', in *East European Communities. The Struggle for Balance in Turbulent Times.* ed. D. A. Kideckel Boulder: Westview Press, pp. 47–63.

Leavitt, J. 1996. 'Meaning and Feeling in the Anthropology of Emotions', *American Ethnologist* 23(3): 514–39.

Liiceanu, A. and Sélim, M. 1999. 'Entretien avec Aurora Liiceanu. De la décommunisation au capitalisme en Roumanie', *Journal des Anthropologues* 77–78: 53–65.

Lutz, C. and Abu-Lughod, L., eds. 1990. *Language and the Politics of Emotions.* Cambridge: Cambridge University Press.

Lutz, C. and White, G.M. 1986. 'The Anthropology of Emotions', *Annual Review of Anthropology* 15: 405–36.

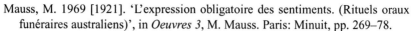

Mauss, M. 1969 [1921]. 'L'expression obligatoire des sentiments. (Rituels oraux funéraires australiens)', in *Oeuvres 3*, M. Mauss. Paris: Minuit, pp. 269–78.

Merry, S.E. 1992. 'Anthropology, Law, and Transnational Processes', *Annual Review of Anthropology* 21: 357–79.

Moore, S.F. 1978. *Law as Process*. London: Routledge and Kegan Paul.

——— 1987. 'Explaining the Present: Theoretical Dilemmas in Processual Ethnography', *American Ethnologist* 14(4): 727–36.

——— 1994. 'Ethnography of the Present and Processual Analysis', in *Assessing Cultural Anthropology*, ed. R. Borofsky. New York: McGraw-Hill, pp. 362–76.

——— 2001. 'Certainties Undone: Fifty Turbulent Years of Legal Anthropology, 1949–1999', *The Journal of the Royal Anthropological Institute Incorporating Man* 7(1): 95–116.

Ortner, S. 1984. 'Theory in Anthropology Since the Sixties', *Comparative Studies in Society and History* 26: 126–66.

Palumbo, B. 1991. '"You are Going Really Deep": conflitti, pratica e teoria in etnografia. Alcune riflessioni a partire dal caso Nzema', *L'Uomo* n.s. 4(2): 235–70.

Popescu, L. 1998. *Structură socială şi societate civilă in România interbelică*. Cluj: Presa Universitară Clujeană.

Reddy, W.M. 1999. 'Emotional Liberty: Politics and History in the Anthropology of Emotions', *Cultural Anthropology* 14(2): 256–88.

Rodotà, S. 1981. *Il terribile diritto. Studi sulla proprietà privata*. Bologna: Il Mulino.

Sampson, S. 2002. 'Beyond Transition. Rethinking Elite Configurations in the Balkans', in *Postsocialism. Ideals, Ideologies and Practices in Eurasia*, ed. C. M. Hann. London: Routledge, pp. 297–316.

Sanjek, R. 1991. 'The Ethnographic Present', *Man* 26(4): 607–28.

Sims, M.M. 1995. 'Old Roads and New Directions: Anthropology and the Law', *Dialectical Anthropology* 20: 341–60.

Smidova, O. 1997. 'Propriété et quasi-propriété immobilières sous le socialisme et leurs mutations post-socialistes', in *Anciens et nouveaux propriétaires. Stratégies d'appropriation en Europe centrale et orientale. Cahiers du CeFRes*, 11f. Prague: Centre Français de Recherche en Sciences Sociales, pp. 129–58.

Stahl, H.H. 1982 [1958]. *Contribuţii la studiul satelor devălmaşe Româneşti*. Bucureşti: Cartea Românească.

Stătescu, C. 1970. *Drept civil*. Bucureşti: Editura didactică şi pedagogic.

Svaşek, M. 2000. 'Borders and Emotions. Hope and Fear in the Bohemian–Bavarian frontier Zone', *Ethnologia Europaea* 30(2): pp. 111–26.

Throop, J.C. 2003. 'Articulating Experience', *Anthropological Theory* 3(2): 219–41.

Verdery, K. 1996. *What Was Socialism, and What Comes Next?* Princeton: Princeton University Press.

——— 1999. 'Fuzzy Property: Rights, Power, and Identity in Transylvania's Decollectivization', in *Uncertain Transitions. Ethnographies of Change in the Postsocialist World*. ed. M. Buraway and K. Verdery Lanham. MD Rowman and Littlefield, pp. 53–81.

Yanagisako, S. 2000. 'Patriarchal Desire: Law and Sentiments of Succession in Italian Capitalist Family', in *Elites. Choice, Leadership and Succession,* ed. J. de Pina Cabral and A. Pedroso de Lima. Oxford and New York: Berg, pp. 53–72.

Zerilli, F.M. 2003. 'Playing (with) Bribery. Ethnographic Images of Corruption from Romania', in *La ricerca antropologica in Romania. Prospettive storiche ed etnografiche*, ed. C. Papa, G. Pizza and F.M. Zerilli. Napoli: Edizioni Scientifiche Italiane, pp. 275–308.

—⟨⟨ⲉ✪ⲋ⟩⟩—

Chapter 4

Postsocialist Ownership: Emotions, Power and Morality in a Czech Village[1]

Maruška Svašek

These people [the inhabitants of Vesnice] should not try to turn the village into an economically prosperous community. This is simply a very beautiful environment in which people should live who can afford to keep a pretty house in a good state of repair, and who won't make a mess and establish factories, breaker's yards, and similar crap. I don't find it necessary for people to live here, and I don't see the purpose. Young people should move to places where they can be educated and find jobs.

Dutch investor who established a pheasant shoot in the Czech village of Vesnice

Is this our home or Mr. Hulshoff's home? As I said earlier, there is an increasing feeling that we are threatened.

A Czech inhabitant of Vesnice

Introduction

The two quotations above indicate that changing property relations can trigger strong emotional reactions. The first speaker is a Dutch investor who, over the past eight years, has been buying numerous buildings and large plots of land in and around Vesnice, a Czech village in the West Bohemian border region. The second speaker is one of the Czech inhabitants of Vesnice, who is extremely worried about the increasing influence of the Dutchman in the village and the surrounding area. As this chapter will demonstrate, both speakers and a number of other persons have been engaged in passionate discussions about the effect of changing ownership on life in Vesnice and the future of the village community. The issue of property claims is further complicated by the former inhabitants of the village, Sudeten Germans who were expelled to Germany after the Second World War. After the end of the Cold War, they began frequently to visit their place of birth, and engage in symbolic acts of reappropriation.

Since the early 1990s, various patterns of changing ownership, including decollectivisation, restitution, privatisation, and property changes resulting from forced migration and ethnic cleansing, have evoked widespread feelings of anxiety amongst many Central and Eastern Europeans (Hann 1998; Leutloff 2002; Svašek 2000, 2001, 2002; Zerilli 2002). This is not surprising because 'having' and 'being' are dialectically related processes. Ownership does not only involve relationships between owners and their possessions but also influences processes of identification and self-perception, and shapes the interaction between different individuals (Miller 1987; see also Zerilli, Chapter 3, and Leutloff-Grandits, Chapter 5 in this volume). This chapter argues that these complexities cannot be analysed without a theoretical focus on the *emotional* dynamics of changing ownership.

The analysis focuses on property, emotions and power, and examines the various ways in which different social actors in the village of Vesnice have used subject-object discourses and emotional dynamics to construct images of self and other that have justified or criticised their own or other people's property-related behaviour. It defines emotions as powerful social forces that play an important role in the shaping and perception of ownership relations. The village is regarded as a political arena in which different actors have struggled for the right to own and use public space. The main interest groups are, firstly, former Sudeten German expellees who, since 1990, have started to visit their 'home village' on an annual basis; secondly, the social democratic mayor and his supporters; and thirdly, a Dutch entrepreneur who has bought large plots of land and numerous buildings, and who has established a pheasant shoot with the help of a British gamekeeper. To reach their goal – the actual or symbolic appropriation of property and space – the three groups have all used particular narrative constructions that have expressed and reinforced specific moral discourses of ownership and self.

Emotions, Property and Self

When analysing emotional dynamics, it is important to examine a number of related processes, including the genealogy of culturally and historically specific discourses of emotions and emotivity (Abu-Lughod and Lutz 1990), the functioning of emotions as forms of interpersonal communication (Parkinson 1995), and the ways in which emotions are performed in contexts of power struggle (Jamieson 2000). Equally important is the realisation that these processes are at least in part grounded in physical experience, and that, therefore, 'emotion' cannot be understood as either 'pure sensation' or 'pure cognition' (Leavitt 1996: 516).

The perspective of emotion as 'embodied experience' (Csordas 1990, 1994; Lyon and Barbalet 1994) problematises the Cartesian split between 'body' and 'mind', and questions rigid distinctions between 'nature' and 'culture'. Embodiment theory regards both direct, 'preobjective' experiences and their subsequent 'objectifications' as inherent elements of human culture. This means that culture is partly formed in the bodily processes of perception which shape and give meaning to representations.

When people, as living organisms that move through space and time, encounter concrete environments, particular sensual interactions, such as being held and breastfed during infancy, produce experiences that can be (but are not necessarily) objectified, interpreted, naturalised and internalised. In this process of objectification and embodiment, complex physical interpersonal experiences are not only translated into discourses and ideologies as the cultural constructionists would have it (see, for example, Abu-Lughod and Lutz 1990). In addition, they also form an inevitable part of 'being-in-the-world', of human perception and engagement, understood as an experiential process that cannot be explained in terms of pure cognition. The latter view was propagated during the 1940s, 1950s and 1960s by phenomenologists such as Maurice Merleau-Ponty (1962; Moran 2000: 391–432), and has become increasingly popular in the anthropology of emotions during the last decade (Csordas 1994; Jackson 1983, 1989).

The perspective of embodied experience undermines straightforward analytical distinctions between 'the individual' and 'the social'. Even though individuals are unique beings locked in their own ageing bodies (disturbingly clear when experiencing pain), the emotional life of feeling and thinking selves is normally marked by past, present and future interactions with others. Remembered, fantasised or ongoing social encounters may make a person smile, blush, or get angry. Even when we are alone, others may affect our moods through their internalised presences, as 'mind is fashioned from without – known from without via identifications with others' (Casey 1987: 244–45; Svašek 2005).

But the question remains: why and how do individuals get emotionally involved in ownership? To answer this question, it is helpful to use William James's (1890) distinction between 'I', the self as knowing subject, and 'me', the self as known object. James convincingly claimed that possessions partly constitute 'the self as known'. Contra Descartes, who had claimed that individual consciousness exists independently of others, he argued that human consciousness is directly built on the existence of other human beings as well as the material world that surrounds us, and that our changing social relations, roles and reputations are an inherent part of the known self (van Meijl and Driessen 2003: 18). James's perspective helps to explain why the prospect of losing property (and the loss of status that may come with it) can be felt as a direct attack on individual or collective identity. Losing something that is 'mine' or 'ours' means a direct transformation of the known self.

From the perspective of embodiment, the process of gaining knowledge about owning selves or others has a clear physical dimension. As human subjects actively engage with their own and other people's material properties, they may use a variety of senses which influence the objectification of their experiences of ownership. Seeing (our house), touching (his clothes), smelling (my dog), hearing (their car) and tasting (her apple pie) all constitute embodied knowledge that situates individuals in networks of subjectively experienced ownership relations. Your house is bigger and nicer than mine. Their car is perhaps more expensive than ours but it is also noisier. And so on.

Sensual experiences are also part of a learning mechanism in which people emotionally 'tune in' as they acquire particular perceptual skills, and develop specific interests and expectations (Milton 2002: 64). Experiences of ownership thus generate emotional anticipation. Whereas *a* tree is normally (but not always) just 'one of many trees', *my* tree may generate rather particular meanings and feelings. I may find 'my' apple tree in 'my' garden beautiful, and the apples tasty. The idea that I have access to my apple tree (or 'my castle', 'my country') whenever I want to can be emotionally satifying or even empowering. The sight of my tree may also remind me of those who possessed it before me, and bring back memories of, for example, my grandmother's perfume, the colour of her favourite dress, and her body as it felt when I used to sit on her lap in the garden when I was a child. As noted earlier, to understand possession and its emotional dimensions purely in terms of 'discourse' would mean to ignore the importance of such embodied experiences.

It must be stressed, however, that human subjects do not only engage emotionally with their own and other people's properties by 'being-in-the-world'. Living subjects *also* operate as symbolising agents, and transform 'owners' and 'their possessions' into a wide range of signifiers and signs that are incorporated into multiple and changing discourses. 'My tree' may, for example, signify 'my country' if that particular type of tree is used as a national symbol. The sign of the tree may then be strategically used to express and evoke nationalist sentiments. As this chapter will demonstrate, objects of ownership are often transformed into emotionally loaded signifiers of personal and collective identities, and subject-object distinctions may completely disappear in discourses of ownership that are based on territorial identity claims.

The Research Setting

Vesnice was established in 1666 in the Habsburg Empire by ethnic Germans, who cultivated the land and exploited the forest. During the second half of the nineteenth century, the inhabitants began to regard themselves as 'Sudeten Germans' whose ideology of blood and soil linked notions of 'collective self' to the idea of a God-given homeland. This idea became more outspoken after the establishment of Czechoslovakia in 1918, when the tensions between Czechs and Sudeten Germans increased, particularly as Hitler came to the political fore in neighbouring Germany. In 1938 most Sudeten Germans, including the inhabitants of Vesnice, welcomed the incorporation of the Sudetenland by Nazi Germany.

After the Second World War, the 1945 Potsdam Agreement stipulated that ethnic Germans from all over Central and Eastern Europe should be expelled from the area and 'return' to Germany. In the case of Czechoslovakia the Sudeten Germans' citizenship rights were annulled by the postwar government between May and October 1945, and most of their property was confiscated. During the next two years, over three million Sudeten Germans were expelled to Germany and Austria, and were forced to leave their homes and belongings behind. The expulsion began as soon as the war ended, a few months before the signing of the Potsdam Agreement, and took almost two years to complete. During the first six months, a period also known as the 'wild expulsion' (*wilde Austreibung*), tens of thousands were terrorised and brutally killed in a spirit of revenge (Hamperl 1996; Staněk 1991).

This fearful and traumatic experience soon generated the emotionally and politically powerful discourse of *die verlorene Heimat* (the lost homeland) (Svašek 2002, 2003). The *Sudetendeutsche Landsmannschaft*, the biggest organisation of Sudeten German expellees with its seat in Munich, defined the confiscated land as 'stolen property', and politicised their claims to the old homeland by demanding *Heimatrecht*, the right to return 'home' and to repossess their personal and collective belongings (cf. Hamperl 1996; Staněk 1991; Svašek 1999).

Immediately after the war, the Czechoslovak government introduced a policy to repopulate its border areas, and the abandoned Sudeten German houses were occupied by Czechs, Volhynia Czech, Slovaks, Roma and others. All cities, towns, and villages were officially renamed or only referred to by their Czech names. During the rapidly unfolding Cold War, the border with West Germany and Austria was transformed into one of the most heavily guarded sections of the Iron Curtain. Numerous border villages were blown up for security reasons, and villages like Vesnice – situated only four kilometres from the border with Eastern Bavaria – were never fully reoccupied. Situated in a remote, peripheral corner of the Eastern bloc, many houses remained empty and were eventually destroyed.[2]

In 1950, a number of Ruthenian families from Northern Romania moved to the village of Vesnice. They occupied some of the houses along the main road, worked in the state-owned forest and in the newly established collective farm. Most of the other houses were knocked down or slowly deteriorated. Over the years, the new villagers were able to buy the houses in which they lived from the Czechoslovak state, and some used their large gardens to cultivate fruit and vegetables for their own use.

I first visited Vesnice in the summer of 1991, as my family had bought a house there from one of the Ruthenian inhabitants. By now, almost all the houses were privately owned, and being mostly smallholdings the villagers depended in part on subsistence farming. The state farm was in the process of decollectivisation. By the time we arrived, the majority of the villagers still consisted of Ruthenians and their children. Other inhabitants included Czechs and a Slovak. The Soviet officers and soldiers who had been based in the village during the Cold War had already been demobilised and returned home. A typically 1960s-style apartment block which had previously housed the officers and their families was now occupied by the villagers, and the barracks had been turned into a home for physically and mentally handicapped children. Nearby there was also a now unused military radar post which was owned by the Czech Ministry of Defence. The village also included a number of larger buildings which had been built by the Sudeten Germans. The church, originally Roman Catholic, was now used by the Orthodox Ruthenians. The school, the parsonage, and the shop had been empty for many years, and were in a state of disrepair.

From 1991 onwards, I regularly visited Vesnice, and between September 1996 and August 1998, I used the village as a base for a research project which mainly dealt with identity formation in the Bohemian–Bavarian border area in the light of political, economic and social changes. As I became more familiar with the locals, got to know more about the Sudeten German history, learnt about the Dutchman's interest in village property, and was confronted with former Sudeten German inhabitants who visited their former *Heimatdorf*, I slowly realised that 'ownership' was one of the key expellee issues (see Leutloff-Grandits, Chapter 5, this volume, for an analysis of emotional ownership discourses by Serbian refugees).

Lost Property, Lost Selves and Symbolic Appropriation

Not surprisingly, after the abolition of compulsory visa requirements in 1990, the Sudeten German expellees displayed an increased interest in their *Heimat*, and many visited their places of birth for the first time in forty years. The visits were highly emotional occasions during which the expellees relived embodied experiences, remembered and reexperienced feelings of loss, fear and anger[3], and symbolically reconstituted themselves as a village community. At least five expellees from Vesnice recounted how they had burst into tears when they had first seen their old family houses or the remaining foundations. One of the Ruthenian inhabitants of the village said: 'They cried, they all cried. They searched the ruins and cried.'

Being able to spend some time in the village was emotionally confusing. 'Especially the first time when we were back in the church, me and my sisters, we all cried', said one of the expellees in 1997. 'I got many childhood memories, but today the village is of course very different from how it was so many years ago. That was hard, but at the same time, it made things easier'. She had felt a sense of relief during that first visit because she could now accept that the clock could no longer be turned back. 'Being-there' in real time and space had partially eroded her post-expulsion memories of 'the lost homeland', and had softened her feelings of frustrated longing.

Interestingly, the call by the *Sudetendeutsche Landsmannschaft* for *Heimatrecht* demanded that the Sudeten Germans should be given back their property, or some form of compensation, enabling them to restore their 'damaged' subject-object relationship. The discourse of 'stolen property' and the related politics of nostalgia engendered a particular image of ownership which portrayed the expellee community as a collective whole with a natural connection to their old *Heimat*. Diasporic nationalist homeland discourses are often politicised and highly moralistic (Skrbiš 2000), producing a cultural logic in which the lost object *is* the subject and vice versa. In the Sudeten German case, some of the more extreme groups, such as *Sudetendeutsche Rückkehr*, claimed that the affected 'deterritorialised' selves of the expellees could only be healed through reunion with the lost *Heimat*.

The expellees from Vesnice, however, were not attracted by the idea of returning, even though they identified themselves with their *Heimatdorf*. They had started new lives in Germany, and their children and grandchildren who had been born after the expulsion often regarded themselves as local Bavarians. Besides, the village itself was in a depressingly poor state. Instead of seeking to legally reclaim their old property from the Czech state, they began to symbolically reappropriate spaces in the village that still had a strong emotional value. From 1993 onwards, they held commemorative services in front of the war memorials and in the church. On the day of the annual service, their presence was undeniable as their shiny cars were parked all over the village, and their voices could be heard as they walked over the village road. Over the years, they also left more permanent marks by restoring the old war memorial and doing up the few remaining Sudeten German graves.

Their emotions, in this regard, were embodied feelings and social forces which motivated specific object-focused activities. Nostalgia and unresolved mourning moved the expellees to organise annual visits to their place of birth which, subsequently, enabled them to have positive experiences in their old village. Even though mistrust and hatred of the Czechs would be remembered and at times reexperienced, they created intersubjective space for reconciliatory feelings which partially blurred the line between their Sudeten German 'collective' self and the Czech aggressive other. With the help of local priests (Svašek 2000), they actively managed and performed more positive emotions in an attempt to open up the possibility for friendly cooperation with the Czechs.

Property as Investment: Subjects and Objects in the Global Market Economy

Over the past thirteen years, the changed economic climate in postsocialist Europe has attracted the interest of Western investors (see also Müller, Chapter 8, this volume). Not surprisingly, capitalist discourses of ownership have differed considerably from the nostalgic and moralistic subject-object discourse of the expellees. To avoid selling off the 'family silver', the Czechoslovak government passed a law prohibiting the sale of land and real estate to foreigners. It was, however, easy enough to circumvent this hurdle by establishing a firm with a Czech director (*jednatel*). Such companies were officially Czech, and were therefore allowed to buy property.

The villagers of Vesnice were suddenly confronted by exactly such a 'Czech' company which had been set up by the Dutch entrepreneur Pieter Hulshoff. Unlike the Sudeten Germans, he was not interested in symbolic appropriation but simply wanted to buy buildings and land, and establish a pheasant shoot and a hunting lodge. To realise his dream, the Dutchman needed to buy buildings which could be turned into living space for himself and his family, a gamekeeper, and the future members of his hunting lodge. Two buildings in Vesnice which could easily be transformed into comfortable living spaces were the old Sudeten German school and the parsonage. Hulshoff managed to purchase them from the Orthodox Church and the Catholic Church within a year.[4]

It would be wrong to imagine the Sudeten German relationship with the village as 'purely emotional', and Hulshoff's attitude as 'purely rational'. The latter was not 'just' looking for investment and long-term financial gain. Hunting had been one of his life-long passions, and his hunting experiences in and around Vesnice contributed to his growing attachement to the place. Embodied experiences – the smell of the air, the sound of the game, his walks though the countryside – also fed his strong desire to establish a quasi-estate in the area.

While the purchase of the school and the parsonage had been relatively easy, acquiring the thousands of hectares of land the Dutchman needed for the shoot, was to prove far more difficult. The fields around Vesnice were still owned by the Czech state, having been collectivised under communism, and had been assigned to a state farm which was eventually privatised in 1992. The new private owners of the farm, which was run by director Jan Nový, were not yet allowed to buy the fields they worked due to the slow transformation of land ownership, as well as their own lack of capital. Instead, the farm rented the fields from the national government body which officially oversees the lease, restitution and sale of state-owned land, known as the *Pozemkový fond*.

Hulshoff contacted Nový, and proposed buying the land on the basis of the restitution claims which he had already purchased.[5] In return Nový would be given a lease contract for a period of twenty years. Nový agreed to the idea because it meant he would no longer need to fear the sudden loss of land were it bought by developers or simply somebody who did not wish to lease it to him. Hulshoff, as the lessor, had first right to purchase the land thanks to the rules of the *Pozemkový fond*. This right, by means of various legal contracts, was to be assigned to Hulshoff.

Restitution was a slow and painful process but his frustration and anger made him even more determined to persevere, to realise himself as an 'estate owner'. This again shows how emotions can be a driving force which empower people to take action. As with the Sudeten German case, Hulshoff's example also demonstrates that people actively manage emotions, and attempt to change other people's emotional states to attain certain goals. The Dutchman tried to create good relationships with key figures in the privatisation process, such as with one of the regional directors of the *Pozemkový fond*, by taking them out for lunches. He admitted to having threatened some 'hopeless' local bureaucrats by telling them that he would contact their bosses in Prague and ensure that they were fired. 'Nice words don't work in this country,' he said. 'The only thing that has any effect is fear.'

Justifying the Right to Buy 'Stolen Property'

The Dutchman knew that his new possessions had once belonged to the Sudeten Germans. Each year, the expellees held their annual ritual in the square between the school and the parsonage, and knocked on his door to ask if they could take a look inside. 'We had whole crowds in our house', he told me. 'They pointed out the class rooms where they used to sit. Well, we are always very friendly to them.' When I asked him whether anyone had ever accused him of living in 'stolen property', he said: 'Yes they did. They are actually always friendly, but once I had a discussion with some of those Germans, and they told me that everything had been stolen from them', and added:

> I told them: 'I don't agree with you. As a German community you lived in Czechoslovakia so you were Czechs (meaning Czechoslovak citizens). Subsequently, you chose to support an aggressive state. The fact that you were punished for that...well, such things have happened throughout history. If you would have won [the war], you would have owned the whole of Czechoslovakia. Unfortunately you lost ... and now the buildings are mine!'

He clearly disagreed with the Sudeten German claim for *Heimatrecht*, and by accusing them of supporting the Third Reich, he justified his ownership of their confiscated properties. He noted, however, that he did understand their feelings of nostalgia, and did not mind their rituals in front of his doorstep. Evidently, his 'liberal' attitude was in line with his own interests. He wanted to avoid unnecessary tensions, and, after all, the Sudeten Germans were just engaged in symbolic appropriation. They did not intend to buy property in the village, and therefore, he did not see them as competitors.

Anger and Resentment

As noted before, property relations are dynamic relations between different social actors who form (changing, conflicting) notions of self and other. As the shoot began to function and Hulshoff started to buy more houses, claim more land, and put up fences, many villagers began to feel uneasy about his presence, and the ways in which the shoot affected their experience of the village space. Those who worked for him (as builders, cleaners, housekeepers, assistants to the new British gamekeeper, and beaters) or who sold property to him, benefited financially from his presence. Yet many, in particular those who did not benefit, saw him as a crude profiteer.

Petr Hedrlin, who had lived in Vesnice since the 1970s argued that Hulhoff's presence had led to the return of the old estate system. He said: 'As happened after the thirty-year war under the domination of the Habsburg aristocrats the Czech lands will soon be controlled by rich foreigners, and once again we'll have a *panstvi*. History is repeating itself.' It is telling that he used the term *panstvi*, which links the concepts of 'estate', 'serfdom', 'domination', 'power', and 'nobility'. The image of an estate visited by members of a powerful aristocracy was reinforced when the future king of the Netherlands, Prince Willem Alexander, came to shoot pheasants in Vesnice in 1999. He was an acquaintance of Hulshoff's brother, a banker, and although the crown prince's presence was 'secret', the whole village soon knew about it.

In Hedrlin's view, the capitalist free-market ideology and its approach to ownership formed the centre of the problem:

> The question is: 'who owns the means of production?' We are now being transformed into a developing country. We will work hard but somebody else will export our products, and God knows who will get the profits. Whichever way you turn it, capitalism is relentless. The only criterion is profit. Evidently, we haven't been prepared for that, and the governments which came to power after 1989 have not shown much interest in our region. By selling out through privatisation we have survived the last decade, and may possibly further survive but the situation will only become worse.

Hedrlin felt threatened by the fact that more and more houses and plots of land in and around Vesnice were falling into the hands of one powerful foreigner. 'We're becoming strangers in our own house', he noted, 'I used to think that this was my home, but now we're confronted with something we never wanted to be confronted with.' One way in which the villagers expressed their resentment towards Hulshoff was through gossip. Gossip is a communicative practice which both shapes and is shaped by changing power relations, and helps people to make judgements and respond to rapid change (Svašek 1997: 115). To most of the villagers, the transformation from state-socialism to democracy meant changing working conditions, economic insecurity, and the confrontation with new socioeconomic hierarchies. Gossip provided a subjective, emotional account of these experiences in relatively fixed narrative structures in which the rich intruder Hulshoff was simply 'the bad guy'. The stories portrayed him as somebody who made huge profits from his hunting lodge while his employees only earned average Czech wages. They also accused him of being a burglar and a drugs dealer, and reported his 'crimes' to the police. Hulshoff, called the stories 'absolutely absurd', and argued that the rumour-mongers were basically driven by envy.

Capitalist Ownership: the Self as 'Patron'

The villagers did not just protest against the disappearance of communal (i.e. state) ownership. Some people complained that Hulshoff's pheasants ruined their gardens, and covered the graves in the cemetery with excrement. In Hulshoff's view, the best way to respond to this was by subsidising a number of communal projects. He explained that 'patronage' was common practice among estate owners:

> In our family, we always had country estates. Having an estate means owning a larger plot of land, and that brings with it social obligations. Normally you do that in consultation with the people who live there. So the first thing I did was to waterproof the town hall. Secondly we renovated the chapel by the graveyard. And then, much against my wishes, we financed a new stretch of asphalt. A gravelled road would have been much more picturesque.

Through his 'help' to the village, Hulshoff clearly intended to construct an image of himself as a willing, caring patron who should be welcomed instead of envied. A number of villagers I spoke with indeed appreciated his concern. Hulshoff, however, was disappointed that his actions did not stop the gossip and the antics.[6]

Several villagers interpreted the Dutchman's 'good deeds' in a different way. One of them remarked: 'Well, the guy is so rich … he's just being strategically nice. In the end he is the one who profits and we are the ones who lose.' Hulshoff objected by saying that the villagers had no idea of his expenses. So far, the shoot had yet to turn a profit. Evidently, he was in a position to take such financial risks. He also admitted that he expected his money to be well spent.

The Dutchman justified his presence in the village as a new owner through a specific subject–object discourse which was based on a mixture of capitalist, perceived 'aristocratic', and kinship values. Firstly, he clearly approved of the functioning of the free-market economy, and regarded buying property in postsocialist Europe as a fundamental right. In his view, life should be enjoyed, and money should be (at least partly) used for that purpose. Secondly, in numerous cases, his ownership directly influenced the life and self-perception of other villagers. Hulshoff tried to pacify them through good deeds which he defined as an inherent component of large private ownership. Thirdly, he regarded his property as an investment which would benefit his children.

The Social-Democratic View: the Village as a Growing Community

The mayor, Jan Veselý, who had himself sold a house to the Dutchman, did not disapprove of Hulshoff's presence in the village. He stressed that it was financially advantageous to the community as a whole, and accepted Hulshoff's claim to patronage. The mayor, a Social Democrat, did not mind that Czech property fell into foreign hands. He did, however, also believe in shared community rights, and noted that the dynamics of capitalist ownership complicated the introduction of a socioeconomic policy which would support the village as a collective. The village community badly needed to enlarge its budget. The roads were in a terrible state, only half of the village was connected to the sewerage system, young people needed housing, and the children had nowhere to play. According to Veselý, the best route to take was to build new houses and increase the number of inhabitants by attracting young people to the village.

Building new houses was restricted because of a nearby freshwater reservoir. Some of the restrictions would be lifted after the completion of the sewerage system, for which the mayor had secured funding. This meant that once the *Pozemkový Fond* agreed to sell the plots of land which were still state-owned, more houses could be built, and the village could grow.

Young families would most likely not have enough money to build new houses, so Veselý looked for other possibilities.

The only large unoccupied building in the village was the old military base that had been used during the Cold War as a radar station. The mayor came up with a plan to turn the building into flats and a children's clubhouse. He thought that the future inhabitants would be willing to pay half of the reconstruction costs. A bank could provide a low-interest loan, which would be paid back in instalments in the form of monthly rent.

The base was still owned by the Ministry of National Defence, but it no longer served any purpose, and in 2000 the Ministry put it on the market for 5,800,000 crowns. This was still far too much for the village community, and Veselý, who was a member of the ČSSD (the ruling social democratic party) used his party contacts to get in touch with the Minister. With a triumphant smile, he recounted:

> When the Minister announced that the ministry wanted to get rid of most of its properties because they cost too much money, I travelled (to Prague) to visit him, and simply used his words. And he personally told me – I have two witnesses, two parliament members who can back me up – that he would give the base to us for free.[7]

As part of his perceived 'socialist-democratic view of ownership', the mayor thus accepted responsibility for the well-being of the village as a community. Like Hulshoff, he used personal networks in the bureaucratic jungle of Czech politics to realise his plans. Yet his political views were based on the notion of communal rights, and not on the paternalistic idea of individual patronage.

Hulshoff ridiculed the plan, and called it 'unrealistic'. More importantly, it went against his image of the village as a picturesque backdrop to his estate. In his words:

> These people should not try to turn the village into an economically prosperous community. This is simply a very beautiful environment in which people should live who can afford to keep a pretty house in a good state of repair, and who won't make a mess and establish factories, breaker's yards, and similar crap. I don't find it necessary for people to live here, and I don't see the purpose. Young people should move to places where they can be educated and find jobs. So the military base … well, you know, nothing will come of it.

The Dutchman justified his view through emotional rhetoric which depicted himself as a neat and environmentally-conscious person who 'knew better' than the irresponsible locals what was best for the environment. About his most recent purchase, the old village shop, he stated in the summer of 2001: 'I only bought the shop because they wanted to turn it into a small factory. And I don't want another dirty, collapsed piece of trash with rubbish all over the place.'

Hedrlin was rather shocked when he heard about Hulshoff's plans, and said that the villagers felt threatened. 'If he wants that, he'll have to move us. So there, we have arrived at the problem. Is this our home or Mr. Hushoff's home? I talked about it earlier, there is an increasing feeling that we are threatened.'

Mixed Feelings in the Village

To get a better understanding of the contradictory feelings Hulshoff's activities evoked among and possibly also within distinct villagers, it is interesting to focus on the opinions of members of the Příhoda family. Honza and Jiřina Příhoda had moved to Vesnice in the 1970s. Jiřina had two sons from an earlier marriage, and together, the couple had two daughters born in 1988 and 1993. Having worked on the state farm until its privatisation in 1992, they decided to use their acquired skills and try their luck in private farming. The couple bought five milking cows, which they kept in a small stable behind the house, and rented the adjacent field from the *Pozemkový fond*.

Honza dreamt of expanding his business but found out that he was restricted by strict environmental regulations. The few cows he had did not provide enough income, and he was forced to take on another job as a road worker. A heavy drinker, he frequently cursed and lamented his fate. Not surprisingly, when Hulshoff entered the scene and managed to set up his hunting lodge in a relatively short period of time, Honza became even more bitter. Jiřina's oldest son Petr was also irritated by Hulshoff's increasing presence in the village. Jiřina, by contrast, argued that she did not really mind him buying property in the village. At least he was repairing the school building, and his shoot might create some jobs for the villagers. Her perception was partly affected by the fact that her marriage with Honza was on the verge of breaking down. Some months later, she planned to move out, and was desperately looking for a place to live and a job to secure her financial independence.

I knew Jiřina quite well, and knew that she had been trying to find employment in Tachov. Yet unemployment was on the rise, and being in her forties, Jiřina was greatly disadvantaged. When I got to know that Hulshoff was looking for a cook/housekeeper, I recommended her to him. Jiřina did not only get the job, she also moved into one of the houses recently bought by Hulshoff. The house, which had belonged to the mayor, was damp and in a bad state. Hulshoff did not use it because he planned to knock it down and build a bigger house on the spot. Yet to Jiřina and three of her children, it was good enough as a temporary solution. On the whole, she was satisfied, and liked her employer, his wife and their children.

In 1998, even though he disliked the idea of a foreigner 'taking over' the village, Petr also started to work for Hulshoff but did not show as much enthusiasm for the pheasants as some other employees. After a few years, he was advised by the gamekeeper to look for other employment.

The different, changing, and ambigious evaluations of Hulshoff by Petr, his parents and the other villagers, and the changing perception of 'Czechs' by the Sudeten German expellees reinforces the view that different 'modalities of intersubjective reasoning are steeped in an awareness that one's humanity is simultaneously shared and singular' (Jackson 2002: 142). None of the actors doubted that 'power' and 'morality' were what linked them as human beings, but there were clear differences as to which moral and legal codes should underly the management and control of ownership.

Conclusion

This chapter has defined emotions as social forces that are grounded in embodied experience, thereby arguing that emotions cannot be reduced to purely mental or physical processes. Specific emotional dynamics have been central to the rapidly transforming property relations in the post-Cold War Czech-German border area. The experience of having lost possessions, and the prospect of losing or gaining property generated particular emotional discourses and performances as people sought to ground a sense of personal and collective identity. Narratives and embodied experiences of 'having' and 'being' reinforced each other, and justified claims to a particular morality. Physical sensations and bodily memories of particular spaces, owned or symbolically appropriated by individuals (self or other) or groups (self or other), were important motivators of the justifying claims.

Three conflicting narratives of ownership and self strengthened distinct moral, legal, and political arguments concerning personal and collective ownership. The expellee discourse of identity was based on the image of a strong emotional connection of blood and soil in which subject (the former owners) and object (the lost possessions) merged into one single unit. The expellees from Vesnice played out embodied memories and emotional discourses in the context of religious ceremonies. On an annual basis they physically appeared as a collective in the village, moving in and out of spaces which they had once owned. With the help of local priests, they symbolically appropriated the village, justifying their actions within the socio-religious discourse of reconciliation. In addition, some also made more regular individual trips to the village, for example to new aquaintances and the old graveyard, thus gaining new embodied experiences in the post-Cold War context.

When the new inhabitants of Vesnice were confronted with rapidly changing property relations after the introduction of a free-market system in 1990, some criticised the capitalist ideology of ownership because it did not give enough rights to the village as a collective unit. It undermined their strong sense of communal self which had been fiercely propagated by the communists even if seldom adhered to. Others felt that their personal – physical and social – space was being invaded by a foreigner who had no moral right to own Czech property, transforming village life according to his own ideas. The mayor, who supported social democratic ideals of 'social justice for all', sought to generate an emotional discourse among villagers who felt resentment and depression with political ambitions of his own. He presented himself as a responsible politician who aimed to protect the village collective by controlling the Dutch buyer's aspirations, and ensuring the growth of the village community.

The Dutch investor used a subject-object discourse of capitalism, environmentalism and patricianesque sentiments. He profited from the weak Czech economy, and thanks to his capital and business acumen was able to transform himself into a transnational estate owner, partly by slowly finding his way within the Czech bureaucratic system. As he spent an increasing amount of time and energy on the development of his estate, he attached himself emotionally to his acquired and desired possessions, and developed a discourse to justify his increasing presence and power in the area. This discourse served to strengthen his own identity as a worldly-wise benefactor who helped to create a happy village.

Notes

1. A slightly different version of this text was published in 2003 in *Social Networks in Movement. Time, Interaction, and Inter-ethnic Spaces in Central Eastern Europe*, ed. D. Torsello and M. Pappova, Šamorín: Lilium Aurum. I would like to thank Lilium Aurum for permission to reprint parts of the earlier text, and Justin I'Anson-Sparks and Davide Torsello for their helpful comments on the 2003 version. In the 2003 publication, I mainly looked at emotional dynamics as discourses and

performances. By contrast, this chapter aims to combine the perspectives of discourse analysis and embodiment theory.

2. A comparison of the numbers of inhabitants before and after the Sudeten German expulsion demonstrates the extent to which the village was affected. At the time of their expulsion, over 1,000 Sudeten Germans had lived in Vesnice. Today the village houses only about 200 inhabitants, 80 percent fewer than before.

3. For a discussion of the distinction between the concepts of 'remembered' and 'reexperienced' emotions, see Svašek 2000b and Svašek 2005.

4. The school was owned by the Orthodox Church, and the parsonage by the Catholic Church. Within a year, Hulshoff managed to buy both buildings, respectively, for 600,000 and 250,000 crowns (about £12,000 and £5,000). He clearly profited from the weakness of the Czech economy, and by hiring cheap Czech and Ukrainian labourers to renovate the buildings.

5. As part of the democratisation process, the Czechoslovak government had designed a law to grant former landowners or their descendants the right to reclaim previously owned land which had been nationalised or collectivised. People who did not want to reclaim land, either because their plot was too small to make it profitable or because they now lived in cities, sold their restitution rights to third parties. Various entrepreneurs such as Hulshoff bought as many restitutions claims as they needed to start particular projects.

6. In Hulshoff's words: 'What I don't understand is that when you are friendly and do nice things, just nice things without any reason, pay things for the community, because the community has never done a friendly thing for me, it only hindered me in all possible ways, but then still you think ... you want to create some goodwill, so on the one hand you buy land, and on the other you try to create goodwill, but also the goodwill, or exactly the goodwill is taken as an opportunity to screw you.'

7. Veselý also received a letter from a Colonel to confirm the promise. He explained that he was now working on an official application, a concrete proposal which would have to be signed by the council representatives.

Bibliography

Abu-Lughod, L. and Lutz, C.A. 1990. 'Introduction: Emotion, Discourse, and the Politics of Everyday Life', in *Language and the Politics of Emotion*, ed. C.A. Lutz and L. Abu-Lughod. Cambridge and Paris: Cambridge University Press and Editions de la Maison des Sciences de l'Homme.

Anderson, D.G. 1998. 'Property as a Way of Knowing on Evenki Lands in Arctic Siberia', in *Property Relations. Renewing the Anthropological Tradition*, ed. C.M. Hann. Cambridge: Cambridge University Press, pp. 64–84.

Attfield, J. 2000. *Wild Things. The Material Culture of Everyday Life*. Oxford: Berg.

Casey, E.S. 1987. *Remembering. A Phenomenological Study*. Bloomington: Indiana University Press.

Creed, G. 1998. *Domesticating Revolution. From Socialist Reform to Ambivalent Transition in a Bulgarian Village*. University Park: Pennsylvania State University Press.

Csordas, T.J. 1990. 'Embodiment as a Paradigm for Anthropology', *Ethos* 18(1): 5–47.

———, ed. 1994. *Embodiment as a Paradigm for Anthropology. The Existential Ground of Culture and Self.* Cambridge: Cambridge University Press.

Hamperl, W. 1996. *Vertreibung und Flucht aus dem Kreis Tachau im Egerland, 1945–1948. Schicksale in Berichten, Dokumenten und Bildern* (I and II). Trostberg: Private publication.

Hann, C.M., ed. 1998. *Property Relations. Renewing the Anthropological Tradition.* Cambridge: Cambridge University Press.

Hoebel, E.A. 1966. *Anthropology. The Study of Man.* New York: McGraw-Hill.

Jackson, M. 1983. 'Knowledge of the Body', *Man n.s.* 18(2): 327–45.

——— 1989, *Paths Towards a Clearing: Radical Empiricism and Ethnographic Inquity.* Bloomington: Indiana University Press.

——— 2002. 'The Exterminating Angel. Reflections on Violence and Intersubjective Reason', *Focaal. European Journal of Anthropology* 39: 137–48.

Jamieson, M. 2000. 'It's Shame that Makes Men and Women Enemies. The Politics of Intimacy among the Miskitu of Kakabila', *Journal of the Royal Anthropological Institute* n.s. 6: 311–24.

Kaneff, D. 1996. 'Responses to "Democratic" Land Reforms in a Bulgarian Village', in *After Socialism. Land Reform and Social Changes in Eastern Europe*, ed. R. Abrahams. Oxford: Berghahn, pp. 85–114.

Leavitt, J. 1996. 'Meaning and Feeling in the Anthropology of Emotions', *American Ethnologist* 23(3): 514–39.

Leutloff, C. 2002. 'Claiming Ownership on Post-war Croatia. The Emotional Dynamics of Possession and Re-possession in Knin', *Focaal. European Journal of Anthropology* 39: 73–92.

Lutz, C. and White, G.M. 1986. 'The Anthropology of Emotions', *Annual Review of Anthropology* 15: 405–36.

Lyon, M.L. and Barbalet, J.M. 1994. 'Society's Body. Emotion and the "Somatisation" of Social Theory', in *Embodiment and Experience. The Existential Ground of Culture and Self*, ed. T.J. Csordas. Cambridge: Cambridge University Press, pp. 248–68.

van Meijl, Ton and Driessen, H. 2003. 'Introduction: Multiple Identifications and the Self', *Focaal. European Journal of Anthropology* 42: 17–29.

Merleau-Ponty, M. 1962. *Phenomenology of Perception.* Trans. J. Edie. Evanston, IL: Northwestern University Press.

Miller, D. 1987. *Material Culture and Mass Consumption.* Oxford: Basil Blackwell.

Milton, K. 2002. *Loving Nature. Towards an Ecology of Emotion.* London: Routledge.

Moran, D. 2000. *Introduction to Phenomenology.* London: Routledge.

Müller, B. 2002. 'Say it in Rhymes. Hits Below the Belt in Czech Village Politics', *Focaal. European Journal of Anthropology* 39: 29–40.

Parkinson, B. 1995. *Ideas and Realities of Emotion.* London and New York: Routledge.

Skrbiš, Z. 1999. *Long-Distance Nationalism. Diasporas, Homelands and Identities*. Aldershot: Ashgate.

——— 2002. 'The Emotional Historiography of Venetologists. Slovene Diaspora, Memory, and Nationalism', *Focaal. European Journal of Anthropology* 39: 41–56.

Staněk, T. 1991. *Odsun Němců z Československa*. Prague: Academia naše vojensko.

Svašek, M. 1997. 'Gossip and Power Struggle in the Post-communist Czech Art World. *Focaal. European Journal of Anthropology* 29: 101–22.

——— 1999. 'History, Identity and Territoriality. Redefining Czech-German Relations in the Post-Cold War Era', *Focaal. Journal of Anthrolopology* 32: 37–58.

——— 2000. 'Borders and Emotions. Hope and Fear in the Bohemian-Bavarian Frontier Zone', *Ethnologia Europaea. Journal of European Ethnology* 30(2): 11–126.

——— 2001. 'The Politics of Emotions. Longing for the Sudetenland'. Paper presented at the workshop 'Theorizing Emotions', School of Anthropological Studies, Queen's University, Belfast.

——— 2002. 'The Politics of Emotions. Emotional Discourses and Displays in Post-Cold War Contexts', *Focaal. European Journal of Anthropology* 39: 9–28.

——— 2003. 'Narratives of Home and Homeland. The Symbolic Construction and Appropriation of the Sudeten German "Heimat"', *Identities. Global Studies in Culture and Power* 9: 495–518.

——— 2005. 'The Politics of Chosen Trauma. Expellee Memories, Emotions, and Identities', in *Mixed Emotions. Anthropological Studies of Feeling*, ed. K. Milton and M. Svašek. Oxford: Berg.

Verdery, K. 1998. 'Property and Power in Transylvania's Decollectivization.', in *Property Relations. Renewing the Anthropological Tradition*, ed. C.M. Hann. Cambridge: Cambridge University Press, pp. 160–80.

Zerilli, Filippo M. 2002. 'Sentiments and/as Property Rights: On the Conflicts Between Tenants and Owners over House Property Restitution in Bucharest', *Focaal. European Journal of Anthropology* 39: 57–72.

Chapter 5

Claiming Ownership in Postwar Croatia: the Emotional Dynamics of Possession and Repossession in Knin

Carolin Leutloff-Grandits

Introduction

During the wars in the Yugoslav successor states in the 1990s, ethnic engineering and ethnic 'cleansing' became a powerful strategy for political actors seeking to reorder the society nationally and socially (Denich 1994; Grandits and Leutloff 2003; Hayden 1996). On all sides of the front lines, hundreds of thousands of civilians from the opposing national groups were expelled and their houses were destroyed or redistributed to members of other national groups. Notions of private or socially owned property were neglected in this nationalistic approach. Houses became national homes, and the land became national territory and homeland. After the end of the war, emotionally loaded conflicts over property and housing rights arose between those who occupied houses that were allocated to them during the war, or immediately after the war, and the owners who wanted to repossess their houses.

Property cases in the region of Knin, a town which falls within the boundaries of the Croatian state (internationally recognised in 1992) in which the war was fought along national lines between Croats and Serbs, may serve to illustrate conflicts over property. Before the war in 1991 the inhabitants of Knin consisted of a large Serbian majority and a Croatian minority, the members of which lived in 1991 either in family houses in private property or in (formerly) socially owned apartment buildings. During the war from 1991 to 1995, Croats were expelled by Serbian extremists and their property was partly destroyed and party redistributed to Serbian coethnics. When in 1995 the Croatian army reconquered the territory, the Serbian population fled to Serbia and other Serb-held territories. As had occurred to Croatian property previously, Serbian property was partly destroyed and partly redistributed to Croatian settlers.

During my fieldwork in the region of Knin in 2000, most local Croats had returned to their houses, and those dwellings requiring reconstruction were rebuilt. Numerous private Serbian houses were still in ruins. Croats from Bosnia and other parts of Croatia had moved into Serbian dwellings, including intact private family houses and socially owned flats. Serbian returnees therefore did not have much choice but to return to houses that had not been occupied by Croats due to their bad condition or their remote location.

Staying in a village near Knin, I was often in the company of one of the few younger Serbian returnee couples. When we talked, they frequently explained that they had returned because they felt connected to the area. Before they were forced to flee in 1995, they had lived their whole life in their home region and perceived it as their ancestral land. They also often mentioned that their biggest tragedy was that they could not return to their own family home, because it was occupied, which forced them to stay in the house of a relative. The couple had already waited three years for their house, and were very angry about the behaviour of the occupiers. They explained that the occupants had only moved into the house in 1997, although the Serbian neighbour and even a Croatian relative, with whom they had good relations, had tried to prevent it. Returning from exile only a little later and trying to settle the case with the occupiers peacefully, the occupiers called the police, accusing the owners of harassment. They were warned by the police to stay away from the house, and were told to leave the present occupiers in peace. Subsequently, the Serbian couple decided to wait for the local housing commission to solve the case, although they had little faith in the process.

Speaking to the occupiers, I discovered that they were about the same age as the Serbian owners. They were warrefugees from Bosnia, and openly accused the owners, the Serbian neighbours, and even some local Croats of having harassed them after moving in, although they had legally received the house from the Croatian state. They justified their occupation by saying that the Serbs lost their right of settling in the area because of the war, and that it belonged to them as Croats. However, the wife said that she lived every day in fear because the Serbs lived nearby, and that she felt lonely and depressed. They planned to leave the Serbian neighbourhood, and waited for the local housing commission to offer them another house in a Croatian neighbourhood in Knin. When I talked about the case with the head of the local housing commission, who was a local Croat from the region, he said that he had sympathy for the young Serbian returnee family, whom he knew well. He was aware that they had waited for a long time to repossess their house, and explained that he had not found an alternative accommodation which met the expectations of the Croatian settlers. He also noted that, being a Croat, he would lose his reputation when publicly defending Serbian rights 'against' the interests of Croats.

This example of a property conflict near Knin, in which Serbian returnees, Croatian settlers and a local Croat were involved, shows that the issues of housing and in particular repossession and occupation of property are highly charged with emotions in the war-torn region of Croatia, as in other regions of former Yugoslavia. The case agrees with Hann's (1998) definition of property relations as social relations embedded in social and political fields (cf. also the chapters of Svašek and Zerilli in this volume), and shows that in Knin, the emotional experiences of the war and of returning to or settling in the area have shaped property-related discourses and actions. The postwar inter-ethnic encounters have thus been framed by nationalist sentiments, which have been formed by the violent collapse of the Yugoslav state between 1991 and 1995, and which have been (re-)produced by powerful political and religious institutions (see Zerilli, Chapter 3, this volume, for the importance of political institutions in shaping emotions). This analysis also argues, however, that certain emotional judgements that have been articulated in private and/or local spheres have undermined nationalist representations that stress ethnic difference and the postsocialist experience of ethnic war. By contrast, these judgements have referred to positive inter-ethnic ideals and experiences during socialist times.

This chapter will examine the emotional judgements made by members of three groups, namely Serbian returnees, Croatian settlers and local Croats. The analysis is based on anthropological fieldwork in the Knin area of Croatia between May 2000 and July 2001. Examining emotional claims for housing and property rights, I shall argue that emotional judgements are constructed in particular social and political contexts (Reddy 1997: 329, 331, Lutz and White 1986: 408, 415, 420, see also Zerilli, Svašek and Skrbiš this volume), and that emotional judgements and claims can be regarded as reactions to past and present social events. As Svašek (2000) has shown, emotional judgements can be strongly influenced by past individual and collective experiences. They are informed by expectations and norms, which are developed in a long process of socialisation, and influenced by dominant politics (Reddy 1997: 335).

In the postwar context of Croatia, emotional judgements are often related to memories of violent events in war, and are strongly affected by authoritative political discourses and propaganda (Denich 1994; Grandits 1998; Jansen 2000; for general theoretical considerations see Appadurai 1998). Public political and religious rituals and festivals which refer to the times of war in the 1990s create an image of nationalist unity, even if the participants also distinguish themselves in ways that cut across ethnic boundaries. Yet individual emotional judgements have been ambivalent and conflicting (Lutz and White 1986: 419), and people's sentimental attachments have partly been shaped by events and norms which refer to the socialist past. Most informants I spoke with grew up during socialism, and the elderly informants in particular regarded some of the conditions achieved during socialism as positive (cf. Humphrey 2002: 12–15). Because many individuals, Serbs as well as Croats, nowadays live under insecure and difficult social conditions, for many the socialist past is a reference frame to evaluate the situation they are in now, and images of the socialist past legitimise current claims. Obviously, how far and in which way informants relate their emotional claims to the socialist past varies from group to group and from person to person (cf. also Zerilli and Svašek, this volume, who deal with interest groups and their presentations of the past for current property claims). While nationalist memories are in line with postwar official policies, non-nationalist sentiments are largely expressed in the private sphere.

My exposition on these topics is divided into four sections. The first section outlines the historical and political context in which emotional judgements about property issues take place. The three sections that follow describe the changing perspectives and emotional judgements of Croatian settlers, Serbian returnees and Croatian returnees towards property claims in the area, focusing on the way in which the prewar and war experiences have influenced their property claims and have shaped inter-group relations.

Historical and Political Context

Until the 1960s the ethnically mixed region of Knin was basically a poor, rural area. With the construction of socially owned factories after the 1960s, this began to change as most people gained employment in the new local industrial sector. Agriculture gradually became a secondary occupation. With growing wealth people built new family houses on private property, and/or they moved to one of the socially owned flats in the town of Knin built after the 1960s. Privately owned houses in particular were seen as a marker of social prestige. At the same time, entitlements to socially owned housing and access to medical care and education were also seen as basic citizen rights that created greater equality in terms of resource- and property distribution. Based on the socialist policy of brotherhood and unity, the meaning of ethnicity and religion successively lost influence in the public sphere (until the 1980s), despite memories of violent clashes along national lines (during the Second World War).

With the dissolution of Yugoslavia, the assertion of Croatian and Serbian ethnic identity in 1990–91 was followed by a chain of violent incidents in ethnically mixed areas, and led eventually to full-scale war in the predominantly Serb-inhabited regions of Croatia. From 1991 to 1993, Serbian forces managed to conquer and control about one-third of Croatia's territory. They established the State of Serbian Krajina with Knin as the capital, but this was never recognised internationally. In the course of the war, the Serbian army as well as Serbian extremists expelled the Croatian population from these regions and destroyed much of their property, private houses and Catholic churches in particular. Most Croats from the Knin area spent their exile in refugee camps in Croatian coastal towns.

The situation changed drastically in 1995, when the Croatian army successfully reconquered the territory. Almost all the Serbian civilians as well as the Serbian army fled to Serbia and other Serb-held territories before the advancing Croatian army. The formerly Serb held territory was reintegrated into the Croatian state and the Croatian government passed laws on housing rights to grant Croats temporary use-rights to abandoned Serbian houses as well as to the abandoned socially owned flats (Law on Temporary Takeover and Administration of Specified Property 1995; Law on Lease of Apartments in Liberated Areas 1995). Media campaigns were launched to attract Croatian settlers to the region.

In the first months after the reintegration of the area by the Croatian army, looting, destruction and spontaneous occupation of Serbian property were general features of everyday life. In the former Serbian-held regions altogether about 20,000 houses were occupied by Croats from other regions, notably Croatian war refugees from Bosnia-Herzegovina; about 70 percent of the Serbian property that was left behind was destroyed or damaged (cf. Svašek, Chapter 4, this volume on similar processes of confiscation, occupation and destruction of Sudeten German houses in Czechoslovakia after the Second World War). The occupation of the formerly socially owned flats in towns made it impossible for most Serbs to return to urban areas.

As a result of pressure from international organisations, a return programme was launched in 1997 (Croatian Programme 1997) and amendments to certain laws were made to enable Serbs to repossess their private property. In the war-torn municipalities housing commissions were created which were to serve as the main agents for solving the conflict between settlers and owners of the houses. But political change on the local level was much slower. When after 1997 more and more Serbs reclaimed their property, settlers were often, at least until 1999, advised by the local authorities to ignore those claims, and were treated as legal holders of housing rights. The issue of repossession of socially owned flats had hardly been discussed by international or by state organisations even in 2000.

Apart from the difficulties in repossessing their property, Serbs also had trouble in obtaining reconstruction funds for their destroyed houses. Between 1995 and 2000 mainly Croatian property owners received state reconstruction benefits, while Serbian houses were left in ruins. A larger involvement of international organisations in reconstructing Serbian houses in the Knin area started only in 1999. Despite the severe difficulties involved in repossessing (and reconstructing) houses and flats, more and more Serbs, with the help of international organisations, returned to their damaged and abandoned houses in the rural areas. This process of return has changed the population structure severely between 1995 and 2000: while in 1995 Serbs made up less than 4 percent of the population in the Knin area, in 2000 they once again were between 30 and 40 percent (although these numbers are strongly contested by UNHCR, the Croatian authorities and Serbian returnee organisations). However, up to the summer of 2000, the average age of Serbian returnees was about sixty years. The very low percentage of young people and children among the returnees (PLUS/UNHCR 2001) did not make the return of Serbs sustainable and it will not take long until the villages are empty again. Moreover, the town of Knin itself was inhabited almost exclusively by Croats, among whom the new settlers very often outnumbered local Croats. Only the rural areas became more and more repopulated by Serbs (UNHCR 2000). The ethnic divide, which manifested itself in an urban–rural divide, also implied a different access to state resources, positions, participation in government and much more. The housing relations of Serbs and Croats were, however, also bound to the economic situation in the war-torn areas of Croatia. As a consequence of the 1991–95 war, nearly all factories in Knin and the surrounding area were closed down and the economic crisis was especially severe. In 2000, official unemployment rates were about 60 percent (*Jutarnji List*, 20 March 2001: 10).

While Serbs had minimal chances of being employed in the local administration, economic competition between Croatian settlers and local Croats for jobs and positions developed. Furthermore, economic differences between settlers and local people (both Croatian and Serbian returnees) grew. Serbian as well as Croatian returnees started working in agriculture again, while settlers were met with constraints when trying to involve themselves in agriculture (see Leutloff-Grandits 2003).

With the death of President Franjo Tudjman in December 1999 and the electoral success at the state level of a coalition of six opposition parties led by the former Communist Party in January 2000, the power of the previously dominant nationalist HDZ (*Hrvatska Demokratska Zajednica*) party diminished in Croatia. Power relations were challenged on the local level too. Local politicians and the administration were forced to collaborate more and more with the new government and finally recognised the rights of Serbian owners to repossess property. However, as alternative accommodation for settlers was rarely available, the implementation of repossession was still very slow. Not surprisingly, in local elections in 2001 support for the Croatian nationalist HDZ party remained strong, while most Serbs voted for Serbian national parties (*Večernji List*, 22 May 2001: 19). In addition to the national parties, however, some party branches based in Knin had a mixed Croatian and Serbian election list. Most people on these lists were locals; Croatian settlers were rare. This gives some indication of the reconciliation and reestablishment of solidarity between local Serbs and Croats under socialism, an experience which reinforced the process of inter-ethnic identification in the public sphere. However, the conflict between Croatian settlers and returning Serbs was still fought along national lines.

Emotional Dynamics of Ownership Claims by Croatian Settlers

Croatian settlers, who mostly came from Bosnia, often stressed that they decided to settle in the region of Knin because they did not have any other place to stay. They stated that they could not return to their home regions in

Bosnia because their house or flat had been destroyed or occupied, because of the nationalist atmosphere or because they did not want their children to be raised in an atmosphere of potential conflict between national groups. In their memories of life in Bosnia, experiences of being pushed out of their homes, of violence during war and living in miserable conditions as refugees dominated the narratives and overshadowed the stories of a harmonious and prosperous life under socialism. They explained that their Bosnian homeland had somehow 'disappeared', and referred to the severe changes caused by the war, ethnic migration and nationalism. Many also had an ambivalent view on the socialist past, as they saw the war as a consequence of the socialist policy.

This was contrasted to the feeling of 'freedom' and power that they would enjoy in Croatia and the hope of regaining control over their lives by moving to the region of Knin (Čapo Žmegač 1999a on similar processes of Croats from Vojvodina settling in Croatia). Belonging to the national majority in Croatia implied for them participation in the government and the control of institutions, the right to express their own thoughts, to speak their 'Croatian' language and to practise their religion. Many settlers expressed feelings of trust towards the 'Croatian state' and nation (Jansen 2000). They hoped that the Croatian state would care for them and compensate them for their individual losses (*gubici*). By leaving their home in Bosnia and moving to Croatia, their national identity became stronger (for transformation of the self after (forced) migration, see Svašek and Skrbiš, this volume).

Many settlers also described how, at the beginning of the settlement of Croats in the Knin area, the atmosphere was marked by enthusiasm (*oduševljenje*). People met regularly in the Catholic church and started helping each other, visiting each other and even marrying each other. Expectations about the positive development of the community were high and sentiments of having found a new home were expressed (Leutloff-Grandits 2002; for the settlement of Croats from Vojvodina in the region of Virovitica, see Čapo Žmegač 1999b). One woman, who together with her husband and two sons occupied three houses, justified her own situation in the following way: 'I think that we deserved this. I think the houses were given by God.' As in this case, the notions of 'God-given rights' to property and territory often supported the ethno-national claims of Croatian settlers (for similar processes in the Sudeten German context, see Svašek, Chapter 4, this volume).

Instead of feeling guilty about occupying one (or several) house(s) and thereby acting against learned standards of respecting private property, the settlers developed a sense of having taken part in the 'ordering' and 'repopulating' of an area that was carrying the wounds of war and thus participating in the construction of the new Croatian nation-state. A settler put it this way:

> Concerning our life here, when we arrived and even later it was ugly and poor. The houses were devastated and burnt; the streets were full of rubbish. Everything had to be cleaned first of all, to be set up and to be moved so that a more or less normal life could be started at all.

One other settler explained this in the following words:

> I think that we as well as all other citizens are needed in these regions, that is, in our beautiful homeland that I consider as my homeland, the motherland of Croatia, and I have deep hopes that we will stay here, that we do not have to move on.

This quote shows the insecurity felt by many Croatian settlers from Bosnia in the region of Knin, and their need to justify their status. In this conviction, many settlers also visibly identified their occupied houses with the words 'zauzeto' (occupied) and 'Hrvat' (Croat), hung a Croatian flag from their house, or painted the Croatian coat of arms and other Croatian symbols (like acronyms of the nationalist HDZ) on the outer walls.

Occupying houses was nevertheless often accompanied by feelings of fear and a strong rejection of Serbs who stayed or returned to the area, evolving despite the fact that many of the settlers had not fought against Serbs in Croatia, but mainly against Muslims in Bosnia. One settler, who was the first to settle in a half-destroyed, largely abandoned Serbian village near Knin, told me about a conversation between him and other settlers at the time of moving into the Serbian house:

> When I decided to move to that [Serbian] village people asked me 'You are going there? What do you want there? They [the Serbs] will kill you there!' But who will kill me; there were twelve or thirteen people [Serbs], all old and only thinking about how they could get firewood for their ovens. Who would kill me? I really do not know why someone would kill me. What did I do that they would kill me?

> But O.K., there was still intolerance between people, fear [strah] in people on the one and other side. But I did not fear anyone. I did not do anything wrong. The house I am staying in is my own possession. I have documents for this. I got my possessions in a very honourable way.

In his utterances, the settler applied two moral orders: one inside his own Croatian we-group, based on trust and solidarity, and one outside, directed at Serbian neighbours and returnees and based on mistrust and fear.

Occupiers often did not let the Serbian owner come close to the house, even into the year 2000. In their logic, Serbs who had lost the war had also lost their rights to the houses (cf. Svašek in this volume, who discusses houses as emotionally loaded signifiers of personal and collective identities).

However, life in the area did not fulfil the expectations settlers had when arriving in the area. All settlers I spoke to in 2000–2001 initially referred to their difficult economic situation. They claimed that jobs were lacking, as most of them were unemployed. Many of them were hardly able to secure a livelihood and had spent all the savings they had brought with them (*Slobodna Dalmacija* 1998). Some mentioned that they did not see any future for their children; they often had trouble simply putting food on the table.

The rising economic problems also changed their position on the occupation of houses: when Croatian settlers questioned the importance of merely solving the housing question, they stressed the simultaneous need for economic development in the area. Settlers also expressed disappointment (*razočarenje*) about the lack of action on the part of their own politicians at local and state levels, and some of the settlers even thought of leaving the area again. Croatian settlers also mentioned that more and more the relationship with local Croats had deteriorated. Facing competition with local Croats for jobs and positions, settlers felt they were being discriminated against. Furthermore, local Croats were seen increasingly as tending to socialise with local Serbs again, and even of developing alliances of locals against newcomers. One settler described this in the following way: 'I see that they [the local Croats and Serbs] have a greater sympathy towards each other than towards us, who settled here in the region. They [the local Croats] would prefer that WE leave, rather than the Serbs.' To explain the sympathy of local Croats towards Serbs, settlers often pointed out that many Croats had Serbian relatives and were therefore not 'real' Croats. Contrasting this notion, they stressed that they belonged to the Croatian people and had fought for the Croatian state.

After the government was replaced in 2000, the legal changes of 1997 that principally enabled Serbs to repossess their property found more recognition and put settlers even more under pressure to rethink their situation and the basis of their property rights. Many settlers had already received an official letter from the local housing commission, which informed them that they would have to return the occupied house to the legal owner as soon as the state could provide them with alternative accommodations. This was followed by diverse reactions and new emotional judgements, although the implementation of these repossessions had usually not been carried out even well into 2003.

Some settlers had a radicalised view and still ignored the repossession-claims of the Serbian owners. Following political changes on the state level in 2000, they feared being overpowered or socially marginalised by returning Serbs. Settlers said that staying in the region was a struggle, a fight for existence (*opstanak*) – a phrase which was taken directly from powerful discourses of the Catholic Church and nationalist institutions, which tried to stop Croatian settlers from moving out of the war-torn areas (Glasnik Sveti Ante 2001: 17–23). Settlers sharing this conviction did not return their house to the Serbian owner, even when they moved out of the area on their own accord, but passed it on to other incoming settlers. This position was based primarily on notions of solidarity among Croatian settlers, because they were convinced that Croats (and especially Croatian settlers) would have to stick together to defend themselves from returning Serbs. They hoped that with a renationalisation of Croatian society, their own rights would again be greater. Still, some of these settlers also expected money from incoming settlers when handing over the keys to the houses, and thus hoped to gain materially from the transaction.

Other Croatian settlers willing to move out of their house were in principle ready to return it to the Serbian owner, but asked to be financially compensated for protecting the house and maintaining it in a good condition, not considering the fact that they lived for years in the house without paying rent to the Serbian owner. This claim was lent strength by the notion that many settlers had already made an investment in or had repaired the house.

Most settlers, however, had no chance of leaving the region. Many of them increasingly accepted the rights of Serbs to their private property, despite the ethnic identity of the owner. Based on norms from the socialist period, in which it was a common and recognised practice to build a private home, they considered houses to be private property since they were built privately. Such norms seemed to gain importance under the new government in Croatia from 2000 on and as more time passed from the end of the war. However, settlers did not express this acceptance of the private property rights of the Serbian owner publicly. Until 2000/2001, public discourse in Knin was still so nationalist in tone that it would have been inadvisable for the settler to discuss it in any other way. One settler put it this way:

> I tell you something in confidence. This is not my house. I did not build it. The owner built it. ... That Serbian woman who asked for her house back might move back in, as soon as the state solves the housing problem for me. The state would have to give us a new place to stay.

In 2000–2001, many settlers argued that Serbian ownership rights could be implemented as soon as social rights of the occupiers were realised, which meant supplying them with alternative accommodation. In this view, the social rights of occupiers had to be placed above ownership rights. Settlers referred to a passage in the law of occupation rights that mentioned the right to alternative accommodation as soon as the owner expressed his wish to repossess the house. However, they were not able to solve the conflict with their Serbian neighbours and owners of the houses themselves but depended on the Croatian state to resolve these property issues and to care for them.

Emotional Dynamics of Ownership Claims by Remaining and Returning Serbs

Most Serbian informants told me that they stayed or returned to the region of Knin out of personal feelings of belonging to this place. Many had spent their entire life there and felt connected to the houses, to their local kin group and neighbours and to the land. Some of the older returnees said that they returned to their homes to die and to be buried next to their ancestors. As decribed by Svašek in this volume, returning to one's 'own' house had a special positively connotated emotional meaning and could not be compared to living in 'a' house. (cf. Verdery 1999 and Skrbiš, Chapter 6, this volume on the importance of historic memories of ancestral places for national identities). Others highlighted that they did not want to live in Serbia because in exile in Serbia they had been discriminated against, perceived as strangers and as poor, rural refugees (Leutloff 2002).

Despite the feeling of belonging to the region of Knin, Serbs, however, very often lacked a feeling of belonging to the state of Croatia, mainly because they felt discriminated against by the Croatian nationalist regime and dispossessed in the new social and political order after this region had been re-conquered in 1995. Serbian returnees had strong feelings of bitterness and loss about fleeing their homes before the advancing Croatian military, leaving everything behind which was then destroyed, stolen or occupied (Nikolić-Ristanović et al. 1996). Those that remained during the military action referred to even worse experiences after the 'fall of the Serbian Republic of Krajina', remembering how they had observed their houses being looted and partly destroyed, and how their lives had been endangered. The fear of such actions dominated at least the first two years after the military operation. During this time, they did not dare to express their own claims, culture or even mere Serbian identity, but tried to live as invisibly as possible. Contacts between Serbs and returned local Croats or even Croatian settlers hardly took place.

Having remained or returned to Knin, Serbs were still confronted with the Croatian public view on Serbian atrocities against Croats, and had to relate their own misery to the suffering of local Croats. Many Serbian interviewees admitted that many Serbian 'extremists' had destroyed and looted the houses of their Croatian neighbours in 1991–1995. They sometimes felt shame for such actions and expressed understanding for the 'revenge' taken by Croats. However, they often denied individual guilt, pointing to Serbian politicians and extremists who were responsible for those developments. Furthermore, they said that it was not necessary *to allow* so many houses of 'guiltless' Serbs (as they considered themselves) to be destroyed after the Croatian military action in the region. They held that the Croatian state authorities had deliberately not controlled outbreaks of violence that led to the looting and destruction of so many Serbian houses after the military action in 1995. At the same time, they tried to rebuild connections with the local Croats in their neighbourhood and region by stressing local similarities and common past experiences. Many people emphasised that they had family links to local Croats; that they had become godparents or even marriage partners in socialist times.

Notwithstanding the feeling of loss for destroyed houses, even stronger feelings of injustice accompanied people whose houses were occupied by Croatian settlers. Again, emotions changed with changing policies and social positions of Serbs in the postwar situation. In the beginning, occupation was seen more as a temporary state, because possession rights, so they hoped, would be easier to reinstate than the reconstruction of a house. However, after a while this hope was shattered, as in practice they often were not able to repossess their property even in 2003. One informant expressed his despair in the following words:

> In an effort to repossess our house, we have been in court against the Republic of Croatia for four years. The court worked fast and gave us the decision for the repossession of our house, but the house is still not empty and we cannot move in.

The fact that occupiers had stronger rights to the occupied property than Serbs as owners themselves had was seen as a great injustice. The Croatian settlers who occupied Serbian houses were seen as invaders and 'enemies' of Serbs who did not respect their property (and other) rights. In this situation, memories of the local context in socialist times were used in considering the loss they had to face after the war, to mark the dissatisfaction about their social position in Croatian postwar society and to reevaluate the rights they had before. Here again, Serbs differentiated between local Croats and Croatian settlers. In their view, most local Croats respected the private property rights of Serbs and shared similar moral norms and social conduct. As referred to in the example at the very beginning, some Serbs, mostly those who had close Croatian relatives due to ethnically mixed marriages in their families, mentioned with pride in their voices that some local Croats protected, or at least tried to protect, their houses and property from being occupied or destroyed by incoming Croatian settlers. Most Serbs also stressed that in socialist times, ethnicity was not important, and that they had been friends with Serbs *and* Croats. They talked about how they as well as local Croats had been employed in the factories and worked on their own agricultural plots, often helping each other. With their hard work they had been able to invest in the building of new houses; the bigger and more modern the house, the better was the reputation of the family in the local community.

But Serbs did not judge all settlers as the same. Observing socially underprivileged settler families with several children, they carefully thought about differentiating social grounds of settler families despite their occupied houses. They understood that it was not possible to force those, who did not even have enough income to feed their own children, out of the houses and onto the street. Instead of accusing these impoverished settler families occupying their houses, they accused the state of being irresponsible in this situation. As with many of the settlers, they were waiting for the state to resolve these issues by supplying alternative accommodation for settlers in difficult social positions. However, this expectation lost force as they were more and more convinced that the state did not have any interest in solving this problem. Furthermore, Serbs were certain that some settlers profited unfairly from the situation. Serbs claimed that quite a few settlers were not refugees at all, but were using the situation to occupy as much property as possible, while they might even have repossessed their own property in Bosnia. Serbian owners felt especially humiliated by settlers leaving the area who passed houses on to other settlers despite the owners' request to repossess the houses, fighting in vain for their homes against settlers who did not follow the legal rules.

On the Serbian side, feelings of powerlessness and despair were overwhelming. People often referred to experiences in which they went several times to the Croatian state institutions on the local and regional levels to argue their case, presenting ownership documents and, as they claimed, all other required proof, but nothing happened in the end. At the same time, they gained the impression that the Croatian administration was purposely not controlling the situation on the ground, not keeping an eye on Croatian settlers who abused their housing rights.

Due to these negative experiences, for many Serbs emotional judgements became increasingly radical. One old woman returnee told me in summer 2001 that she would have preferred her house had been destroyed rather than to have it occupied. This was, on the one hand, due to very pragmatic reasons, as getting reconstruction funds in 2001 seemed to be easier (although still difficult) to achieve than the repossession of a house. While the woman tried by all means and on all levels to find a way to repossess her occupied house, her neighbour, whose house was destroyed, received reconstruction benefits. On the other hand, this also had an emotional effect. It was still easier, as the woman pointed out, to see a destroyed house, than to pass by her house every day, knowing that other people were using her possessions and humiliating her by harassing and yelling at her. By giving up the hope that she would achieve the repossession of her house soon (before she died), she was thinking that it might be better to destroy her own house just to have peace of mind.

In general, living conditions for Serbs, both those who remained and those who returned, were much worse than under socialism. Like most of the Croatian settlers, those few young Serbs who returned to their home region felt frustrated at not having a chance to build a future. Still, they did not express solidarity with the settlers. Being unemployed, they used agriculture as a survival strategy and were proud to work on their own land, comparing this with settlers who mostly did not work at all. As they said, settlers only depended on state social benefits, drank coffee several times a day and were lazy. Serbs felt closer to local Croats, not only because many of them respected the private property of Serbs, but because of personal kinship and friendship ties to them and because of many similar everyday practices; for example many local Croats worked the land in the same way as Serbs.

But the relations with local Croats could not be reestablished the way they used to be in socialist times. Serbs who stayed or returned felt abandoned and lonely because they missed many family members and friends and they were discriminated against by Croatian institutions. The growing disappointment in and mistrust towards Croatian authorities encouraged a hidden resistance against them and laid the ground for Serbian nationalist parties active in the locality of Knin and in Croatia.

Emotional Dynamics of Ownership Claims by Local Croats

Like Serbs, local Croats recalled in their narratives the experiences of violence and expulsion during war from 1991 to 1995. Fear, insecurity and the curtailment of freedom dominated their everyday lives in those times. Some explained that they had not even felt secure in their own houses, so that the notion of being at home was fragmented. When they had to leave their houses and home region in 1993 (and sometimes earlier), they left – as many said – everything behind. One Croat remembers this in the following way:

> First of all we were attacked. Our people were locked up. It was horrible. My husband and I slept for a whole month in the house of a stranger. Then my husband went to Split to see the children. He could not return, not at all [because Serbs had blocked the roads], so that I stayed here alone, together with two neighbours. At that time I slept sometimes in their house and sometimes in the house of neighbours on the other side. I did not dare to sleep in my own house. I feared my [Serbian] neighbours down the other side. They harassed me. ... It was very difficult for us. Then in 1993 they [the Serbs] moved us out of the houses completely. They gathered us together. I left my house open and went away. Without anything.

Like this woman, local Croats often highlighted that they had feared local Serbs, among them their own neighbours or (former) friends. This was accompanied by a change from trust in Serbian neighbours, relatives and friends to mistrust in them. The feeling of mistrust was long-lasting and the experiences of violence prevailed as trauma.

As with the Serbian narratives about exile, most local Croats also remembered their exile, spent in Croatian coastal towns, in negative terms. They said that the local community received them as strangers, always making them feel as though they were second class, and that they had lacked material and economic resources as well as social contacts. Local Croats stressed that they felt emotionally connected to the region, being socialised in Knin and having their houses, land and work there. Here they should feel free again (for the yearning for homeland in places of exile, see also Skrbiš and Svašek in this volume). Their expectations about 'home' were, however, different from what they had found after their return. Many Croat informants noted that they had found 'nothing'. Their houses were looted and partly destroyed, and the local economy was completely desolated. Their descriptions showed similarities to those by the Serbs, and also to those by the settlers who had felt the shock of entering a devastated area. One local Croat put it this way:

We returned in 1995 after the *Oluja* [the local term for the Croatian military intervention]. We had some sheep after we returned, nothing else. No one helped us. No one came to us. ... Windows were destroyed, doors missing. God, everything was destroyed and so it stayed until today. Many things were stolen: doors and windows and bricks. What we left we did not find. Nowhere. No one from our government came and asked if we needed anything. Nothing, absolutely nothing. So we helped ourselves little by little. So we worked hard. It is very difficult for us.

As pointed out by this Croat, many local Croats were disappointed about their situation and accused the Croatian state of not helping them enough to re-build their livelihood. The reconstruction benefits, which they received from the state ministry, if at all, were often represented as a drop in the ocean, although people generally extended their houses during reconstruction and were able to use more living space. Young people who returned moved into formerly socially owned flats used by Serbs in Knin. This gave many of them for the first time the possibility to establish their own household apart from their parents. But due to the atmosphere of social and economic deficiency people first of all saw the difficulties they had to bear. Many other younger Croats did not return at all, but stayed in the towns in which they had spent their exile. For them, the notions of a 'lost home' diminished in consideration of the depressive state in the former war regions (for similar processes of Sudeten Germans who visited their home villages after the fall of the Iron Curtain, see Svašek, this volume).

Like their Serbian neighbours, as well as like Croatian settlers, local Croats who returned felt socially isolated and left alone with their sorrows and needs. When strolling around on the main street in the first days of their return they often hardly recognised anyone. Most people they saw were Croatian settlers, who were strangers to them. While local Croats were few in numbers already in 1991, the number of those who returned permanently in 1995 was even smaller. The vast majority of local Serbs had fled and many local Croats avoided socialising with the few who had stayed behind. In addition to feelings of mistrust and of having been victims of Serbian aggression, relations towards Serbs were marked by feelings of being morally superior. They often argued that Serbs had started the war against Croats, and that they (the Croatian army) did not destroy Serbian Orthodox churches when liberating the area, even though the Serbian side destroyed their Catholic churches.

In this sense, local Croats expressed (more or less strongly) nationalist emotions. After the Croatian army 'liberated' the area, as they explained, they could for the first time put their feet back on the local ground that, occupied by Serbs during the war, now was Croatian territory again. Connecting their memories of having been ruled and even forced violently out of their homes by their Serbian compatriots, they also felt the need to protect themselves from a possible future Serb domination. When the Croatian flag was flown above the castle in Knin and in other public places to mark the town's belonging to the Croatian state, local Croats (as much as Croatian settlers) felt secure, protected by the demonstrated integrity of the Croatian state. The settlement of Croats into the region was therefore also seen as a form of protection against possible Serb rebellions in the future, as guarantors of being stronger than Serbs (in numbers and in political representation). In the first months after *Oluja*, they mostly did not restrain themselves and sometimes even told incoming settlers which were Serbian houses (as Serbian houses have the same appearance as Croatian houses).

However, next to the nationalist view on war and violence, there was always the other side: the memories of good relations with their Serbian neighbours, friends and even kin in socialist times, which were silenced in public but not forgotten by individual actors. Some local Croats felt the moral obligation to try to protect houses of Serbian family members (mixed couples, godparents, etc.) or neighbours against incoming settlers and had therefore to cope with the emergence of conflicting moral orders. They felt pressured from above to maintain a nationalist point of view, but might have been forced to show commitment based on local ties too. One informant expressed this conflict in the following way: 'Why can't we [local Serbs and Croats] come together again? Why did it all happen? Why? When the states quarrel, what do we peasants have to do with it? Is it not like that?'

Back in the private context, they very often soon took up personal relationships with Serbs following the moral order of kinship, friendship and neighbourhood (although in some cases, these relations were destroyed by the war) and based on the many similarities in the organisation of everyday life, most of all in the realm of agriculture. As time passed, after the reintegration of the region into the Croatian state and with the growing disappointment about the meagre social and economic conditions in Knin, such contacts with local Serbs were reestablished more and more. At the same time, local Croats experienced many differences towards Croatian settlers in the organisation of everyday life, as the latter had been socialised in Bosnia, followed their own habits and norms, and mostly did not work in agriculture. They often did not succeed in establishing friendly relations with them, but rather developed relations of mistrust.

Local Croats often accused settlers of having taken part in looting after the war or of not respecting private property rights while occupying Serbian houses. Regarding themselves as morally superior natives of the region, the locals claimed special privileges in ruling the town, for example by occupying the position of the mayor and heading the regional court and other commissions. Their perception of Croatian settlers as 'non-belongers' indicated a fear of being overpowered by them as they built up the majority in Knin after the war (see Svašek in this volume for the fear of locals of being overpowered by strangers or settlers), as well as a shift from national to local sentimental attachments. As with nationalist sentiments, however, feelings of local belonging have been contextual and fragmented.

Conclusion

In the Knin example, it can be seen that housing and ownership claims in the postwar situation were initially influenced by emotional judgements that were mainly based on war experiences. Being deprived and dispossessed in all possible respects, and being confronted with economic devastation throughout the war and the postwar period, generated sentiments of loss and despair which dominated all groups. These sentiments were integrated into the claims for property and housing rights in the postwar period.

The emotional judgements of Serbs, Croatian settlers and Croatian returnees, however, were not based on an image of shared experience. By contrast, members of the different groups regularly accused other groups of being the source of their suffering. On the local level this resulted in the alienation of former neighbours and the building up of mutual hostile emotions while dependency on forces at the national level grew. Memories of inter-ethnic violence continued to captivate the people in Knin, and these perceptions framed, patterned and politicised their emotions (Appadurai 1998; Kalb 1997).

This was even more the case because claims to property inherently positioned individuals and families in the postwar social and political power structure, which was mainly shaped by dominant political discourses of the authoritarian Croatian government and other organisations. Through these agencies the reading of past experiences was mostly presented in an ethno-national context. Croatian settlers who had left their own homes behind and occupied houses of Serbs justified the occupation by highlighting the outcome of war in which Serbs were seen as aggressors, while they stressed their own belonging to the Croatian national group. Croatian returnees highlighted their victimisation through war by Serbian aggression, and claimed reconstruction funds and access to powerful positions. Conversely, Serbs had to relate their claims to repossess their own houses against the resistance of the powerful Croatian nationalist discourse. They tried to highlight notions of their deprivation of property rights along Serbian national lines.

But these emotional judgements along national lines were not the only ones. Alternative judgements based on norms and experiences of prewar times, like the notions of private property rights and social rights to property, were especially articulated in the private sphere. Relating to norms and experiences from socialism, people could distance themselves from nationalism, and sometimes recognise the position of others and even to associate partly with them. In other words, they deconstructed discourses of nationalist belonging, and depoliticised sentimental images of ethnic purity, replacing them with images that acknowledged the existence of inter-ethnic ties and responsibilites.

These alternative emotional judgements were also promoted by non-governmental political actors and a changing political climate. With the pressure of international organisations to implement private property rights from 1997 on, and the change in political power structure on the state level in 2000, national property rights were more and more challenged. Reflecting the new social and political situation, Croatian settlers put forward claims to housing rights that were more and more related to social rights and demanded that alternative accommodation should be provided to them. Serbs recognised the social need for accommodation for some of the settler families and waited for the state to resolve these issues. Local Croats shifted very often between the competing discourses about national and local belonging, depending on the situation and the context in which they found themselves (see the concept of switching by Elwert 1995). In general, individuals made conflicting emotional judgements relating to different prewar and war norms and political concepts.

However, being dependent on the state, many members of the three groups felt that the state had not fulfilled its promises. While Croatian settlers were disappointed because the promised possession rights were not secured, Serbs were frustrated by the fact that they had to wait for years for the repossession of their property. Like settlers and Serbian returnees, local Croats were disappointed in state representatives who did not seem to care about the problems in the devastated region. In general, the postwar community was highly marked by mistrust, both amongst people and towards the state. In a situation of migration and war, insecurity and severe social changes in which political discourses were authoritative and often not realistic, feelings of trust and mistrust frequently alternated within the different communities. In this situation of insecurity and continued tensions, it has remained difficult for 'democratic' powers to compete against nationalist ones.

Acknowledgements

This paper was first published in a slightly longer version in 2002 in *Focaal. European Journal of Anthropology* 39. The fieldwork was part of a Ph.D. project supported by the Max Planck Institute for Social Anthropology in Halle/Saale, Germany. I would like to thank Barbara Cellarius, John Eidson, Hannes Grandits, Chris Hann, Andreas Hemming, Renata Jambrešić Kirin, Don Kalb, Deema Kaneff, Maruška Svašek, Fillipo Zerelli and John Ziker, who read and commented on various versions of the paper. Naturally, I am responsible for its shortcomings.

Bibliography

Appadurai, A. 1998. *Modernity at Large. Cultural Dimensions of Globalization.* Minneapolis, London: University of Minnesota Press.

Čapo Žmegač, J. 1999a. '"We Are All Croats. It Is Not Our Goal To Be Set Apart From Our Own People". A Failed Attempt at Firmer Incorporation of Croatian Migrants', *Ethnologia Balkanica* 3: 121–39.

———— 1999b. 'Constructing Difference, Identifying the Self – A Case of Croatian Repatriates From Serbia'. Manuscript presented at the sixth MESS meeting, Piran 1999.

Croatian Programme for the Re-establishing of Trust, Accelerated Return, and Normalization of Living Conditions in the War affected Regions of the Republic of Croatia. Zagreb 2 October 1997.

Denich, B. 1994. 'Dismembering Yugoslavia: Nationalist Ideologies and the Symbolic Revival of Genocide', *American Ethnologist* 21(2): 367–90.

Elwert, G. 1995. 'Boundaries, Cohesion and Switching. On We-groups in Ethnic, National and Religious Form', *Bulletin of the Slovene Ethnological Society* 24: 105–20 (Ljublijana: Mediterranean Ethnological Summer School).

Glasnik Sveti Ante, Glasilo Samostana i Župe Sv. Ante Knin, God. I/II., Božic 2000, Br. 1, Sv. Ante 2001, Br.1 (2).

Gledhill, J. 1994. *Power and Its Disguises. Anthropological Perspectives on Politics.* London: Pluto Press.

Grandits, H. and Leutloff, C. 2003. 'Discourses, Actors, Violence: the Organization of War-Escalation in the Krajina-Region in Croatia 1990/91', in *Potentials of Disorder: Explaining Conflict and Stability in the Caucasus and in the Former Yugoslavia*, ed. C. Zuercher and J. Koehler. Manchester: Manchester University Press, pp. 23–45.

———— 1998. 'Über den Gebrauch der Toten der Vergangenheit als Mittel der Deutung der Gegenwart – Betrachtungen zum Krajina-Konflikt 1991–1995', in

Anthropologie der Gewalt. Chancen und Grenzen der sozialwissenschaftlichen Forschung, eds J. Koehler and S. Heyer. Berlin: Verlag für Wissenschaft und Bildung, pp. 179–86.

Hann, C. 1998. *Property Relations. Renewing the Anthropological Tradition.* Cambridge: Cambridge University Press.

Hayden, R.M. 1996: 'Imagined Communities and Real Victims: Self-determination and Ethnic Cleansing in Yugoslavia', *American Ethnologist* 23(4): 783–801.

Humphrey, C. 2002. 'Does the Category "Postsocialist" Still Make Sense?' in *Postsocialism. Ideals, Ideologies and Practises in Eurasia*, ed. C. Hann. London and New York: Routledge, pp. 12–15.

Jansen, S. 2000 'The Violence of Memories: Local Narratives of the Past after Ethnic Cleansing in Croatia'. Paper presented at the workshop '*Intersecting Times: The Work of Memory in South-eastern Europe*', Swansea, June 2000.

Jutarnji List. 2001. Nezaposleni Kninjani žive od sakuplijana limeki i zelježa, 20 March, p. 10.

Kalb, D. 1997. 'Identity-politics, Globalisation and the National State', *Focaal, Tijdschrift voor Antropologie* 33: 251–64.

Law on Temporary Takeover and Administration of Specified Property. 1995. *Official Gazette* 73, Zagreb.

Law on Lease of Apartments in Liberated Areas 1995. *Official Gazette,* Zagreb.

Leutloff, C. 2002. 'Im Niemandsland. Kollektive Identitäten von Krajina-Serben in der Emigration in der BR Jugoslawien', in *Umstrittene Identitäten. Ethnizität und Nationalität in Südosteuropa,* ed. U. Brunnbauer. Frankfurt am Main: Peter Lang Europäischer Verlag der Wissenschaften, pp. 149–72.

Leutloff-Grandits, C. 2002. 'Housing Relations After Ethnic War: National and Social Dimensions of Home in the War-torn Region of Knin/Croatia', *Ethnologia Balkanica* 6: 95–116.

——— 2003. 'Coping with Economic Devastation. Agriculture in Post-war Knin', in *The Postsocialist Agrarian Question. Property Relations and the Rural Condition,* ed. Chris Hann et al. Muenster: Lit, pp. 143–70.

Lutz, C. and White, G.M. 1986. 'The Anthropology of Emotions', *Annual Review of Anthropology* 15: 405–36.

Ministry for Public Work, Reconstruction and Construction – Office for Displaced Persons, Returnees and Refugees (ODPR). 2001. *Repossession of Property. The Revision of Decisions on the Law on Temporary Take-Over. Final Revision Results.* Zagreb.

Nikolić-Ristanović, V. et al. 1996. *Žene krajine, rat, egzodus i izbeglištvo.* Belgrad: Midlim Print.

PLUS 2001. *Market, Media and Public Opinion Research 2001: Survey on Returnee Population in Croatia.* Zagreb.

Reddy, W.M. 1997. 'Against Constructionism: the Historical Ethnography of Emotions', *Current Anthropology* 38(3): 327–51.

Sahlins, M. 1972. *Stone Age Economics.* New York: Aldine de Gruyter.

Slobodna Dalmacija. 1998. 'Doseljenici igračka političara', (29 April 1998, p. 20.

Svašek, M. 2000. 'Borders and Emotions. Hope and Fear in the Bohemian-Bavarian Frontier Zone', *Ethnologia Europaea* 30(2): 111–26.

UNHCR. 2000. *Number of Returnees and Remainees According to Village, Municipality and County*. Knin

Večernji List. 2001. 'Neslužbeni rezultati izbora za županijske skupštine i gradska viječa'. Izbori 22 May 2001.

Verdery, K. 1999. 'The Political Lives of Dead Bodies', *Reburial and Postsocialist Change*. New York: Columbia University Press.

──᷿ᴄᷓᴇⰔᴏᵌᴕᷓᴖ──

Chapter 6

'The First Europeans' Fantasy of Slovenian Venetologists: Emotions and Nationalist Imaginings

Zlatko Skrbiš

Introduction

Nationalist historiography cannot fully be appreciated without taking into account the political realities that fuel the need for the reevaluation of specific ethno-national histories. In this chapter I illustrate the convergence between the new political realities and the accompanying need to redefine the identity of a nation, by elaborating on the case of Venetological theory among Slovenians, a theory that emerged in the mid-1980s. Venetologists, the advocates of this theory, sought to rewrite the history of the Slovenian nation by arguing that Slovenians are indigenous to the European continent and thus unrelated to any surrounding ethnic groups.

During this period, the state of Yugoslavia, of which Slovenia was a part, confronted a serious economic crisis, which was compounded by emerging political and national divisions in the Yugoslav Communist oligarchy and by the global weakening and gradual demise of socialism as an alternative to liberal-democratic forms of governance. The two defining elements of the post-Second World War political order, Yugoslavism and communist ideology, were on a path that would eventually lead to their violent implosion. The withering away of the final reminder of their ideological mystique generated a void that eventually engulfed Yugoslavia in a delirious and contradictory mixture of democratisation, authoritarianism and nationalist orgy.

I had been aware of the Venetological theory since its beginnings in the mid-1980s but it was my fieldwork among Slovenians in Australia in the 1990s that sparked my further interest (Skrbiš 1999). I found that books exploring the Venetological history of Slovenians were often treasured possessions in migrants' homes and, although often left unread, they were constructed as outward signs of the migrants' ethnic and national consciousness. Having one of these books in their possession fuelled patriotic emotions among diaspora Slovenians, flagged their patriotically inspired curiosity and has generally been interpreted as a sure sign of apparent openness to the true glory of Slovenian history and heritage. What makes the Venetological interpretation of Slovenian history interesting is its relative recency, the social and historical context in which it emerged and the existence of a relatively limited network of supporters and advocates for the theory. The Venetological theory is an exemplary illustration of the genesis and evolution of nationalist historiography, in terms of its dissemination network, its ideological premises and intellectual content. The purpose of this interrogation of the Venetological theory is not to examine the validity of its claims, or whether it attempts to reconstitute a nation on real or imagined foundations of memory (Fentress and Wickham 1992). Instead, it aims to examine the extent to which it imbues history with emotionally charged, and nationalistically tailored, ideas about Slovenian history and identity. (On the political significance of emotional nationalist narratives and performances, see also Leutloff-Grandits, Chapter 5, and Golanska-Ryan, Chapter 7, this volume).

Emotional Excesses of Nationalist Historiography

When Ernest Gellner (1997: 90–101) asked the famous question, 'Do nations have navels?', he was pointing to the crucial aspect of nationalist narratives, commonly captured by the idea of 'chosen peoples' and 'national election' (Akenson 1992; Smith 1999). The idea of the navel metaphorically captures the essence of nationalist historiography. Ideally, the navel should not only be clearly discernible but should be able to connect the present with a remote and hard-to-imagine past. As Anderson (2001: 39) ironically remarked: 'the older the Past the better'. The stronger the real and imagined linkage between the distant past and the present, the stronger the claim to a righteous slice of the future. The ambiguity of the relationship between nationalist historiography and the past is replicated in its relationship with territories. The territories occupied by ancestors thus become transformed into meaningful places of significance. The imaginary homeland becomes 'a repository of historic memories and associations, the place where "our" sages, saints and heroes lived, worked, prayed and fought' (Smith 1990: 9). It is because of their capacity to deliver suitable meanings that the nation's past and territory are held central to any nationalist historiography.

Nationalist history is not the source of identity pure and simple. From the perspective of nationalist politics preoccupied with pressing and immediate concerns it is also a symbolic investment of a very special kind. It transforms history from science into a precious commodity. In the ideal world of nationalist historians, the uncovering of an ever more authentic past would always be coupled with an ambition to make the past conform to political aspirations of the present. The establishment of continuity with the distant and suitable past is the key ambition of romanticising nationalists, and the tools of their trade are quite specifically sharpened with the view of generating a specific emotional dynamic. They appear to be less preoccupied with issues of 'scientific objectivity' and 'emotional distance' then their 'non-nationalist' counterparts who claim to be unbiased, although, quite clearly, the line between objectivity and bias is often blurred when it comes to the reconstruction of historical narratives from sketchy and fragmented historical evidence. No group of historians is immune from drawing speculative conclusions, but nationalist historians tend to put them, quite intentionally and openly, in the service of the nation.

The ultimate measure of success of nationalist historiography is not so much scrupulous attention to facts as it is the pleasure derived from the discovery of the glorious past and drama of the ancestors. Nationalist historiography is time- and context-sensitive and usually proliferates in periods in which old certainties are collapsing and new realities are all too slowly taking shape. The new, supposedly more authentic history is then offered as a firm ground from which the people can obtain a tighter grip on the future. The most important task of nationalist historiography is to provide the new foundations for national identity and to provide a new base for identity construction.

The purpose of nationalist historiographies is to emotionalise the past, provide dramatic narratives, and recall catastrophic events and heroic stories of 'survival against the odds', as well as of conquest. Nationalist historiography is never far away from emotional excess and its core characteristic is its capacity to generate and energise emotions. A rather misguided reputation of nationalism as something impulsive, and indeed irrational, allowed emotions to be seen as an implicit, yet rarely scrutinised, part of nationalist discourses. Consequently, the studies of nationalism have been somewhat exempted from attempts to 'bring-emotions-back-in' that have characterised recent shifts in the broader fields of sociology (Barbalet 2001) and anthropology (Lutz and White 1986).

This chapter affirms the centrality of the politics of emotions in nationalism in general, and nationalist historiography in particular. Emotions play an indispensable role in the 'economy of nationalist sentiment', a field representing a conglomerate of suitably imagined constructions about the national past, that are built around the ideas of national purity, election and distinctiveness, and intermixed with projections about the future. Emotions are embedded in nationalist projects, and in this chapter I add two specific dimensions that have emerged out of my initial approaching of the Venetological theory from a diasporic perspective. First, this chapter examines a diasporic environment as a specific and to some extent 'controlled environment', which is particularly susceptible to nationalist emotionalisation of the past. And second, I argue with reference to Bourdieu, that the Venetological theory embodies the kind of emotional capital that is commonly sought in, but not exclusive to, specific diasporic environments. These dimensions are integral and implicit to the discussion of Venetological reinterpretations of Slovenian history.

Slovenian Romance with Nationalist Historiography

The broader context and genesis of the Yugoslav crisis has been extensively discussed elsewhere (Pavković 2000; Ramet 1999). The crisis, with its mix of economic hardship, an ideologically divided communist elite, and a blossoming national stereotype, produced circumstances that were interpreted by some Slovenians as requiring redefinition of Slovenianism. The existing economic nationalism of Slovenians (Connor 1984) thus began to incorporate additional motives and take on an increasingly pronounced ideological, political and nationalist dimension. By the second half of the 1980s, the quest for assertion of Slovenian national identity and independence became a site of both political and symbolic struggle. The need for symbolic distinction from other ethnic groups in the former Yugoslavia was never greater. Slovenian nationalists have based their grievances on the belief that Slovenians were exploited by the 'Southerners' who, in sharp contrast to Slovenians, were known for 'their proverbial laziness, Balkan corruption, dirty and noisy enjoyment, and because they demand bottomless economic support, stealing from Slovenes their precious accumulation by means of which Slovenia could already have caught up with Western Europe' (Žižek 1990: 55).

It was against this emotionally charged background that in 1985 a Slovenian newspaper in Vienna published the first discussion paper on the Venetological origin of Slovenians by an economist, Jožko Šavli (1985). Eventually, his efforts were compounded by two other amateur historians: Matej Bor, the poet, and Vienna-based Slovenian priest, Ivan Tomažič. Their first joint work was published in the German language in Austria with the title *Unsere Vorfahren – die Veneter* but was soon translated into Slovenian (Šavli et al. 1988).

The Venetological theory is not the first attempt to reinterpret Slovenian history. Štih (1997) reveals that theories propagating Slovenian European indigeneity began to emerge particularly strongly at the time of the nineteenth-century Romantics, when they were used as a tool of national emancipation. For example, the nineteenth-century publicist, Trstenjak (1817–90), argued that Slovenians had occupied their present-day territories since time immemorial and that Slavs had ruled all three continents of the old world. Henrik Tuma (1858–1935) also argued in favour of Slovenian indigenous status in Europe, claiming that Slovenians were the first human occupants of the European continent. These indigenous theories experienced a resurgence in the 1960s when a Slovenian political exile, Franc Jeza, published a thesis about the Scandinavian origin of Slovenians, based on similarities between some Swedish and Slovenian words. And, around the 1970s, a theory about the Etruscan origin of Slovenians began to be advocated by Matej Bor, Ivan Rebec and Anton Berlot. Interestingly, none of these authors were historians, but they shared a common ambition to show that Slovenians were the original European inhabitants and therefore distinct from other Slavs.

In contrast to the predominant academic opinion that Slovenians are Slavs who migrated to Europe from the region around the Carpathian Mountains in the sixth century AD, Venetologists put forward the thesis that Slovenians are the descendants of the proto-Slavic Venets who emerged around 1200 BC. According to the theory, by the eighth century BC the Venets had spread between the Alps and the Adriatic Sea and inhabited a large part of Europe. They were known by various names, such as Veneti, Venedi, Winidi, Wendi, Sloveni – names that are, in different European languages and contexts, in use even today. Venetological theorists argue that most European nations have inherited the culture of Venets and so, for example, Venetological heritage is claimed to represent a substratum for two-thirds [*sic*] of Germans (Šavli 2001). Proponents of the theory also assert that it is modern Slovenians who are the direct descendants of Venets and who today are the most important repositories of Venetic tradition and culture, as best exemplified by their similarities in language, tradition and folklore. For Venetologists, the Slovenians are the autochthonous European population and this quintessential Europeanness makes them the first builders of the European community (Šavli et al. 1996). One of Venetological theory's boldest claims is that the Slavic origin of Slovenians was a fabrication and a conspiracy, designed initially by German nationalist historians and later adopted by the Communists. The sole purpose of this conspiracy was to deprive Slovenians of their rightful status as Europeans *par excellence* and to keep them in the superficial political union with other Balkan Slavs. Additionally, these newly discovered ancestors of Slovenians are presented in the Venetological literature as repositories of unprecedented heroism that warrants pride. As one of the key texts boldly puts it, the famous forebears of the present-day Slovenians must be 'designated as "victorious"' (ibid.: 82) whenever compared to other ethnic groups.

Venetological theory's protagonists find the evidence for the link between Venets and Slovenians in practices such as the non-standard method of reading inscriptions on ancient monuments and artefacts. They also seek proof for their theory in Slovenian folklore and myths, or by identifying similarities in the sound of non-Slovenian toponyms in places such as Austria, Italy, Germany, Switzerland and as far away as the Near East (Šavli et al. 1996: 189). The case of Switzerland is illustrative:

> You would probably laugh if we said that Slovene was spoken in Switzerland. But we can not avoid facts. I am not saying that the contemporary Slovene used to be the Swiss language. There are proofs, however, that the Swiss original language was very similar to Slovene but it disappeared under external influences (Tomažič 1990: 68).

This statement is followed by a substantial list of toponyms which Tomažič claims that 'only Slovenians can understand' (ibid.). Upon examination it becomes clear that the listed toponyms can only be understood by the more imaginative speakers of Slovenian. Venetologists interpret signs and letters liberally and often suggest that a certain sound could be written with various combinations of signs. This allows them to manipulate Venetic inscriptions until they find a suitable combination of sounds that could then be recognised as Slovenian in origin. Such a procedure clearly breaks the fundamental rules of palaeography (Grafenauer 1988: 387–96) and phonology (Lenček 1990). There is no doubt, however, that this liberal use of the imagination in interpretation of foreign words makes Venetological science appear democratic, for it removes the important barrier that exists between lay and scientific communities: the knowledge of interpretative methodologies and scientific methods. As one of the contributors to a recent conference on Venetology put it: 'I have always been interested in history but I am not an historian. I also don't have time to study [history] with scientific scrutiny. However, I have my own views on some questions and I would be glad to have them either accepted or rejected by scientific arguments' (Babič 2001).

The removal of strict scientific criteria from Venetological endeavours means that anyone can participate in a grassroots effort to recreate the glorious past of the Slovenian forebears. The Venetological research outcomes are therefore easily attainable and the communitarian nature of this endeavour guarantees success. Not surprisingly, a housewife, a poet, a dentist, an economist and a priest – to name but a few real-life occupations of Venetological protagonists – can enjoy the journey of Venetological self-discovery with equal passion and credibility. Venetological scientific efforts appear, in principle, to be democratic and non-discriminatory and resemble popular nationalism as represented in Applegate's (1990) study on the idea of *Heimat* in the region of Pfälz. Applegate demonstrates how Pfälzers almost collectively responded to the call of enchanting beauties of their homeland and began to enthusiastically celebrate its local virtues. This was done by collecting museum pieces, preserving the folklore, boasting of natural beauties, or simply by resorting to – as Applegate puts it – a 'George-Washington-slept-here' version of history. Although very different in practical terms, and difficult to be paralleled with the ethnological zeal of Pfälzers, the invitation to such grassroots enthusiasm is also clearly contained in the Venetological efforts to rewrite Slovenian history.

Before I turn to a discussion of the key claims of Venetologists, I wish to describe those who tend to contribute to Venetological historiographical discoveries and present two exemplary constituencies that operate as recruiting grounds for Venetological theory supporters.

Producers ...

One of the interesting features of the Venetological theory is that initially it emerged outside Slovenia, for two of three initial protagonists; Jožko Šavli and Ivan Tomažič, lived in Italy and Austria respectively. The third protagonist, the late Matej Bor, a distinguished poet, lived in Slovenia but was in his old age almost completely alienated from the academic community due to his adventurous historiographical ideas. Venetological theory therefore emerged on the geographical margins of the Slovenian nation and on the fringes of the scholarly community. This double marginality remains a defining feature of Venetological theory to this day, as most of its production, translation of texts, dissemination and consumption continues to take place in diaspora and outside the Slovenian borders, although this has been changing as of late. At the 2001 first international conference dedicated to Venetological scholarship, entitled *The Veneti within the Ethnogenesis of Central- European Populations* held in Slovenia, almost half of all participants were from outside Slovenia (Perdih and Rant 2001). Although Venetological theory is broadly based and open to contributions from a range of individuals, the production of Venetological theory is still limited to a relatively small group of dedicated researchers. I would estimate that the core number does not exceed forty, although there are more who participate in the Venetological discussions marginally through Internet discussion forums.[1]

Early attempts by Slovenian academic linguists (Šivic-Dular 1990) and historians (e.g. Grafenauer 1988) to engage in a dialogue with Venetologists failed. While the academic side was persistently emphasising Venetological passion for adventure and complete disregard for scientific methods, the Venetologists were in turn accusing scholars of ideological and political corruption, a disregard for truth and pro-Yugoslavism. The key Venetological texts are widely available in Slovenia, but the theory lacks widespread support and has not been granted domicile in the mainstream historiography. The quantitative parameters of the Venetological phenomenon are difficult to establish. There is no real data available on how many people actually favour Venetological interpretations over the 'official' ones, although the widespread availability of Venetological texts in bookshops in Slovenia is a good indication of the existing market for this literature.

Nationalist historiographies do not necessarily attract a massive following, but their existence usually penetrates public awareness effectively. This applies to Venetological theory in Slovenia, but also to Iranian theory in Croatia and Rigvedic theory in modern India, to give but a couple of cursory examples. It is no contradiction to say that nationalist historiographies attract both the intense support of their followers and public ridicule. They effectively turn public ridicule in their favour, presenting it as the last line of defence of desperate intellectual and political supporters of an established order. The defenders of nationalist historiographies usually see themselves as defenders of truth, visionaries and martyrs who need to endure criticisms and threats in order to allow the hidden truth finally to emerge. It is not surprising then that Venetologists perceive themselves as the mediums through which Slovenian national destiny announces itself to the ideologically blinded and ignorant. They are a self-constructed elite, who believe in their insight and moral capacity to speak the truth about the 'real' origin of Slovenians.

… and the Market

It is much easier to understand the production side of the Venetological theory than to establish the size of the market of its consumers (i.e., readers and believers). In this section I suggest that there are two key constituencies that have proven likely to generate supporters. The first is represented by the segments of the Slovenian diaspora and the second by a loose group of moderately right-wing nationalist Slovenians in Slovenia, as exemplified by a group associated with the Slovenian World Congress (SWC).

Slovenian Diaspora

Even though Slovenian diaspora settings differ from one state and continent to another, they nevertheless provide a highly specific, and in some ways 'controlled' environment when it comes to the dissemination of information and generation of ideas and emotions. 'Controlled' should not be understood in any deterministic fashion but instead refers to a specific conditioning that takes place in a diaspora environment. In short, the more tightly organised the diaspora community, the more likely it will approximate the idea of a 'controlled' environment, whereby responses to certain questions, issues and ideas are less diverse and more predictable than in the homeland environment. For example, the Venetological reinterpretations of history are promoted and sold through the widely respected Slovenian-Australian Catholic press, which enjoys broad support among immigrants. It is not that the Slovenian Catholic Church in Australia openly advocates the Venetological position, but that the very promotion of Venetological texts in the Catholic press lends the theory a degree of legitimacy. In addition, they both share the tendency to promote the homeland as inherently worthy of emotional investment. The translator of some key Venetological texts into English confirms that the situation is similar in Canada, where 'the church oriented Slovenians are the key readership group', although the situation in the United States is quite different since the majority of the readership is primarily working class and approaches the theory through an interest in genealogy (Škerbinc 2001: 209).

As Svašek (2000) rightly argues, emotions are always 'embedded in contexts' and the diaspora setting is one such clearly defined setting that successfully amplifies emotions. In short, the emotional effect of Venetological theory is dependent upon the theory's inherent capacity to generate and exploit the emotional capital. The Venetological theory is to be seen as embodying the kind of emotional capital that tends to be sought after in a diaspora context. Just as in Bourdieu's (1984: 39) work, in which a given class location implies a certain aesthetic predisposition, the diasporic location in itself implies a rather well-defined predisposition for an emotionalised capital. To put it differently, what the diasporic position requires is precisely what Venetological theory has to offer. After all, the emotional potential of the Venetological arguments is not an accidental side-effect of the theory but rather an integral part of the theory's design.

Slovenian diaspora is quite heterogeneous and only parts of the diaspora have shown a distinct enthusiasm for the Venetological theory. The most pronounced receptivity for the theory is to be found among those members of the diaspora who were prima facie negatively disposed towards communism and who, even today, have a pronounced propensity to toy with the idea of communist conspiracy. These are generally people comprising a spectrum between the politically disillusioned, the academically marginalised and those with an inclination towards right-wing political tendencies. For them, the Venetological theory becomes more than a theory – it is their cause. I have discussed the issues of the diverse constitution of the Slovenian diaspora elsewhere (Skrbiš 1999, chap. 2) so it is sufficient to say here that many of the Slovenian diasporic communities in Australia, South America, North America and elsewhere that emerged after the Second World War managed to nurture an anti-communist and nationalist impulse by discreetly, and moderately successfully, moulding their membership according to pro-nationalist and pro-religious, as well as anti-communist and anti-Yugoslav sentiments. It is not that the Slovenian diaspora can be seen as overtly nationalist, but this ideological conditioning in diaspora communities has led to the promotion of certain type of values, most clearly exemplified in the development of diaspora sentimentality that encourages members to see the homeland through the prism of ethnic and national symbols. The homeland – short, that is, of its political regime – was viewed as inherently worthy of nostalgic celebration and glorification. Migrants were thus discreetly encouraged by diaspora institutions to view themselves as repositories of those Slovenian values that were constructed as being under threat of extinction in communist Yugoslavia.

This produced a situation whereby, for example, Slovenian national costumes were elevated to the pedestal of national pride and honour, and featured in almost every diaspora communal celebration. The appearance of national costumes in Slovenia itself, however, was, at the same time, seen as a remnant of the past, and hardly ever used in the sphere of public display. Such symbolic discrepancies were, then, used by the diaspora to show that it is a repository of everything truly Slovenian. In other words, the diaspora setting was readily generating, accepting and disseminating ideas, processes and events that were designed to carry on the Slovenian tradition and consciousness, and which held at least the remote promise to celebrate the achievements of the Slovenian spirit.

I have discussed this phenomenon elsewhere (Skrbiš 1999, chap. 4), referring to it as 'the distant view' by showing how the intensity of symbolic imagining is amplified in the diaspora by virtue of distance from the homeland. There is no denying that contemporary borders and spaces are permeable to an unprecedented extent. However, the 'distant view' approach does not refer to the physical distance but rather to the symbolic distance that accompanies dislocation, uprootedness and life away from the original social and cultural milieu. This situation produces circumstances that are conducive to *amplified receptivity* to ethno-national myths and propaganda.

The Slovenian World Congress (SWC) and Co-option of the Diaspora into the Slovenian National Project

In the period between 1945 and the late 1980s the homeland and diaspora settings could be seen as two rather discrete units characterised by an almost diametrically opposed concept of Slovenism. However, the process of political liberalisation in Slovenia, which began around the mid-1980s and culminated in the proclamation of Slovenian independence from Yugoslavia in 1991, was based on the idea of global Slovenian solidarity, that aimed to transcend historically conditioned political divisions among Slovenians. To put it rather simply, the main idea behind this programme of national reconciliation was to overcome the differences between pro- and anti-communists that had emerged during the Second World War, and which later resulted in the massacres of anti-communists and pro-Nazi Slovenian formations as well as the mass exodus of those who happened to find themselves on the losing side of the Second World War conflict.

This idea of universal Slovenian solidarity, which emerged in the dying days of socialism, informed the establishment of the SWC, an institution designed for the purpose of fostering a Slovenian national community as a transnational project. The SWC was established during the process of Slovenian independence in June 1991 and one of its aims was to bring about national reconciliation, in the hope that this would help to overcome differences between pro- and anti-communists dating back to the Second World War.

The SWC-assisted incorporation of the diaspora into nation building played an important symbolic role in the process of a transition to democracy. It was certainly in sharp contrast to the post-Second World War period, when it was often portrayed by the Yugoslav state as an historical reject consisting of people who were negatively disposed towards the Yugoslav state and out of touch with contemporary Slovenian identity and reality. The diaspora saw the end of communism in Slovenia as an opportunity to materialise their political agenda and it positively encouraged the diaspora to imagine itself as a coherent and legitimate symbolic space. It was the late 1980s that gave the diaspora a sense that its political dreams and reality had collapsed into one. And nothing fed these dreams better than a heroic narrative about the newly discovered and authentic truth about their nation's past and uniqueness. The historical momentum thus became a typical site of tension between the rational and emotional (Lutz and White 1986).

This bipolarity between diaspora and homeland settings still persists today, although it might be thought of as unnecessary. After all, communism in Europe has collapsed, Slovenia was proclaimed an independent state in 1991 and, following a decade of successful democratic and economic development, it is now a stable parliamentary democracy that joined the European Union in May 2004. However, the gap between the diaspora and the homeland is still considerable because the diaspora finds comfort in the time warp in which it exists. It is not so much that it refuses to acknowledge the change but, rather, is unable to cope with the idea of it. This position finds its homeland-based equivalent in those political parties which exploit the rhetoric of continuity between communism and postcommunism and insist that the contemporary social and political ills in Slovenia are due to the lack of a radical break from the communist past.

Since the establishment of the Slovenian independent state, the SWC not only lends its support to political parties located right of the centre of the political spectrum, but is also the strongest public supporter of the Venetological theory in Slovenia. It is dedicated to making a contribution to finding 'the historical truth about [Slovenian] origins' and this dedication prompted it to organise the 'First International Topical Conference, *The Veneti within the Ethnogenesis of Central-European Populations*, as part of the long-term project "Origins of the Slovenians"' (Perdih and Rant 2001: 8).

The Slovenian diaspora and the SWC are two core constituencies providing support for Venetological theory, although enthusiasm for the theory is far more diffuse. There is little doubt, however, that the enthusiasm for the theory is directly correlated to the promises that Venetological theory implicitly or explicitly makes. Most significantly, in contradiction to established theories of Slovenian Slavic origin, Venetologists do not make Slovenians blend into historical processes – they make them stand out. Venetological theory offers everything that nationalists could dream of: a narrative about their nation as a nation with dignity, history, heroic tradition and rich culture. What is also appealing is the fact that Venetologists speak the language of the common people, by defying the rules of academic conventions, building their arguments on commonsense notions and providing explanations that everyone can understand and relate to. In other words, Venetological theory is transformed into a tool of communication that cuts across various geographical locations and provides a sense of an imaginary community of belonging.

The following section organises the Venetological claims into six key areas, all of which reveal how and why the Venetological theory productively taps into the economy of nationalist sentiment.

Venetological Promises to the Slovenian Nation

Symbolic Frontiers

Venetologists argue that Slovenians no longer need to view themselves as coming from 'the Trans-Carpathian swamps' (Šavli et al. 1996: 10). The Venetologists reassuringly tell Slovenians that they 'do not accept the proposition about Slovenians being part of the South Slavic "one race and blood"' (ibid.: 9). They commonly claim that established historical science portrays Slavs less than favourably: as people who aimlessly wandered around, lacked firm organisation and sought refuge in forests. In contrast, they dissociate Slovenian ancestors from this portrayal totally. Slovenian ancestors, they say, 'did not dwell in swamps and forests ... Rather, they settled on hills and sunny sides in full view of their potential enemy' (ibid.: 14). The 'swamps and forests' metaphor is designed to produce a rather predictable reaction of revulsion and disgust and evoke specific emotions.

By identifying the metaphoric zone of 'swamps and forests', Venetological theorists identify some places as being best kept at a distance, for too close an alignment with them may cause symbolic pollution. In other words, the more effectively the habitation of Slovenian ancestors in swamps and forests can be disproved and habituation on the sunny areas asserted, the purer the form of Slovenism. In order to achieve this distancing from life in 'swamps and forests', Venetologists fortify the Slovenian national entity behind the symbolic frontiers which provide basic guarantees that Slovenians are different from everybody else and unquestionably assured of primacy in Europe.

To understand the processes of symbolic frontier construction, it is worth remembering that this practice is not uncommon in this part of Europe and, as I have explained elsewhere, is strongly present in a diaspora context (Skrbiš 1999: 118–28). Similarly, in a more general discussion of the imaginary nationalist frontiers of the Balkans, Žižek (1992: 39) writes:

> For the right-wing nationalist Austrians, this imaginary frontier is Karavanke, the mountain chain between Austria and Slovenia: beyond it, the rule of Slavic hordes begins. For the nationalist Slovenes, this frontier is the river Kolpa, separating Slovenia from Croatia: we Slovenians are Mitteleuropa, while Croatians are already Balkan, involved in the irrational ethnic feuds that really do not concern us.

This is not, of course, where it all ends. Further south, one encounters the frontier between Croatian Catholicism and the Serbian Eastern Orthodox collective spirit, which cannot grasp the values of Western individualism. And Serbs then, finally, conceive of themselves as the last line of defence of Christian Europe against the polluting hordes of Muslims (ibid.: 40).[2]

Venetological emphasis on Slovenian distinctiveness when compared with the surrounding groups fits the well-established nationalist practice of construction of nationalist symbolic frontiers. But the emphasis on difference and unrelatedness also gives the promise of continuous assertion of this difference. This difference is not neutral and inconsequential. Rather, the entire symbolic capital of the Venetological position rests on it.

Historical Memory and the Indigeneity Theory

Venetologists claim that Slovenians should rightfully see themselves as indigenous to the European continent. They have not come to Europe from anywhere else but have occupied the European continent since time immemorial (e.g., Šavli et al. 1996: 200, 521). The term 'immemorial' puts the question of national origin outside any measurable frame. Immortality is traditionally appealing to nationalists and it symptomatically prefaces Venetological texts again and again, reassuring people concerned of their right of domicile. When Venetological theory promised to inaugurate a radically new understanding of Slovenian ancient history, this idea was embraced particularly quickly by the diaspora Slovenians. After all, it promised to add substance to an already selective romantic and folkloristic portrayal of Slovenian ethno-history.

The Slovenian Predisposition for Things Spiritual

The Venetological texts emphasise that Slovenian Venetian ancestors stand out of the conglomerate of other ethnic groups by having a particularly well-developed sense of spirituality. The acceptance of Christianity by Venets is not an historical accident but rather a logical consequence of the fact that their pre-Christian spirituality resembled the basic tenets of Christianity. Tomažič (1990: 9) wrote that 'Venets were afraid of the afterlife. This means that they had a sense of responsibility before God. What inevitably followed from that was the belief that a person must do good deeds and avoid bad ones.' It was this heritage of Venets that predisposed Slovenian ancestors to embrace Christianity and furthermore to excel in its defence. Not surprisingly, we read that:

> From the 15th century on, the southern Slovene regions of the Hapsburg Monarchy (present-day Slovenia) were repeatedly victimized by Turkish raids. It was mostly the Slovenes – without outside help [sic!] – who bore the brunt of those recurring invasions. It was the Slovenes who suffered and lost most, fighting in the first line of defence for the freedom of Europe (Šavli et al. 1996: 523).[3]

The Internet site dedicated to Venetological discussions that is moderated in Australia features a contribution from one of the founders of Venetological theory (Šavli 2001). He argues that the name of India comes from Vindia, which supposedly indicates a clear relation to Venets (Venets = Vindia = India). This discussion also includes a section on the spiritual impact of Venets in India (Šavli 2001). The argument goes that when Venets combined with Aryans and penetrated into the river valley of the Ganges in around 1000 AD, their spiritual impact was as follows:

> The religious and spiritual force of Indian Wends or Veneti was *unbelievable*. For centuries, their religious cast of Brahmans governed in all the principalities that evolved in the territory of Hindustan. Such a spread of religion, philosophy, poetry and storytelling, that was caused by the Veneti in India, was never seen by the world before. Theirs are the famous Vedas, poetry Mahabharata, remarkable

Upanishads and also the much appreciated Ramayana, even though it appeared much later, but it originates from the Venetic tradition. So let us refer to just some of the *unbelievable spiritual legacy that does not come from Aryans but from Wends or Veneti*. (ibid.: my emphases)

In other words, Slovenian Venetian origins are inherently connected with a strong spiritual dimension.

Slovenian Peacefulness and Missionary Enthusiasm

Despite obvious bravery and – what we would call today – imperialist exploits, Venets were never brutish and violent. Quite the contrary, 'the Venets did not leave their settlements but acquired new areas in a totally peaceful way by their "missionary" enthusiasm' (Tomažič 1990: 9). Even when military force was used, it was never done to '… enslave other peoples, but to bring them the new faith and firm social organisation …' (ibid.).

The belief in the ability of the Venets to conquer half of the world in a completely peaceful manner directly corresponds to a popular Slovenian nationalist myth that – in direct opposition to other Southern Slavs – Slovenians are not a warring nation. This myth was commonly reiterated to me when I was undertaking research among Slovenians in Australia (e.g., Skrbiš 1999: 127). Through the prism of Venetological theory, the idea of a peace-loving, gentle Slovenian nation finally receives its historical justification.

Venetologists versus Corrupt Scientists

Venetologists present themselves as rebels with a cause. Their mission is to liberate Slovenians from the chains of a corrupt academic establishment whose ambition is to push Slovenian ancestors outside Europe, deprive them of European indigenous status and identify them, without distinction, with other Slavic people. Venetologists argue that they have uncovered the truth about the origin of Slovenians and, more than this, they claim that their theory *is* the truth, which is also ideologically unbiased because it has no connection with Slovenian academia and parties who are recognised as forces of communist continuity. Venetologists emphasise two categories of people whose objective position dictates that they resist Venetological theory. The first group consists of Slovenian academics who were supposedly brainwashed with ideas of South-Slavic unity, Yugoslavism, Germanic primacy in Europe, and who turn Slovenians into diminutive players in world history. The second category consists of French, English 'and other history writers [who] merely copied German anti-Slavic intentions' (Šavli 1996: 492). The theory about Slavs being the latecomers to Europe is presented as a German plot which was designed to 'clear the way for the political powers to carry out Germanization of the West Slavs' (ibid.: 200).

This mistrust of established science gives the Venetologists important credentials, particularly in the diaspora. Pursuing the truth for the sake of truth and against the mainstream is praiseworthy and a sure sign of true intellectual independence. Their mistrust of science and politicians is appreciated by people who are inclined to be sceptical about the establishment. This quality is something that the diaspora population finds particularly appealing because of the historical baggage attached to their position and because of their traditional mistrust of mainstream Slovenian academic and political processes.

Honour and Shame

The sixth and final point brings us to the central promise of the Venetological endeavour. The protagonists of Venetological theory argue that the theory has an extra-scientific dimension. When asked whether their theory 'embodies a wish to establish in Slovenian lands an affirmation of its history and Slovenian presence from the beginning of the civilization' (Šavli 1996: 492), the answer was: 'Yes, absolutely, and more! The essence of "Venetic theory" is to correct the wrongs committed against the Slovenian nation – the disfiguring of its origin and its early history' (ibid.).

In a different context, Tomažič puts it no less clearly that while Slovenian youth are taught in schools 'the misleading theory about the arrival of Slovenians in the sixth century from trans-Karpatian swamps, Slovenians are going to be ashamed of their own ethnie' (quoted in štih 1997: 36). The only way out of this shame, it is argued, is to teach them to recognise themselves as the 'descendants of the famous paleo-Venets' (ibid.).

These statements not only refute the claims by Venetologists that they are pursuing an unbiased view of Slovenian history, but also put them in the service of a romantic notion of Slovenian nationhood. Their effort thus becomes a matter of national pride, unfailing love and honour which official history denies to them. Lenček's (1990: 84) accusation that Venetologists are 'wandering into romance' is nowhere more obvious than when they speak about the need to give Slovenians back their honour. The notion of honour is upheld against the background of fear of being continuously associated with the 'other' of nationalist imagining. The main source of shame appears to be the formal association that Slovenia enjoyed with other

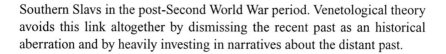

Southern Slavs in the post-Second World War period. Venetological theory avoids this link altogether by dismissing the recent past as an historical aberration and by heavily investing in narratives about the distant past.

Conclusion

Although it is an opportune child of the demise of the communist project, Venetological theory remains firmly faithful to the principles of nationalist politics. It continues to preoccupy those who take the interests of their nation to be their ultimate task in life, those who long for an imagined and imaginary glory of their forebears, and those with a taste for historical drama tailored to political need. In short, it preoccupies all those who keep the evils of communism and its associated imaginary alive in spite of the reality that fails to conform to the products of their imagination. Through their fondness for amateur politics, Venetologists wage a war against the evils of another era, the era of now bygone communism. They see Slovenia as being run by old communist and anti-Slovenian forces, which are facilitated by inaccurate interpretations of Slovenian history (Škerbinc 2004). Their suggestion for ending this state of affairs is as simple as it is effective: the work on Slovenian ethno-genealogy must be encouraged (Lenarčič 2001).

The Venetological explanation shows some of the classical attributes of national myths such as unrelatedness, separateness from surrounding groups, and autochthonous existence from ancient times. It accentuates the distinctiveness and uniqueness of the Slovenian people and follows the ambition to establish – as Hobsbawm (1997: 1) puts it – the 'continuity with a suitable historic past'.

The Venetological quest for a new history of Slovenians is not simply an exercise in truth-seeking, but should be viewed in a broader historical context, which is externally defined by the dramatic changes that took place in Europe in the last fifteen years of the twentieth century, and internally by the nationalist inspirations of its authors. The Venetological theory attempts to increase the symbolic capital of the nation by dissociating itself from its neighbours and emphasising its uniqueness, its ancient roots and cultural heritage. Furthermore, one of the key attributes of Venetological theory is its emotional capital, masked behind the quest for solidification of symbolic frontiers, honour, reinvention of historical memories and spiritualisation of the past. It has the potential to make a radical impact on the economy of nationalist sentiment by providing emotionally charged narratives that purport to overturn established ideas about the nation's past and – implicitly

– the future. Most of this historiographical innovativeness takes place in a relatively self-assuring market of producers and consumers of Venetological ideas. The Venetological re-interpretation of Slovenian history is fundamentally a search for collective emotional anchorage and emotional gratification. And nationalist historiography performs this task far better than a science of history ever could.

Notes

1. For example, visit the Internet discussion forum at http://forums. delphiforums.com/VENETI
2. To uncover further complexities of this dialectic of otherness-building, see Meštrović (1994: 61).
3. Venetologists might be surprised to learn that we find an almost identical statement in recent Croatian nationalist historiography. The Croatian writer Horvatić (1994: 3) reproduced a statement made by a Croatian politician in 1916: '... the Turks could never ever advance on Zagreb, never break Croatian resistance! ... Croatia has never been defeated ... Croatia is one of the oldest, if not the oldest, state in Europe, dating back to the seventh century.' To this, Horvatić added: '... and between the fifteenth and the eighteenth centuries the state of Croatia, although reduced to "reliquiae reliquiarum olim magni et inclyti regni Croatiae" [the relics of the relics of the formerly great and glorious Kingdom of Croatia], nevertheless stood as the "antemurale christianitatis", the shield of Christianity, that is, Western civilization.' (ibid.)

Bibliography

Akenson, D.H. 1992. *God's Peoples: Covenant and Land in South Africa, Israel and Ulster*. Ithaca and London: Cornell University Press.

Anderson, B. 2001. 'Western Nationalism and Eastern Nationalism', *New Left Review* 9: 31–42.

Applegate, C. 1990. *A Nation of Provincials: The German Idea of Heimat*. Berkeley: University of California Press.

Babič, Š. 2001. 'Neprekinjenost krščanstva v Sloveniji', in *Proceedings of the First International Topical Conference 'The Veneti within the Ethnogenesis of the Central-European Population'*, ed. A. Perdih and J. Rant. Ljubljana: Jutro, pp. 201–4.

Barbalet, J.M. 2001. *Emotion, Social Theory, and Social Structure*. Cambridge: Cambridge University Press.

Bourdieu, P. 1984. *Distinction: a Social Critique of the Judgement of Taste*. Cambridge MA: Harvard University Press.

Connor, W. 1984. 'Eco- or Ethno- Nationalism', – *Ethnic and Racial Studies* 7(3): 342–56.

Fentress, J. and Wickham, C. 1992. *Social Memory*. Oxford and Cambridge: Blackwell.

Gellner, E. 1997. *Nationalism*. London: Phoenix.

Grafenauer, B. 1988. 'O autoktonističnih teorijah (etruščanski, venetski itd.) v zvezi s pojavom slovenskih prednikov v novi domovini v 6. stoletju', in *Zgodovina Langobardov,* Pavel Diakon. Maribor: Založba Obzorja.

Hobsbawm, E. 1997. 'Introduction: Inventing Traditions', in *The Invention of Tradition*, ed. E. Hobsbawm and T. Ranger. Cambridge: Cambridge University Press, pp. 1–14.

Horvatić, D. 1994. 'The Contribution of Croatians to Western Culture I', *Klokan* 5(1): 3-6.

Lenarčič, A. 2001. 'Conference on Slovenian "Ethno-Genealogy"', *Delphi Forums*: http://forums.delphiforums.com/VENETI. Accessed on 7 January 2004.

Lenček, R. 1990. 'The Linguistic Premises of Matej Bor's Slovene-Venetic Theory', *Slovene Studies* 12(1): 75–86.

Lutz, C. and White, G.M. 1986. 'The Anthropology of Emotions', *American Review of Anthropology* 15: 405–36.

Meštrović, S.G. 1994. *The Balkanization of the West:* the *Confluence of Postmodernism and Postcommunism*. London and New York: Routledge.

Pavković, A. 2000. *The Fragmentation of Yugoslavia: Nationalism and War in the Balkans*. London: Macmillan.

Perdih, A. and Rant, J., eds. 2001. *Proceedings of the First International Topical Conference 'The Veneti within the Ethnogenesis of the Central-European Population*. Ljubljana: Jutro.

Ramet, S.P. 1999. *Balkan Babel: The Disintegration of Yugoslavia from the Death of Tito to the Insurrection in Kosovë*. Boulder, CO: Westview Press.

Skrbiš, Z. 1999. *Long-distance Nationalism: Diasporas, Homelands and Identities*. Aldershot: Ashgate.

Smith, A.D. 1990. *National Identity*. London: Penguin.

——— 1999. 'Ethnic Election and National Destiny: Some Religious Origins of Nationalist Ideals', *Nations and Nationalism* 5(3): 331–55.

Svašek, M. 2000. 'Borders and Emotions: Hope and Fear in the Bohemian-Bavarian Frontier Zone', *Ethnologia Europaea* 30(2): 111–26.

Šavli, J. 1985. 'Veneti – naši davni predniki?', *Glas Korotana* 10: 23–125.

——— 2001. 'Vindia: Veneti med Evropo in Indijo', *Delphi Forums*://forums. delphiforums.com/VENETI. Accessed on 7 January 2004.

Šavli, J. Bor, M. and Tomažič, I. 1988. *Veneti: naši davni predniki*. Maribor: ČGP Večer.

——— 1996. Veneti: First Builders of European Community. Vienna and Boswell: Editiones Veneti and Anton Škerbinc.

Šivic-Dular, A. 1990. 'Na rob venetsko-slovanskim razpravljanjem Mateja Bora', *Arheo* 10: 90–93.

Škerbinc, A. 2001. 'Angleška izdaja knjige 'Veneti'', in *Proceedings of the First International Topical Conference 'The Veneti within the Ethnogenesis of the Central-European Population'*, ed. A. Perdih and J. Rant. Ljubljana: Jutro, pp. 208–13.

———— 2004. 'Distortions of Slovenian History', *Delphi Forums*: http://forums. delphiforums.com/VENETI.

Štih, P. 1997. 'Avtohtonistične in podobne teorije pri Slovencih in na Slovenskem', in *Karantanien - Ostarrichi*, ed. H. and M. Založba, A. Moritsch. Klagenfurt and Ljubljana, pp. 25–49.

Tomažič, I. 1990. *Veneti naši davni predniki: Matej Bor, Jožko Šavli, Ivan Tomažič,* Ljubljana: Editiones Veneti.

Žižek, S. 1990. 'Eastern Europe's Republics of Gilead', *New Left Review* 183: 50–62.

———— 1992. 'Eastern European Liberalism and Its Discontents', *New German Critique* 57: 25–49.

Chapter 7

Strategies of Resistance in the Polish Campaign against EU Membership

Justine Golanska-Ryan

Because of its economic and political advantages, integration with the European Union (EU) seems to be, a priori, a good thing for the postcommunist states of Eastern Europe. However, even if EU membership is seen in this way by the main political parties and the majority of the population, there is, almost invariably, some resistance. Although Poland is the largest of the countries that joined the EU in May 2004, approximately 23 percent of the population (with the right to vote) voted against the accession. This was disregarded by the proactive parties as unimportant, and yet it means that almost 4 million people with the right to vote (over eighteen years of age) opposed membership.

This chapter examines the discursive practices and strategies of resistance in the Polish campaign against EU membership, and focuses on two opposition groups in Silesia, the Union of Realistic Politic (the UPR) and the League of Polish Families (the LPR).[1] The first is an ex-parliamentary party now attempting to get reelected, and the second is a parliamentary party of increasing social support. These groups can, however, be placed in the national context, as they do not necessarily focus exclusively on the local problems of Silesia.[2] Both groups claimed to be using a specific way of forwarding their arguments. The LPR purposely aimed at 'calling on people's hearts' (*odwołanie do uczuć*), evoking nationalist sentiments and fear of moral decline in an attempt to convince their audiences. The UPR, by contrast, was explicit about informing people about the advantages and disadvantages of EU membership as its priority. They identified their campaign as 'informative' (*informowanie*), and claimed not to be strategically appealing to people's emotions.

Criticising the UPR's claim to rational politics that are purely based on objective facts, this chapter argues that political processes are inherently emotional, and that the opposition between 'rationality' and 'emotionality' is itself a political myth (Svašek 2002). As this chapter will demonstrate, both parties' campaigns were involved in deliberate acts of emotional management, and the rhetoric of *informowanie*, employed by the UPR, was a clever strategy which in itself reinforced the image of 'purely rational politics'. It reproduced the underlying idea that 'showing of emotions' signifies irrationality and loss of control, implying that the public display of emotions is unsuitable for serious politicians. Yet, as the analysis will make clear, the UPR 'cunningly' used emotional strategies (even though they denied this), and played down their political importance. The LPR, by contrast, went to the other extreme by suggesting that emotions, which were openly expressed and evoked by the Party representatives during the campaign, signified their serious concern for the Polish people, and demonstrated a sense of political responsibility that proved the party's moral righteousness. As with the UPR, however, the LPR denied that emotional management was a crucial strategy to improve their own election results.

This chapter not only demonstrates that 'reason' and 'passion' are certainly not mutually exclusive categories in politics, but also emphasises the fact that politicised emotions have become a powerful source of power in postsocialist Poland. The dynamics of political change, in this case EU membership, served as a political tool in the reinforcement of the nationalist sentiments, and emotions, in particular feelings of disillusionment and mistrust, have been deployed by both opposition parties in their political campaigns opposing global processes. Both parties played out emotionally sensitive themes in their campaigns, and used emotional management in attempts to gain power.

The Referendum as Field Site: Discourses, Strategies and Resistance

My fieldwork was conducted between 15 May 2003 and 10 July 2003 in Southern Poland, in the region of Lower and Upper Silesia. In the context of the EU referendum held in Poland on the 7 and 8 June, Silesia was the place to go to observe strong campaigns for and against, and particularly the material dimensions of such campaigns – banners, placards, mass meetings, debates and marches. The first half of my fieldwork covered the time of the hottest EU/non-EU campaign. Before the referendum I took part in the numerous meetings and actions, marches, demonstrations, debates and consultations held by the two groups. The second half of my fieldwork covered the time after the referendum when I participated in both parties' meetings about their further policies. Having lost the referendum, they had to take on a new approach to the situation and decide on the implementation of new strategies.

Contemporary theories of emotional discourse (Abu-Lughod and Lutz 1990), in particular in the postsocialist states (Svašek 2002), have emphasised the inherent importance of emotions to politics. In this chapter, I examine the connection between Polish discourses of resistance to EU accession and the political deployment of emotions. The concept of resistance itself has been widely employed and investigated in anthropology (Abu-Lughod and Lutz 1990; Comaroff 1985; Routledge 1996). As the analysis will show, discursive practices of resistance in Poland's case have been constructed around notions of a mythical national identity (see Skrbiš, Chapter 6, this volume for an analysis of nationalist myths of Slovenian origin). The UPR and the LPR have both used nationalist myths in an attempt to strengthen mistrust in the pro-EU government and scepticism about the future of Poland in the EU (see also Chapter 9, Kalb and Tak, this volume).

The UPR: the Discourse of *Informowanie*

During my fieldwork, it became soon apparent that the UPR's 'No' campaign had two alternating strategies: informative and emotional. Even though the party denounced the LPR approach as 'playing on emotions' (*granie na emocjach*), and emphasised that their own purpose was to convince people through factual information, *informowanie*, they did actively respond to people's insecurities and fears. They did, however, underplay the importance of emotional dynamics in an attempt to distance themselves from their political rival.[3]

The UPR campaign can be analysed in terms of its efforts to challenge 'the myths' about the EU forwarded in the official, pro-EU, campaign. By explicit emphasis on the priority of informing in their campaign, they wanted to show that what the government told the Poles about the EU was not true. 'The myths about the EU' then, were understood by the UPR as 'all the so-called good, unlikely to happen, things that the official campaign uses in their propaganda to convince the Poles to support EU membership.'

My first encounter with the UPR in action, during their 'No' campaign, was at a lecture entitled 'Freedom or European Union' in the University of Silesia. Announced via the Internet (the UPR official website) and leaflets distributed at the university and around the town, the lecture gathered a crowd of approximately 150 students. Some of the students were standing, some sitting; the hall was overcrowded. Representing the UPR was a former leader of the party, and three other members of the Silesian faction of the UPR. There was only one poster with the slogan 'NO TO EU!' displayed at the back of the lecture hall, and a party flag, with blue, white and black colours, tied together with the Polish red and white national flag. Since it was aimed at challenging myths about the EU, this lecture was meant to convince Silesian students that what they were told by the government was not true. A professional approach involving the lecture at the university and some juggling of the information, numbers and statistical data, was meant to act against governmental propaganda. The speaker drew charts and graphs on the board, making associations between the poor economic situation in the EU and EU membership as a bad choice. Statistical facts describing the declining economic situation in Europe included the slump in economic growth, growing unemployment, high taxes and many other examples. He wrote the numbers on the board and spoke about the situation in Europe:

> If the economic growth of Ireland was +7% per annum in 1996, it was only +1% in 2002. The same with Germany, their growth reduced to -1%. If we compare Eastern Germany, that was a socialist country too, we get -6% economic growth and 26% unemployment. And they, as a matter of fact, joined the EU after the wall had fallen. And all the troubles they have now, despite 900 bn euro of subsidies from the European Union. Not only Germany does so badly, France has gone bankrupt as well. The French pension system is struggling and they have no way of improving situation other than by getting new markets – that is why they want *us* to work for them. Do you realise that the EU plans to bring the working age up to 65 for women and 75 for men? Well, somebody will have to pay their pensions. This is the truth about the EU. Why should we join an organisation that is falling apart?

The UPR: Polish Victimhood

Despite the claim purely to provide objective information, the UPR evoked emotional memories of Polish victimhood. As well as on economic facts, the ex-party leader drew on the historical past: 'We have to realise that history repeats itself, we face the powers of Europe, Germany, France and

Russia, working together again. We encounter an axis as in the past: Paris, Berlin, and Moscow – this should tell us the truth about the EU.' He stressed the importance of this comparison with a silent pause in his speech. 'Yes, once again in history, we have to face the unity of our nation being endangered by outer powers. The EU is like the Third Reich, unscrupulous in taking advantage of the weaker countries.' The comparison to the Third Reich was made twice more. First, when he spoke about the effects EU membership would have on Polish independence:

> Our accession to the EU is like another *Anschluss*, we will lose our independence again, there will be no self-determination, there will be, instead, more bureaucracy, and all decisions will be taken in Brussels. Imagine having to do what you are told. You don't like it, do you?

The second time he mentioned the Germans, was when he spoke of the land regained in the West of Poland after the Second World War,[4] and the Germans attempting to get it back. He tried to keep all these historical remarks as digressions only to the mainstream of his thought but deliberate attempts to evoke emotions in his audience through references to the past were used every few sentences to strengthen the impact of his speech.

Another example of this emotional strategy concerns his comparison of the EU to the USSR:

> What else, if not another form of the USSR, is the European Union? I am asking *you*. You remember the bureaucracy of Soviet rule in Poland – do you? You are probably *too young* to remember. The EU is just a better, well, let's put it like this, enhanced, version of the USSR and its socialist mechanisms of power. Do you want a proof? Don't we live in a common European market? Or, rather, won't we live in one common market? Does it not sound to you like 'the common soviet market'? They have just changed their masks.

At the end of his lecture, questions from the audience were invited. Most of them concerned the economic situation in Europe, the UPR stance if they lost the referendum, and their relationship with the LPR. The UPR spokesman rejected any similarities with the LPR. He emphatically denied being an extreme nationalist who used emotional arguments to convince people, as Roman Giertych (the leader of the LPR) was.

The UPR: Factual Realism versus Emotional Extremism?

Aiming at informing society of the real consequences of EU membership, the UPR organised a stand in the city centre of Katowice at the end of May[5] which displayed books on EU accession, their own party flags and Polish national flags. Party members were present to provide inquirers with information on the EU. They met with public approval and great interest. Passers-by were stopping and asking about the party and their arguments: why did they not want Poland to join the EU and what was their standpoint? This type of approach gave them an opportunity to be asked the questions and to provide answers. Their discreet display of only the party and national flags, with no banners or posters condemning the EU (unlike the LPR), helped them to avoid being perceived as radical opponents. Having good insight into much detailed information unknown to the average citizen, they could impress people with their knowledge of economic and political matters with regard to Polish membership of the EU.

A professional approach to their image (wearing suits and ties, as 90 percent of the members are men) helped them to evoke the impression of being a well-organised and well-informed party. Their strategy was not only based on demonstrating their dissatisfaction or scepticism about Polish membership of the EU. They also tried to convince the public of their rights in a so-called informative way. The UPR drew on their party name (the Union of *Realistic* Politics), assuring people of their never-changing priority of being realistic about politics and economics in any situation. They informed people of the potential consequences of Polish accession to the EU, like an increase in VAT, or an increase in unemployment by a certain percentage, juggling information (e.g. 'If our VAT on building materials is 7 percent now, in May 2004 it will increase to 21 percent') in their efforts to challenge the 'myths' about the EU. However, they again evoked nationalist sentiments in an attempt to convince their audience.

> The unemployment in Germany increases, why should it then fall in Poland, or even worse, why should the Germans employ the Poles? Do not believe in what the government tells you. Their argument that our children will be able to work and study abroad is ridiculous – we have been able to do so since the fall of communism and *without* the EU. (A party member talking to a passer-by)

In a similar vain, another member of the UPR picked up on a discussion with a disillusioned woman in her forties, stirring up feelings of distrust in the government:

> Yes, you are right in what you say, government do not care about people. Why? It is because the government represents the interests of the EU in Poland rather than Poland in the EU. It becomes even more suspicious, if we consider that the person responsible for the promotion of EU in Poland is an ex-first secretary of the KC PZPR[6], Jerzy Wiatr. All they are considered about is their own business and future employment in the European Parliament; post-communists forgot that it is Poland that matters.

The woman shook her head with great approval: 'Yes, we were never really cared for. Whoever gets to Parliament forgets about us ordinary people.' The discussion continued, as the young men kept telling her about more lies by the government about future prosperity in the EU. This strengthened her feelings of mistrust.

UPR *and* LPR Slogans: 'European Union – No', 'UESR = USSR'

The trial referendum in Głuchołazy was preceded by two days of party presentations on stage, discussions and debates. Sunny weather brought big crowds, enjoying themselves and trying to learn more about the EU. Various stands of supporters and opponents were located around the town square. Local TV and radio (RMF FM) were involved in broadcasting the news from the event. The town square was full of European blue and yellow starred flags, balloons and Polish national flags.

Because they had similar priorities, the UPR and the LPR were located in neighbouring stands. The UPR displayed its own flags, alongside the Polish flags. This time, they had also prepared leaflets, posters and banners with slogans like: 'Poland – YES, Europe – YES, European Union – NO!', 'Union VAT – economic executioner' (it rhymes in Polish: *VAT – kat*). To be noticed they had to make themselves visible, so they took part in the LPR marches around the square, shouting: 'Poland YES, Union NO' and 'Yesterday Moscow, today Brussels'. Such an approach strengthened observers' view of them as a party associated with the radical right wing. I heard a person saying: 'I thought the UPR was more serious. I never knew they were going to end up with the LPR. It's not like them to march around and shout.'

On stage, each party was given twenty minutes to present their stance. The UPR went on stage at 5:40 p.m. Four party members talked for over twenty minutes about the 'real' picture of the EU as they saw it. As one of them said:

> It is not true that the EU guarantees Poland security and sovereignty. The EU is becoming a federation and accepting an even more socialist model of the state. This results in strong centralisation and techniques of control unnoticeable to the average citizen. If foreign policy, military policy, monetary policy and passports, the basic features of sovereignty, are going to be held in common and governed by the EU, then we will be treated as second-class citizens. Our state will become dependent on the centralised structures of the EU. The structure of evil in the EU and in Russia is the same. The aims are similar too. The only things

that differ are the techniques of power – there was terror in Russia; here, in the EU, there is so-called 'democracy'. The 'masters' from Brussels do not kill and terrorise, they steal and defraud, keep order by means of bureaucracy and rules that have to be obeyed. The EU is a structure similar to the USSR. It even uses the same propaganda as the Soviet Union did: in the socialist era children were waving Russian flags with the red stars … now the only thing that has changed is the colour – like the colour of the SLD.[7] The quasi socialism of the EU, with its quotas and directives to be obeyed, will not help our economy. The EU as a socialist organisation does not allow the state to achieve economic wealth on its own but aspires to dividing the wealth already achieved among its members.

This comparison of the EU to the USSR was supported by shouts from the crowd gathered below the stage: 'Yesterday Moscow, today Brussels.' People from the UPR waved their banners with the slogan, 'ZSRR = ZSRE (in English, USSR = UESR; United Soviet Socialist Republics = United European Socialist Republics).

Another party member provided a different example of how emotional management was employed in their campaign:

One of the greatest myths,[8] which our President tries to use to convince Poles about the benefits of EU membership, is the national security that the EU is supposed to provide for Poland. He said: 'EU has provided Europe with peace for the past fifty years.' It is not true. Where was the EU in 1956 when Hungary needed help, in 1968 when Prague was struggling, or in 1981 when Poles fought for freedom? Let's be honest about it, the EU does not care about our security. It is NATO, Mr President, not the EU that we should rely on. There was too *much* grief in the history.

The presentation strategically finished with the singing of the national anthem. This conclusion engaged all the people gathered there, both opponents and supporters, as everyone stood up to show respect and sang.[9]

The last, and only official, chance the UPR had to take part in a discussion in the public media was a television debate held on the Polish Programme One the night before the referendum. Party members (approximately ten) were very well prepared and well able to discuss complex economic problems with the supporters of EU membership. Trying to convince the audience to vote 'no' in the referendum was only one of the targets to be achieved. The aim underlying their actions was focused on forthcoming elections and their appropriate self-presentation to the potential electorate. Their campaign clearly served their political aim of coming back onto the political stage.

The UPR after the Referendum

The referendum resulted in 77.44 percent votes for the accession, and 22.55 percent votes against EU membership, with a turnout of 58.85 percent. Afterwards, the party leader, Stanisław Wojtera, thanked people for voting 'no' in the referendum in an official statement on the party website. He also announced the beginning of preparations for party members to stand in the European Parliament elections. Such a policy is recommended by the UPR, as crucial for maintaining Poland as an independent state. This is the only way in which Poles can gain the right to influence the decisions made in Brussels.

The meeting of the UPR leaders and members, which I attended on 24 June in Warsaw, was called: 'Aims and future of the UPR after the referendum'. It attracted approximately fifty people, all of them men, from twenty to fifty years old. Wojtera gave clear directives on how to reach the potential electorate, recommending that the slogans for national independence were dropped. Instead, he argued that issues relevant to most potential voters, such as unemployment, taxes and insurance, should become central in the UPR programme. Only then, he believed, would the UPR be convincing. The party tried to convince people that the EU would not solve their problems, and that it was necessary to find 'Polish' (i.e. UPR) solutions for 'Polish' problems – unemployment, corruption, poverty and indebtedness. These were issues that had a strong emotional resonance for many Poles, faced with increasing insecurity.

The example of the UPR shows how a campaign, which claimed to be 'informative' and thus rational, in fact shifted between different discursive strategies, depending on the circumstances, audience and aim to be achieved. Sophisticated emotional management was clearly one of the tools employed to convince potential voters.

The LPR: Calling on People's Hearts

While the UPR denied its use of emotional strategies, the LPR openly called on people's hearts. Not surprisingly, the latter made even more frequent references to memories of Polish victimhood than the former. Identification of the EU with Nazi Germany and the USSR was intended to stirr up old fears, and references to a tradition of fighting for freedom were intended to reinforce the romantic ideal of Polish national rebellion.[10] The LPR also warned against the probability that the EU would bring total secularisation and kill the moral spine of the nation, thus triggering the loss of Polish identity.[11] Such an approach evoked feelings of anger and the need for organised self-defence.

The LPR started its campaign on 8 May under the banner of patriotism and protection of national identity and sovereignty. The LPR members and sympathisers marched and demonstrated carrying Polish flags and banners. The usual way of conducting their 'No' campaign was by means of public demonstration of their stance – usually very loud and conspicuous. The choice of place was crucial in their campaign. Polish town and city squares have proved to be the best places for being noticed and heard in their campaign, bringing also the necessary feeling of history in which they are immersed. What was very particular about the LPR's campaign was the involvement of graphic, written and printed materials alongside the effective use of music and songs. The songs were of national origin and the opponents were united in the proud singing of the Polish national anthem and other, so-called, independence songs from the times of German or Russian occupation. Of particular interest was the song written in 1908 called 'Rota', which says:

> We will not abandon the land from where our ancestors come,
> We will not let our language be forgotten,
> Poland is our nation, Poland is our home,
>
> …
>
> We won't let the Germans spit in our faces,
> And we won't let them Germanise our children …

(My translation)

The gathering had the importance of a pilgrimage to the place from where the independence of Poland can be saved. Numerous banners and flags were visible to the other passer-bys, who were showered with the home-printed leaflets. Ear- and eye-catching watchwords could not pass unnoticed as they were written on numerous posters and banners and were shouted out loudly and repeatedly:

> Poland YES – Union NO
> Yesterday MOSCOW – Today BRUSSELS
> Anschluss of POLAND again: Do you want to lose your LAND?
> I AM A POLE – I SAY NO!
> ENDANGERED LIFE – ENDANGERED LAND – ENDANGERED IDENTITY!
> EU – NO MORALITY, NO SOVEREIGNTY!
> WAKE UP THE NATION AT RISK! THE CHOICE IS YOURS!
> USER = USSR – United Socialist European Republics!
> NEVER MORE TOTALITARISM

The way of composing the slogans and press headlines recalls socialist slogans exhorting people to work and obedience. We get, then, a biased choice of words and juxtaposition of meanings seemingly unrelated but clearly referring to emotional themes. For example, EU accession will be called 'incorporation' rather than 'membership', with an emphasis on outer powers acting against the will of the nation. The motifs triggered two main emotional responses: fear of victimisation and rebellious pride.

LPR Rhetorics: Love for the Homeland

On 22 May, an anti-EU rally was organised in Wroclaw City Square that was entitled 'EU – the real picture'.[12] It was advertised on leaflets, handouts and websites as 'a rally of independence with the participation of all eurosceptic organisations'.[13] The rally attracted approximately three hundred people, mostly aged between forty and sixty, and was led by Prof. Dr hab. Jerzy Robert Nowak,[14] who appeared to be one of the spiritual leaders of the party. His speeches triggered off applause and were met with the unanimous approval of the crowd.

Every party attending the rally had an opportunity to present their stance on the EU (always against), and each speech was followed by a song. These interludes introduced the emotional element of unifying mission to save the nation. The material dimension of their campaign included posters, banners, Polish and party flags, self-printed leaflets, books and cheap brochures. Party members wore blue t-shirts with nationalist slogans:

NO to EU! God, Honour, Homeland, Nation!
I say NO! I am a POLE.

People carried Polish flags with the European stars on them and NO printed in the middle. A man in his fifties, who carried a flag with a Polish eagle pictured in the middle of a map of Europe, told me how proud he was to be present when the future of Poland was discussed. The atmosphere of important national mission could be felt. Gathering at the historical whipping post[15] put even more emphasis on how important this meeting was. People were standing proudly, listening carefully to the speakers and singing songs. Before the speakers started, a man with a guitar (the LPR's representative) struck up a song, and the crowd joined him:

Our homeland is our pride
We will not let anybody take our freedom
We suffered pain and captivity
We will stand by our country

This is our duty

People sang and raised their palms with their fingers formed in the V (victory) sign, strengthening their emotional disposition through collective bodily action.

The LPR: Memories of Polish Suffering

Nowak spoke as the first of the party representatives. His task was to present the LPR stance on the EU and to spur people on to vote 'no'. His speech intended to use a choice of themes and problems that would trigger mistrust of the government amongst the crowd. He spoke loudly and with strong emphasis:

> My dear friends! We are gathered here today to talk about what is so painful for us as Poles. We have been betrayed again. Our cheating government, full of post-communists, red apparatchiks and other politicians who cannot be trusted any more, decided to betray us again and sell our country for euros and good jobs in Brussels. They tell us what they want to keep us stupefied. The Polish nation has always been abused and taken advantage of. We've always been the victims of history and the geopolitical position. Our elites never really cared for us. Voting 'yes' we vote for Miller's government! Voting 'no' will be our clear disapproval for his government! We have to vote them out of the government!

This last sentence evoked great applause and people were shouting: 'Poland in the EU is Miller's Poland'[16], 'Poland of freedom, not thieves and soviet agents', and '*Komuchy* to Moscow'[17], chanting repeatedly until Nowak managed to calm them down. He continued, hinting at the horrors of the Second World War.

> By joining the EU we will lose our independence and European legislation will become superior to the Polish constitution. EU membership means political and economic dependence on Germany. Can you imagine that the treaty, signed by our government, allows foreigners, and that means mostly Germans, to buy our land and businesses and we have nothing to say about it? It will be totally uncontrolled.

People started shouting: '*Anschluss*! *Anschluss* again! Union, Union über alles – and an empty plate for the plundered ones.' Nowak carried on, 'Yes, you are right. It is another *Anschluss*. Did you hear what Gerhard Schroeder said in Berlin on the 3 September 2000?' He paused, building up tension. 'He said exactly' (and he read out from his notes) "Pomerania, Prussia, Silesia, Sudeten, Gdańsk and Wrocław are: part of our national and cultural heritage. Soon, Poland, the Czech Republic and Hungary as member countries of the EU will open, for our children and grandchildren, the possibility to return to their land. They will be entitled to engage in the political, economic and social life of Poland. Don't tease the victim that wants to be captured itself. Believe me! I will hand you over the East lands in such a way that will make Poles be thankful for becoming Europeans." People started to shout: 'Save Poland. Save Poland. Save Poland!' Nowak waited for this reaction. 'This is true. 600,000 people in these lands have a right only to lease their land, they do not have ownership. The European Tribunal will give these lands to the Germans.' A woman next to me, seeing me writing, asked if I had heard on the radio what Schroeder had said.[18] When I said I had not, she told me that she had a piece of land near the border and was afraid of losing it. She believed that her mother had been given this land just on the basis of a lease after the Germans had left, so there was no proof of ownership.[19]

The problem of land was a very sensitive one in the campaign. By comparing German claims for land to historical occupation the LPR invoked the emotional attachment to land, drawing on fears of the repetition of history (see Svašek, Chapter 4 and Müller, Chapter 8, this volume, for similar feelings in the Czech Republic). Nowak continued, strengthening even further feelings of mistrust and fear:

> We have always been underdogs in Europe, vulnerable and weak, and so naïve. Every country has abused us. They sold us at the Round Table in 1989 as they did in Yalta in 1945. We should have learnt from history, but we haven't. We are weak in Europe but we are not as a nation. So let's stand together for our freedom and say 'no' to new conspiracy against Poland.

The Germans were presented as the main culprits of all the crimes and ills. It was seen as suspicious that they were the main supporters of Polish membership in the EU:

> We have always been treated as the country to be used for somebody else's advantage. Haven't we? This is why the Germans want us to join the EU: they need somebody to rule, somebody to take advantage of. They will take over not only our land, they will buy out our businesses and companies. What is a nation if it has no land? It equals the loss of independence. We haven't fought for freedom to lose it so easily. We should stand strong against the new germanisation of our nation.

The crowd shouted 'Yes, Yes, Yes,' and Nowak continued, 'It is time for us to decide on Polish matters in this country, not in Berlin or Brussels. It is in your hands to save the country of your fathers. We don't need the scraps from the German plates.'

The man with the guitar struck up another song with strong emphasis on the sentence, 'We will not give away our land'. People grabbed the Polish flags and held them proudly high above their heads. Other songs were sung by only some of the protesters, but this particular one, as well as the national anthem, got them all singing. Many of them put their hands on their hearts, in a gesture of solidarity coming from the depths of national pride. Many stood up straight, following Nowak, who put his hand on his heart and stood to attention.

The LPR clearly drew on emotional themes, seeking active responses. Painful memories and discourses of recurrent victimhood were used to support their 'no' campaign. These strategies dominated almost every meeting, rally or demonstration I attended. At the trial referendum in Głuchołazy, the motif 'comparing the EU to the USSR' took over. I listened to an LPR member talking to a group of sympathisers:

> I believe you all remember our '*membership*' in the USSR, don't you? [He put a very ironic emphasis on 'membership'.] Our membership in the EU is advertised as sweetly as our 'membership' in the USSR was, as a 'brotherly friendship'. And who encourages us to join the EU? Communists themselves! Let us not be fooled, dear friends. The EU is like the USSR, a bureaucratic machine, with no possibility of leaving it. Do you remember what communists were telling us about socialism? Everyone is equal and everything is held in common. Don't we have a common market in Europe? Is not the government trying to convince us that life is good in the European Community? Do not believe in that. They want you to believe that the EU is like a wonderland, where everything is just perfect. Didn't the Soviets say the same thing? Didn't we suffer enough?

The Polish experiences with the Soviet Union were so painful that memories of betrayals, expulsions to Siberia, the Gulag, the lies of the communist past and lack of choice were stifled for forty-five years and cultivated only in private. This strict censorship, however, had brought ambiguous results. It was an amputation of historical consciousness for a few generations, but for those who, despite it, knew a little about the recent past, it presented a challenge. The LPR used the experience of the Soviet past as an example to trigger a feeling of fear about the future. Marek called to people in Głuchołazy: 'Do you believe in having a choice? Did you have a choice in communist Poland? You will not have any choice in the EU either.' Some people started to shout, 'Down with the new Soviet occupation. Red USSR, red Union.' They became silent only when one of the LPR members stood on the high chair and shouted,

> We are a nation of 40 million brave, intelligent and independent people. There
> are 20 million Polish people living abroad and we can't be defeated! We will win
> in this referendum and we will not let the new occupant take over our proud
> nation. Poles have always been proud and fought for freedom so why should we
> lose it now? We can't let the atheistic, spoilt, immoral West rule our country and
> tell our children what to do.

The 'lack of moral spine in Europe' motif was used as another strategy
of resistance. On the one hand, the LPR told people about all the drawbacks
of EU membership, like 'the homosexual marriages and secularisation of
life', 'promotion of abortion', and, on the other hand, they played on the
motif of Poles as the defenders of the morality of Europe. As Roman said at
one of the meetings, 'It is our responsibility as a nation, as it has always
been, to defend the Christian nature of Europe.' He drew on the history of
Poland as a defender of Christianity, and described Poles as proud and
relentless defenders of a Catholic nation.

Behind the Scenes: Emotions as a Source of Political Power

As the leader claimed, the LPR wanted to win the referendum, but lack of
proper access to the media, now in the hands of the postcommunist
government, made this impossible. However, he noted that the main reason
why people had voted 'yes' for EU accession had been their hope for a
better future. He was convinced that admission to the EU would quickly
change their outlook, because the reality would become even more painful.
This vision convinced him that the future for Eurosceptic parties, such as
the LPR, was promising. Even though the LPR's election campaign for
2004 emphasised the necessity of leaving the EU, in interviews he admitted
that the desire to leave was unrealistic, and served mainly as an emotional
trigger to win support. The LPR would also stand for the European
Parliament, and he believed they would profit from increasing
disappointment in the present government and the disappointing reality of
EU membership. He argued that it was important to play on these feelings:
'The campaign has to be targeted precisely, hitting people's emotions,
listening to what might work ...'

The emergence of radical nationalist right-wing parties and
organisations, such as the UPR, also demonstrated how cultural heritage
and history was evoked in order to fashion the new ideals of the nation-state
and relevant group identities (Kurti and Langman 1997). In the postsocialist
context, the recreation and affirmation of identity often comes with

references to the glories of the past or to the injustices suffered under the foreign occupation of the Germans or the Soviets (Hayden 1995; Jedlicki 1999). Political parties and movements use history in order to present their vision of the future of their societies. Emotional reinforcements are then reciprocal, and the spiral of national enthusiasm and fighting spirit may easily awaken latent memories of former sufferings. Such stereotypes arouse fears, but also generate complacent confidence in the rightness of one's cause.

Conclusion

The Polish case discussed in this chapter demonstrates how transnational processes, such as the planned EU membership of Poland, can stir up emotions that can be played out by local and national politicians. Looking at discursive strategies of resistance, and the strategic significance of emotional rhetorics and action in the 'No'-campaigns, the analysis showed how the UPR and the LPR managed emotions in an attempt to influence the result of the referendum. Claiming that they were using either informative or justifiable emotional behaviour, they both expressed and evoked emotions in particular strategic ways, depending on various factors, such as audience and place.

The party representatives actively selected and reinterpreted history and memory, and reshaped images of national identity to serve their political aims. Juggling terms, meanings and facts, the leaders created particular pictures of Poland, its past, present and future. Both parties focused on sensitive historical issues that almost automatically triggered emotional memories to persuade people that the future could become a repetition of the past. Playing on existing feelings of social disillusionment and mistrust in the government, they also attempted to manage emotional dynamics by reinforcing the fear of a worsening situation. Emotional management was thus strongly embedded in the social and political multiplicity of strategies of resistance against the integration of Poland in the European Union, and played an important role in local, national and transnational politics.

Notes

1. For clarity I shall use the Polish abbreviation for these parties: the UPR and the LPR.
2. Placing Silesia in context, as a region it is a place of special significance for the evocation of Polish identity and national issues, due to its own historical struggle to belong to Poland. For this reason it acquires an importance – as any border region

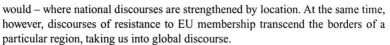

would – where national discourses are strengthened by location. At the same time, however, discourses of resistance to EU membership transcend the borders of a particular region, taking us into global discourse.

3. Because of its opposition to EU membership, shared with the LPR, the UPR became associated with the nationalist right wing. Such views did not satisfy the party members, as they wanted to distance the UPR from the radical voices of the LPR.

4. The issue of the land regained by Poles in the West and North of Poland after the expulsion of the Germans was one of the main concerns for the opponent groups in their 'No' campaign. Expulsion was, however, never mentioned in contrast to the fear of losing their own land.

5. Katowice does not have the kind of square common in Polish cities and towns, but instead has a commercial centre with a walking-only area of shops and cafés. This is the place where most of the meetings, marches and protests were held.

6. The governing Communist Party, 1945–1989.

7. The SLD is the post-Communist party, ex-KC PZPR, which now is called the Union of Democratic Left.

8. I do not discuss all the 'myths' that the UPR was challenging. The choice of them for this chapter reflects their relevance for the shifts in their campaigning.

9. Another 'myth' the UPR tried to counter was that of Poles being able to work and study abroad. It was of particular concern during the television debate held on the last day before the referendum (6 June from 9 p.m. to 12 p.m.). The UPR sat on the opponents' side of the studio altogether with the LPR, Młodzież Wszechpolska (the Polish Youth Organisation), Samoobrona (the Self Defence Party) and the SKL (the Conservative-Liberal Party). Marcin, from the UPR, considered the argument about working and studying abroad to be the worst example of propaganda, having nothing to do with reality: 'If the official campaign encourages the Poles to vote "yes", in order to be able to travel, study and work abroad, it sells us the freedom that we have already gained with the fall of communism. On the other hand, it does not take into consideration the facts: the transition periods for the workers adapted by most of the EU countries, and the fact that studying abroad has been possible for years. The EU is not necessary to make this happen. Besides, if there is increasing unemployment in the EU how will they manage to employ all the Poles, Czechs, and Slovaks? Where is the economic reality?'

10. An analysis of resistance in Serbian protest with the recognition of three motifs – victims, underdogs and rebels – was presented by Jansen (2000). The motifs appear universal – with individual argumentation lying behind them – if we take into consideration the situation of defiance and the emotional employment of arguments concerning identity and history in order to resist global powers in postsocialist states (and elsewhere). In the case of the Polish 'No' campaign, however, resistance was an element of defiance in the face of new powers, which endangered newly regained independence.

11. The LPR appeared on the Polish political stage as a party of the electorate disillusioned with the political and economic reforms of the previous governments. It is a young party that arose in the context of the failure of economic reforms in Poland and the increasing disillusionment of society. Members of the party are of nationalist origin with a strong right-wing ideology and a Catholic background.

Registered in 2001, they gained seats in Parliament after four months on the political stage. The party continued gaining support on the basis of growing social disappointment and a perceived need for change. This is a situation somewhat typical in the postsocialist states, where the economic and political reforms have not always been favoured by all citizens. The LPR aims at the older section of the society, who are less educated and strongly attached to the religious and moral identity of Poland as a Catholic state. Most party members are middle-aged or older people. They have experienced history and are susceptible to the rhetoric of national identity and fears of dangers from behind both borders, east and west.

12. The other events included: Saturday, 23 May, a rally advertised as ' Standing up for Polish independence'; 25 May, a trial referendum in the City Square; 30 May, folks' gala under the name of 'Poland – YES, EU – NO' held on the Wroclaw's stadium.

13. These euro-sceptic organisations included: the LPR, the UPR, the SKL (the Conservative-Peasant Alliance), Młodzież Wszechpolska (The United Polish Youth Organisation).

14. The use of academic titles is one of the strategies employed by LPR, aimed at the increase of credibility. 'Prof. Dr hab.' is an accumulation of all the academic titles possible to obtain in the Polish academic system.

15. This is where all the meetings of historical importance in Wrocław have always been held.

16. Leszek Miller was the prime minister in Aleksander Kwaśniewski's government and one of the postcommunists in power. The LPR campaign also voiced disapproval of the government at the time of referendum.

17. *Komuchy* is an offensive name for communists in Poland.

18. There was strong support for the LPR's 'no' campaign from the Catholic Radio Maryja.

19. During the campaign, it was never mentioned that the Germans had been expelled. Expulsion was justified on the basis of historical justice for all the suffering experienced under the Germans.

Bibliography

Abu-Lughod, L. and Lutz, C.A. 1990. 'Introduction: Emotion, Discourse, and the Politics of Everyday Life', in *Language and the Politics of Emotion*, ed. C.A. Lutz and L. Abu-Lughod. Cambridge: Cambridge University Press and Paris: Editions de la Maison des Sciences de l'Homme, pp. 1–23.

Adler, N. and Gerrits, A. ed. 1995. *Vampires Unstaked: National Images, Stereotypes and Myths in East Central Europe*. Amsterdam: Royal Netherlands Academy of Arts and Sciences, Amsterdam.

Comaroff. J. 1985. *Body of Power, Spirit of Resistance*. Chicago: University of Chicago Press.

Hayden, R.M. 1995. 'The Use of National Stereotypes in the Wars in Yugoslavia', in *Vampires Unstaked: National Images, Stereotypes and Myths in East Central Europe*, eds N. Adler, and A. Gerrits. Amsterdam: Royal Netherlands Academy of Arts and Sciences.

Jansen, S. 2000. 'Victims, Underdogs and Rebels: Discursive Practices of Resistance in Serbian Protest', *Critique of Anthropology* 20(4): 393–420.

Jedlicki, J. 1999. 'Historical Memory as a Source of Conflicts in Eastern Europe', *Communist and Post-communist Studies* 32(3): 225–32.

Kurti, L. and Langman, J., eds. 1997. *Beyond Borders: Remaking Cultural Identities in the New East and Central Europe.* Westview Press.

Lutz, C. and Abu Lughod, L. 1991. 'Introduction', in *Language and the Politics of Emotion*, ed. C.A. Lutz and L. Abu-Lughod. Cambridge, Paris: Cambridge University Press.

Routledge, P. 1996. 'The Third Space as Critical Engagement', *Antipode* 28(4): 399–419.

Svašek, M. 2000. 'Borders and Emotions. Hope and Fear in the Bohemian-Bavarian Frontier Zone', *Ethnologia Europeae* 30(2): 111–26.

——— 2002 'The Politics of Emotions. Emotional Discourses and Displays in Post-Cold War Contexts', *Focaal. European Journal of Anthropology* 39(1): 9–28.

Chapter 8

The Misgivings of Democracy: Personal Resentment and Alternating Power in a Czech Village

Birgit Müller

The distinctions between right and left, between political objectives that are pro-market or pro-communism are blurred in Czech village politics today. Political fights there are intensely linked to relations of love and hatred dating far back into the communist era and to moral convictions and material interests going beyond conventional political-ideological boundaries. Having 'a communist past' as well as being at present a member of the Communist Party matters in the unfolding struggle for power in the village, but it does not correspond to political convictions generally attributed to communism, such as a critical attitude towards privatisation, markets and foreign multinational companies. In the village Mokrovousy in the Český Kras, former communists strongly supported the take-over of the local quarry and limestone factory by foreign companies, while the local dissidents discovered themselves as ecologists and went into organised opposition. The intense fight between the two factions for political power in the village, which I will analyse here, plays with the political categories of communism and democracy. It is characterised by a complex blend of political traditions and newly emerging interests and preferences, mixed with personal feelings and resentments.

This dynamic finds a pointed expression in anonymous poems written in 1994 after the communists had lost the local elections. The opposing factions hung them up for everybody to read in front of the village administration. These poems will be the starting point for unravelling the complexities of postsocialist village politics and the emotional involvement with the main political actors. I am particularly interested here in examining how the expression of personal resentment in public space is linked to social and political judgement and political engagement. What does it tell us about the significance of emotions in the period of postcommunist transformation?

Politics always involves emotions and emotions have played a central and controversial role in political theory. On the one hand, they were considered contrary to reason and thus damaging for a reasonable public order. In *The Republic*, Plato wanted to ban poets from the ideal city because they provoked emotions like fear, sorrow, and pity that should not be encouraged among reasonable people. On the other hand, emotions never entirely disappeared from enquiries in the social and political sciences. Despite rationalisation, most authors acknowledge that affective bonds are necessary for creating and sustaining society.

During the rise of capitalism, between the seventeenth and the eighteenth centuries, – and contributing to its expansion – the notion of passion was replaced by the notion of interest (Hirschman 1977). Emotions and feelings, known then as passions, came to be perceived as noxious to the proper orderly conduct of political and capitalist affairs. While passions came to be associated with unruly human impulses that would lead to social conflict and economic decline, interest became synonymous with rationality and the ability to rein in the irrational. What was initially a normative projection by a number of thinkers including Adam Smith – that 'negative' passions should be checked and replaced by virtues or 'positive' passions and transformed into interest – was later standardised as the principal assumption of economists and political scientists: humans are rational beings motivated by the pursuit of self-interest (Smith 1976).

However, commitment to social norms necessarily involves emotions. Without emotional involvement man becomes indifferent to his environment (Nietzsche, quoted in Habermas 1981: 355). All value judgements contain emotions and those provide the meaning and the orientation to life that allow man to act (Elster 1995: 48). In social movements the political awakening is always also accompanied by an emotional response. Insult and anger at secrecy and political duplicity, an empathetic striving for justice establish connections between personal experiences and events of global consequence (Berglund 1998: 113).

Also, in reverse, social norms influence the expression of emotions and sometimes the emotions themselves. The expression of political commitment to a cause or a conviction, for instance, without the display of a certain degree of emotional involvement, makes it appear untrustworthy in the eyes of the public. Or, as Paperman pointed out, the absence of emotions in circumstances that are socially defined as highly meaningful, such as elections or debates on moral principles, can be regarded as an offence (Paperman 1995: 152–96).

Emotions are thus vital for political life and in particular for a lively democratic system. It is impossible to protect democracy entirely from the antagonisms and even hostilities that are part of political life (Mouffe 1994: 11). Democratic politics always consists in domesticating potential antagonisms, without eliminating passions or relegating them back to private life. To perceive politics only as a rational process based on negotiation between individuals means to neglect the dimension of power and conflict of the political and thus to be mistaken about its nature (ibid.: 151). Conflicting emotions and opinions have to be given a forum where they can be expressed and acted out. There is a convention, however, in most democratic societies to avoid in public political discourse criticism *ad hominem* and the relationship of offence and aggression it establishes (Thévenot 1995: 150).

In the particular context of postsocialist village politics, emotionally loaded attacks *ad hominem*, however, play a decisive role. In the sudden power vacuum after November 1989, individuals fight for political power, economic gain and career opportunities. At the local level, slander attacks happen simultaneously with appeals for social justice and economic well-being that cut across the ideological divide. Political engagement seems to go together with crusades against others, while disengagement is justified on the grounds that it is necessary in order to live in peace with one's neighbours. Gossip thus becomes an instrument for settling personal and political accounts that are inextricably linked. As even those villagers who don't want to take sides in political conflicts engage in gossip about their fellow villagers, it is an important tool for defining and redefining the social position that the individual – and especially the prominent one – occupies in the community. Blame-gossip (Svašek 1997: 102) is here inseparably linked to praise-gossip. To what extent, however, does gossip strengthen the social bonds in the village, as Max Gluckman (1963: 308) argues, and to what extent does it enable the village to act together in the face of adversity? Can it dissolve or exacerbate the tensions and divisions that the postsocialist transformations bring about?

Political Morality and Economic Need

In the period of deep social and political change that the Czech Republic has been going through since the Velvet Revolution of 1989, the values advocated by communist ideology, such as the principles of equality and solidarity and the principle of absolute truth incarnated in the Communist Party, have been replaced in the official discourse of the new democracy by values such as liberty, plurality and competition. However, this change in the official normative system encounters a complex reality at the local level (see also Svašek, Chapter 4, this volume). Protagonists of the communist regime find themselves seeking protection and support from multinational companies, while opponents of the regime now require regulation of economic activities from the state. Neither of them fits entirely into either of the opposing normative systems.

One of the reasons for this seeming contradiction is linked to the fact that in communist times the village was unable to maintain its infrastructure and services with what it received through the central distribution. It was thus in the interest of the village and its inhabitants to go beyond the channels of centralised distribution while paying lip service to the official discourse on socialist distribution. The official ideology appeared as a mere chimera, as a means to please the powerful. No village could expect to get a fair share in modern infrastructure if the members of the village council did not succeed in establishing close personal links with bureaucrats and party officials on the regional and national level in order to manipulate the regional investment plans to their advantage.

Taking materials and tools from work to use for community projects, using equipment of collective enterprises for special tasks in the community brigades, was considered part of a positive engagement for the community and thus highly valued. A close formal or informal link between the local enterprises and the village council was indispensable to advance what most villagers saw as the primary interest of the village, for example the modernisation of infrastructure.

The link that the communist mayor of Mokrovousy, Stepan, still in power in the beginning of the 1990s, tried to establish with a German company that wanted to build a large cement factory near the village, was in the same pragmatic spirit. Surrounding Mokrovousy is a nature protected area, the Český Kras, famous among geologists for its geological formations and coveted by foreign investors for its reserves of pure limestone. The factory was to be built next to an extended quarry and limestone factory that had been exploiting the limestone since the middle of the 1960s. Environmental activists from inside and outside the area objected that the planned cement factory would accelerate the depletion of the precious limestone resources and pollute the air. However, for the inhabitants of the surrounding villages it also promised an inflow of new resources, jobs and money in a time when financial resources were extremely scarce at the local level.

The local population were thus divided in their support or opposition to the factory. The communist mayor, Stepan, supported the project wholeheartedly as it appeared like the realisation of a dream from communist times when, in the 1970s, a gigantic cement factory had been planned by the Czechoslovak state to tower over Mokrovousy. Nobody had objected to this project at the time. In the 1990s, mayor Stepan had set hope in the new project. He expected the foreign company to provide the village with financial help because the new Czech state devolved new responsibilities to local communities without granting them the necessary financial means. He counted on the foreign investor to assume some of the functions the new Czech state had failed to take over from the socialist one. He wanted the company to finance the gas piping, get the waste-water system under way and equip the school with badly needed teaching materials.

The villages around the quarry were poor in spite of the fact that precious limestone was extracted from their territories. The possibilities for action at the local level were limited as only a few financial resources were devolved from the state to the local communities. The laws about the extraction of raw materials that dated back to communist times attributed only a small portion of the already low tax on raw materials to the local communities. The institutional reforms after 1989 did not introduce a democratically elected government at the regional level of decision making as an intermediary instance between national government and the local communities.[1] Financial resources for infrastructure, schooling etc. distributed at the regional level to the communities were thus attributed on an entirely administrative basis.

The opponents of the factory project saw the foreign investor and his communist supporters as continuing the old system when decisions about the future of the local communities were taken behind their backs and imposed on them by the bureaucrats in Prague and Beroun. What made the investor especially unpopular was the fact that he had initially ignored the opinion of villagers and had not consulted them about the investment project. In addition, the fact that the company had its headquarters in Germany stimulated suspicion and revived memories of the Second World

War, when the Czech heartlands were a German protectorate and its productive capacities were to serve the German war effort (see also Svašek, Chapter 4 and Golanska-Ryan, Chapter 7, this volume, on negative perceptions of Germans as former aggressors). The opponents of the cement factory argued that the Germans were exploiting the beautiful Czech countryside to keep their own 'Bavarian landscapes' intact. 'You would never have such a project in Germany', was an often-heard argument. The issue was taken up by the two most important ecological groups on the national level and received wide coverage in the newspapers. A nation-wide petition was circulated against the cement factory, and solidarity concerts were organised around the quarry. The cement factory became known as a symbol for the destruction of the beautiful Czech countryside by foreign capital. The area of Mokrovousy became famous in the Czech political landscape after 1989, for its capacity of determined resistance.

The conflict about the investment project was in full bloom when the nationwide local elections were scheduled in the autumn of 1994. In the three villages surrounding the quarry the citizen initiatives set up their own electoral lists and defeated the lists set up by the communist mayors. The majority of inhabitants of Mokrovousy supported the citizen initiative. However, not all of them did so because they had strong ecological convictions.

The two factions that opposed each other in the local elections had their supporters in different sections of the village population. The communist mayor, Stepan, was supported mainly by the families in the village that had had for generations a tradition of limestone mining and chalk burning or whose members had been manual labourers in agriculture. He had been a tractor driver in the agricultural cooperative before dedicating most of his time to politics and joining the Communist Party. After 1989 he changed the designation of his profession from tractor driver to 'agricultural technician', an embellishment laughed about by his opponents. He was popular among his supporters; they counted on his well-established relations from communist times to the regional administration in Beroun. To have him as a mayor was seen as a safe bet, as a warranty for continuity in spite of all the upheavals.

The citizen initiative led by Bina was supported by inhabitants from old peasant families and by the newcomers who had settled in the village because of its relative proximity to Prague. They were attracted by the attention the initiative received in the regional and national media. For them it represented the new times when open criticism could be voiced and when the old power structures were shaken and questioned. Although they opposed fervently, or for the most part moderately, the building of the cement factory, their opposition was like an attempt to explore whether opposition and also change were possible in the new political system. The idea of change became an aim in itself and had no tangible purpose attached to it.

When the challengers obtained a five-seat majority of the nine seats in the village council they had to choose the mayor from their ranks. This proved a problem because most of them were working during the week outside the village. Also the head of the citizen initiative, Bina, came home only at weekends, as he was working for a company installing telephone wiring all over the country during the week. The choice fell on Brany, the owner of one of the two local shops, who had arrived in the village as a member of a work brigade of forced labourers – the Black Barons (*černý barony*) – thirty years before.

Mirror Images: the Poems

A month and a half after the elections, in December 1994, the first anonymous poem appeared on the notice board next to the village council and the post office, fiercely attacking the newly elected mayor. A few days later a second poem was hung up, this time supporting the new mayor. The poems read:

After Elections

By the supporters of outgoing mayor, Stepan
December 1994

People are staring with amazement
How the people on the post of the mayor are changing
We cannot see a difference
After a while we will judge it all

What about the mayor, dear people
For how long will he be laughing?
He does not know
He has remote control

Dear buddy, hold yourself firmly in the saddle
So that none of the affairs can move you
There are enough troubles waiting for you
To the joy of the grey eminence[2]

He will manage to give you advice

He will manage to play the devil
He will help even the widow
He is a big scrounger

He has no good intentions with you
He waits until something goes wrong
Then he will step in, juchhu
We will have eunuchs in command

So there is one good advice for you
Learn how to count, learn how to greet, be correct in the shop
Or it will soon happen that your customer will hit you
If you can't be advised
Even the impartial Cada can't help you
Tell to yourself:'isn't it in me,
Even the Děti Země[3] won't help.'

Now there will be only a lot of work, little time
There will be no time for poems, before it was easy to laugh

After Elections 2

By the supporters of the head of the citizen initiative, Bina December 1994

Communists are staring with amazement
How the people on the post of mayor are changing
A big change it really is
The used-to-be mayor was from the manure

The used-to-be mayor, dear people
Already will not be laughing any more
He did not know, he had no idea
He had remote control

He was keeping firmly in the saddle,
He thought that no-one could get he out
He had enough troubles
To the joy of the opposition

The grandfather who knows everything controlled him
But he was an old bear
Over the fish pond on a nice hill
He was giving advices in his little house

He had good intentions with him
But he did not know that something would go wrong
He was a big StB agent[4]
And also a big swine

That's why there is one good advice:

Learn how to not be envious, learn how to control yourself
The mayor knows very well how to sell
You are worse than him
Wake up a bit
Even mister Cada will help him
Any advice will be good.
Despite your hate
We will have a good time, communists

Now there will be only a lot of work to put everything back into order
To fix up their work, so that we will be able to laugh.

The two poems, *After Elections* and *After Elections No.2*, are striking in their similarity, creating mirror images of mutual personal accusations. They do not refer to any of the political and ideological arguments used in the environmental struggle that sparked off the election result. In spite of what divided the ecologists from the communists, they used the same level of language and argument. Their elaborate world views seem to disappear behind emotions of hurt pride, envy and hatred. Both sides direct their attacks against the person of the opponent, trying to hurt him in his personal pride and ridicule him in front of the village. Claiming moral superiority, the authors of the poems offer incipient advice to the protagonists of the opposing groups. They pretend to speak in the name of the whole village and to know the hidden axis of power.

The poem *After Elections* addresses the new mayor as an incompetent, unfriendly shop owner manipulated by the head of the citizen initiative, Bina. It is written in the form of an ultimatum, encouraging the mayor to take an independent stance and to conform to the ways of politeness prevalent in the village, thereby integrating himself into the network of personal relations that govern the village affairs. If he won't conform, so the poem menaces, he will be all alone and nobody in the village will support him.

The issues raised are indeed central to the ambivalent position of the new mayor in the village. He arrived in the 1960s as a member of a work brigade that included political opponents and petty criminals declared inept and untrustworthy for military service. A 'rebel' at secondary school, he had to leave school without a degree and was not allowed to study or go into advanced professional training. Instead of military service he was then constrained to do the worst jobs in the quarry.

He broke with his parents, who were convinced communists, and married a girl from the village whose family name he adopted to mark the rupture with his family background. After 1990 he became the first private entrepreneur in the village, setting up a shop, which entered into competition with the cooperative store that the villagers had built in the 1970s. A neighbour and confidant of the equally rebellious but intellectually superior founder of the *Občanské forum* (citizen forum) in the village, Bina, he had stood in his shadow until he became mayor in 1994.

When elected, the mayor Brany was confronted with the difficulty of understanding the decision-making processes and administrative procedures necessary to run village affairs. The old secretary who had previously served the communist mayors was of no great help to him, as she clearly supported the outgoing mayor. She was not prepared to help Brany, who had been regarded as an enemy of the state and an asocial element in communist times. Feeling himself surrounded by enemies, Brany replaced the old secretary with the wife of Bina, the head of the citizen initiative.

The main target of the poem is indeed Bina, the outspoken aggressive head of the citizen initiative, also called *Bertík* by his enemies. This name, (which referred to the word *Čertík*, meaning 'small devil'), was given to him because he was disguised as a devil for a protest action on the 6 December 1994, when the protesters in costumes of Mikuláš, devil and angel, distributed leaflets against the cement factory. A fervent anti-communist, he systematically answers the phone: 'Here anti-communist centre Mokrovousy!' By referring to Brany as a 'eunuch in command', his opponents tried in a clumsy way to appeal to his male pride and provoke a split between the two men that would make the mayor more vulnerable and easier to influence.

The style of the poem *After Elections 2*, written as a reply, is no more sophisticated in style and content than the first one. The communist mayor is ridiculed because 'he is from the manure', from the farm, and was once a simple tractor driver in the agricultural cooperative. The authors present him as the tool of the secret police (StB) in communist times, though they don't dare to claim that he collaborated knowingly and directly. Such an assertion would have been equivalent of accusing him of a crime that excluded him from holding public office. The term 'communist' is used as an insult here.

The outgoing mayor owed indeed most of what he had achieved in life to the communist regime. Originating from an extremely poor family, he had started as a young boy to earn his living as an agricultural labourer on a private farm. The setting up of an agricultural cooperative greatly improved his economic and social condition. The position of a simple agricultural worker was in communist times an honourable one. Workers were – not only according to the official ideology – the leading class of the communist state and encouraged to take up political office. Stepan was thus promoted from a representative on the local council to a councillor on the regional level. For Stepan, the loss of his political position in 1994 meant also loss of the social status he had acquired.

Both poems address the issue of agency; the authors seem to imply that their favourite was brought to power by the majority of the inhabitants, while some manipulating grey eminence stood at the back of his opponent and pulled the strings. It is the issue of support or isolation in the village community that stands out most clearly in the argument. While the supporters of the new mayor insist that there is strong support for him from all sides, and claim that he is bringing about big changes, his opponents depict him as potentially isolated and unable to make a difference.

The Troubles of a 'New Democracy'

As anonymous expressions of slander the poems are a cowardly form of gossip. The slanderer is safe, as he or she does not even have to draw another person into his/her confidence. These poems would not qualify for what Jim Scott (1990) calls 'hidden transcripts', that is discourses that the powerless develop among themselves about and against those in power and that are only voiced behind their backs. The two factions of the village were almost equally powerful and their protagonists were in open opposition to one another. The fact of keeping the poems anonymous avoided the outbreak of open hostilities. Although everyone in the village could guess who might have written them, the authors could benefit from the doubt, and were able to continue to interact normally with both factions in the village on a day-to-day basis. However, at the same time a spiral of hate was set in motion as gossip moved, with the open exposition of the poems, into the public space and replaced the exchange of political and practical argument.

The controversy between the two opposing factions of the village, based on personal attacks, illustrates the problems involved in learning how to make democratic representation work at the local level. The election of

1994 in Mokrovousy was the second democratic election in the village since 1990 but it was the first one to oppose clearly defined factions and to have been preceded by a full-fledged electoral campaign. The election's outcome posed problems for the losers, who had been 'keeping firmly in the saddle' for over forty years, to come to terms with their loss of power, and for the winners to reach out from the high moral ground from which they advanced their criticisms to problem solving on a day-to-day basis.

The priority of the faction linked to the citizen initiative was a moral renewal in the village through a settling of accounts with the past. The change of regime raised high expectations among those disadvantaged by the previous regime. They were therefore morally outraged that communists could still wield power. By cooperating with citizen initiatives on the national level, in a committee that studies the files of the communist secret police StB, Brany and Bina wanted to perpetuate the memory of what 'the communists did'. Only if the past was not forgotten could the new political regime become a more open and transparent one. In his fight against the foreign investor and his supporters, Bina resented bitterly that again 'the truth' was covered up and distorted, and that deliberately false information was given to the public. Involving the media and legal councel, the group that constituted itself as an opposition to the communist mayor denounced his pragmatism as amoral, accusing 'the Communists' of seeking alliance with power whenever it served their interest and no matter where it came from. Their accusation against the communist mayor Stepan, however, of having cooperated with the StB agent in the village, lacked factual evidence, as many of the StB accusations did. As StB archives were neither complete nor access open to the public, an accusation of collaboration could rarely be entirely proved or disproved. The lists of alleged informants circulated at the beginning of the 1990s created a seedbed for rumours and hearsay emotionally loaded with suspicion and fear.

On the other side, the supporters of the communist mayor Stepan saw the action of the ecologists against the investors as fanatical, unrealistic and contrary to the common good. In another poem stuck to the notice board, they enticed the new mayor to:

Keep your analysis to yourself
Don't get the donors involved

Instead of continuing to criticise, so his opponents told the new mayor, it was now up to him to show some concrete results and to solve the dire problems of the village.

Start to build
And thanks to that
Let the water pipes lead
From nowhere to somewhere

After you start to do something
Then it will be hard
Be so severe to yourself
Like you are to others.

His opponents disputed with the new mayor Brany on his own high moral grounds. They challenged him to prove that his practice could face up to his own standards. It turned out, however, that the new mayor and his supporters were strangely disoriented when they finally obtained power. In the face of the need to take action their ideals were non-operational guidelines. In order to solve day-to-day problems, which were most of the time trivial and only rarely of a fundamental nature, the mayor had to step down from his high level of self-righteousness and sit down with his opponents to negotiate and to achieve compromises and common solutions.

Throughout his term of office, however, the new mayor continued to inscribe his actions in terms of opposition and moral expiation. High on his agenda, apart from the resistance to the construction of the cement factory, was the retrieval of property formerly owned by the village and now administered by the regional authorities. The apple of discord became the manor house of the village, which had been transformed in the 1980s from an old people's home into a home for mentally handicapped adults. Mayor Brany launched a campaign against the manager of the hostel, accusing her of maltreating the people under her care and of mis-using funds for the maintenance of the building that she had at her disposal to the advantage of befriended entrepreneurs. He claimed that control over the building should be devolved to the exclusive authority of the village. The issue caused outrage in the village and beyond, when it was published in the regional media. It mobilised the parents of the handicapped persons against the mayor, as they suspected him of wanting to get rid of the handicapped people in the village and use the manor house for other purposes. The women working for the hostel, who were mostly from the village, also stood against him, because they felt he was discrediting their work. As far as I can judge, after having visited the hostel and spoken to many people about it, the accusations Brany proffered had been motivated at least to some extent by the fact that the director of the hostel had been a communist under the previous regime and influential in the regional administration in Beroun.

The scandal around the manor house caused such uproar in the village that the four councillors opposing Brany resigned from the village council only ten months after he had taken office, thus prompting new elections, which the ecological faction lost.

Brany's term of office was later described as a disaster by those who opposed him and also by many of those who had voted him in. His style of leadership was described as authoritarian and uncommunicative. As he was unfamiliar with the decision-making processes on the regional level he had to rely entirely on Bina and his wife to be able to cope even with the simplest of administrative procedures. He was at a clear disadvantage compared to his communist predecessor, who had been able to count on excellent contacts at the regional level as he had served on the regional council in communist times. Stepan had been able to use his old networks of influence, as persons who had worked there during the communist period continued to occupy key positions in the administration. Good personal relations with the administrators were then – and continued to be – of crucial importance in order to obtain financial resources, undertake infrastructure projects or get construction permits.

Brany, on the other hand, had with most members of the regional administration a purely formal relationship. He was suffering from what Herzfeld (1992) would call the social production of indifference. Administrators ignored him, were late in informing him, and made him pass all the procedural obstacles they could possibly apply. They showed him that he was an outsider who was not playing by the informally set rules of establishing links that would be of mutual interest.

The social norms that regulate (at least to a certain extent) the political confrontations on the local level were controversial in Mokrovousy in 1994. No explicit or tacit agreement existed among the opposing factions about what would be appropriate behaviour for members of a democratically elected village council. It is the precondition of a functioning democracy, though, that the loser of the elections accepts that the other party has won and continues to work nevertheless for the community; and that the winner takes into account the opinions of the minority that lost the elections, developing a sense of responsibility for the community as a whole. In Mokrovousy the debate over diverging political opinions and material interests was outweighed by emotions of envy and hatred. After the elections of 1994 the two opposing factions acted as if these had been the last that would ever be held in the village. The idea of an elected office that could be gained and lost at the whim of the majority had not yet become part of the political habit. Political power was still seen as a total force, not as the result of a communicative act (Arendt 1986: 62). The public space was thus the home of attacks *ad hominem* and not the forum for an engaged exchange of ideas and opinions. This led many villagers, who had been interested and active at the beginning of the 1990, to withdraw again from the public arena into their private lives, observing and commenting on what was going on in the village council from afar.

Since 1995 things have calmed down in Mokrovousy. Stepan is now vice-mayor and shares with the new mayor the salary that the council pays for this job. The wife of Bina has been laid off and now fights against this decision in the courts. The faction opposed to the cement factory no longer participates in collective actions to embellish the village. They are organising instead their own activities, like cleaning once a year the nature protection area close to the quarry of rubbish. Brany is an elected councillor but hardly ever goes to the council meetings, whereas Bina tries not to miss a single meeting in order to monitor, as he says, what is discussed in the village council. Uncompromising in his political views, he gets actively involved outside the democratically elected structures where more radical positions get prominence in the media. He finds larger networks of supporters on the national and international level for his environmental concerns and remains the troublemaker on the local level who tapes the discussions on the village council and wages legal battles even about trivialities.

Conclusion

In the open confrontation of two value systems and in the reversal of the relations of dominance between them lie the roots of the intense emotional outbreaks after 1989. Norms imposed through the consistent and regular constraints of daily life and social interaction cause persistent fear, and at the same time they convey also a feeling of security (Elias 1976: 325, 447). When the coercive normative system changes, this fear transforms itself into aggression and insecurity. The humiliation that the opponents of the communist regime suffered, even in aspects of their daily lives, affected the future course of political relations and loaded them with emotions. The desire for vengeance for past humiliations and the settling of accounts made them look for a public process that would draw a thick line between the victim and those accountable for the injustice, thus reestablishing their dignity (Borneman 1997: 103). As this public settling of account did not take place, the undercurrent of hatred remained.

On the other side, the claim of the opponents to the cement factory to have a higher moral standard enraged the communists, who had had for decades the monopoly of morality and truth in society. Their ideological viewpoints being contested, they made the material well-being of the local community their point of moral reference and demonstrated that their opponents were unable to care for it and thus remained outsiders without the means to influence society.

The political debate *ad hominem* reflects an aspect of the democratisation process that puts in the forefront feelings of hate and envy and a desire for vengeance. Bringing down the enemy at all costs and by all means then becomes an end in itself. The use of anonymous poems in public space avoids direct confrontation between people, but instead of dissipating tensions in the public space, it heightens them because no effective exchange of points of view takes place. For a democracy to function effectively emotions and passions do not need to be suppressed but rather need to go beyond the personal level to the level of ideas and concepts about society. Only if different standpoints about society and the common good are openly expressed and passionately discussed in public without fear of personal reprisal – be it from public authorities or fellow villagers – can a democratic society flourish.

In an article that found an echo among social and political scientists, Piotr Sztompka (2000) attests that postsocialist society has a difficulty in establishing democratic institutions, because 'people are not yet democrats at heart, still trapped in the legacy of civilisational incompetence' brought about by forty years of socialism. Having to deal with the communist system, people learned to use double standards in talk and deeds and to avoid straightforwardness in political interactions. For democratising socialist society he puts his hope in the salutary influence of elite actors who have already escaped the grip of 'real-socialism' or have never succumbed to it, in multinational corporations that impose ready-made patterns of modern civilised business organisation, and in the values and norms spread by the process of globalisation. I have assumed the counter-position to this argument here, showing that the political behaviour of former communists is neither more nor less civil than that of their opponents, that multinational corporations have no salutary influence on democratic structures but fit in with the mechanisms of favouritism and clientelism they find in place, and that passionately practising democracy is the only way to learn (Müller and Kohutek 2002).

Acknowledgements

I wish to thank my colleague Petr Kohutek for accompanying me throughout this fieldwork and for all his interesting comments and ideas. A slightly different version of this paper was published in 2002 in *Focaal. European Journal of Anthropology* 39. I would like to thank Maruška Svašek and the *Focaal* reviewer for improvements to the original manuscript.

Notes

1. Regional parliament came into effect in 2000 as a part of fulfilling the conditions for entry into the European Union.
2. The person meant here is the head of the citizen initiative Bina
3. Děti Země (Children of the Earth) is an environmental organisation opposing the quarry and the cement factory
4. StB (Státní Bezpečnost) was the Czechoslovak secret police in communist times.

Bibliography

Arendt, H. 1986. 'Communicative Power', in *Power*, ed. D. Lukes. Oxford: Blackwell.

Berglund, E. 1998. *Knowing Nature, Knowing Science*. Cambridge: The White Horse Press.

Borneman, J. 1997. *Settling Accounts. Violence, Justice and Accountability in Postsocialist Europe*. Princeton: Princeton University Press.

Elias, N. 1976. *Über den Prozeß der Zivilisation*. Frankfurt: Suhrkamp.

Elster, J. 1995. 'Rationalité, émotions et normes sociales,' in *La couleur des pensées*, ed. P. Paperman. Paris: EHESS.

Gluckman, M. 1963. 'Gossip and Scandal', *Current Anthropology* 4(3): 307–16.

Habermas, J. 1981. *Erkenntnis und Interesse*. Frankfurt: Suhrkamp.

Herzfeld, M. 1992. *The Social Production of Indifference. Exploring the Symbolic Roots of Western Bureaucracy*. Chicago: University of Chicago Press.

Hirschman, A. 1977. *The Passions and the Interests*. Princeton: Princeton University Press,

Mouffe, C. 1994. *Le politique et ses enjeux*. Paris: Édition de la Découverte.

Müller, B. and Kohutek, P. 2002. 'Engaging the New Democracy. The Power of Participation in the Post-Communist Czech Republic', in *Focaal. European Journal of Anthropology* 40: 67–82.

Paperman, P. 1995. 'L'absense d'émotion comme offense,' in *La couleur des pensées*, ed. P. Paperman. Paris: EHESS.

Scott, J. 1990. *Domination and the Arts of Resistance. Hidden Transcripts*. New Haven and London: Yale University Press.

Smith, A. 1976. *The Theory of Moral Sentiment*. Indianapolis: Liberty Classics.

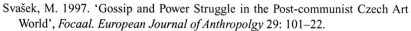

Svašek, M. 1997. 'Gossip and Power Struggle in the Post-communist Czech Art World', *Focaal. European Journal of Anthropolgy* 29: 101–22.

Sztompka, P. 2000. 'Civilisational Competence: a Prerequisite of Post-communist Transition' www.ces.uj.edu.pl/sztompka/competence.doc.

Thévenot, L. 1995. 'Émotions et évaluations dans les coordinations publiques', in *La couleur des pensées*, ed. P. Paperman. Paris: EHESS, pp. 145–74.

Chapter 9

The Dynamics of Trust and Mistrust in Poland: Floods, Emotions, Citizenship and the State

Don Kalb and Herman Tak

In July 1997 a heavy downpour hit Poland and the Czech Republic. Followed by continuous rainfall, it caused the flooding of alluvial areas and the breaking of dikes, in particular in the mountains and swamp areas of Lower Silesia.[1] In Poland, 1,358 villages and towns – 2.1 percent of the national territory – were flooded, 160,000 people fled their houses, and fifty-four casualties were registered.[2] This calamity made headlines in the European media for weeks. National governments sent help, and the European Commission offered financial support. A collective panic spread in Poland. The outside world got the impression that at least half the country was flooded. In Poland itself the flood became wrapped in almost biblical imagery. The waxing waters took both the population and the authorities fully by surprise. On 9 July, for example, the local authorities declared the inhabitants of the town of Opole to be safe that night, but waking up they found their houses surrounded by flushing waters.[3]

The Polish flood of 1997 occasioned a social drama that revealed important off-stage properties of state-citizen relationships in this 'successful transition country'. We will take the flood and associated social and governmental processes as a starting point for a situational analysis (Handelman 1996) that will help us perceive the political and sociohistorical contexts which crucially shape popular cognitions, expectations and emotions. These popular emotions pervade social interactions within formal institutions and between these institutions and citizens in contemporary Poland. Popular emotions are embedded in moral discourses and therefore can weaken as well as reinforce power relations. We aim to show that interactions between Polish citizens and governmental institutions are, compared to what is idealised as 'the West' (i.e., Western Europe and the U.S.A.), marked by problems of trust and trustability between actors. Trust, defined as 'confidence in the reliability of a person or system' (Giddens 1990), is indispensable to stable collective life, while a culture of distrust prevents cooperation and destroys community. This has already been analysed by Banfield (1967) in the 1950s for Southern Italy, where he observed a 'pathological distrust of the state and all authority'.

Trust can be understood as one of (many) basic emotions, such as fear, rage, panic and expectancy etc., 'which have evolved to enable us to cope with specific situations' (Milton 2002: 60) and which need not be seen as irrational, i.e., as opposed to something rational. Trust and distrust should thus not be conceived of as ideas as such but as emotions which, just like interest, are involved in the production of knowledge of daily existence, and which in this sense are naturally strongly determined by earlier experiences. Trust is real but constructed, and of course also contested (Leavitt 1996).

Contributing to the present volume, which is devoted to the relation between politics and emotions, we argue that emotions are constructed, i.e., emotions exist but they do not determine their own and other cultural meanings. Emotions are embedded in sociocultural and political-economic practices. They are produced within discourses which define what they are and how they operate. In this paper we focus on a particular type of (basic) emotion called trust and on its counterpoint, mistrust. Both belong to the most important and widespread emotions in the political postsocialist landscape. And both play important roles in the perception and shaping and reshaping of political relations and political cultures, i.e., the attitudes, beliefs, norms and symbols that legitimate such relations.

The degree of trust or distrust of average citizens in politics and politicians (as representatives of the political power) is based upon the relation between, as Max Weber analysed it in his lecture *Politik als Beruf* (1919), the 'ethic of responsibility' (choice between various morally unacceptable solutions) of politicians, and the 'ethic of conviction' rooted in absolute and ultimate ends of citizens. However, in an apparently quite apathetic society, such as postcommunist Poland, the political 'ethic of responsibility' can raise violent emotions among citizens and considerably damage their trust in national and regional politics. Arguably, the fall of communism in Eastern and Central Europe (ECE) encouraged trust in the newly elected governments, but this enthusiasm soon turned out to be relatively short-lived. The decay of trust and its consequences for citizens, citizenship and political culture constitute an important aspect of most postsocialist societies. This change of heart among ECE societies took place due to a public awareness of spreading corruption, nepotism and favouritism, and expressed itself in the retreat from the liberal discourse of agency towards a discourse of fate (Sztompka 1999).

In Eastern and Central Europe distrust is directed especially towards the state and its institutions, and its expressions fluctuate between anxiety/apathy and anger/resistance. Distrust underlies various forms of citizens' behaviour and reactions. One of these reactions is emigration, demonstrated in Banfield's study of Southern Italy, which also has had a long history of migration. Apart from voting with feet (read: emigration), we see also poor turnout at election (electoral abstention) combined with extra-parliamentary political actions accompanied by intensive emotions, such as strikes, road blockades, demonstrations, marches and occupation of public places (e.g. occupation of the Polish Ministry of Agriculture by peasants).

Distrust of public institutions can be seen also in the growing private health care and private education sectors. Research results suggest that distrust of the state also underlies the fact that a small majority of the Polish population lives with a feeling that their living conditions were better under communism than at present (Sztompka 1999: 167). From the socioeconomic perspective, the postcommunist societies are described as 'waiting societies', as shown by 'conspicuous spending on consumer goods, to the neglect of investing and saving' (Sztompka 1999: 165). In the case of Poland civic distrust of governmental institutions knows just a single exception, namely the military (Sztompka 1999: 168). By contrast, the overwhelming distrust of politicians (and political parties) is recurrently kindled by corruption scandals, which creates ground for populist nationalistic political leaders with their desire to capitalise on public dissatisfaction and anxiety.

Mistrust forms the downside of problems of democratic consolidation, as discussed by political scientists such as Linz and Stepan (1996) and Offe (1996). It should also be seen as that everyday aspect of social relations on which the rising tide of ethno-national, exclusivist, and parochial ideologies, as studied by Tismaneanu (1998) and evoked by Jowitt (1992), is based (Niedermueller 1999). Poland occupies an unsteady place in such accounts, since the gravest reservations about democratic transition spring from the experience of the ex-Soviet 'inner empire', ex-Yugoslavia, and the

Balkans. This is also true for the much more sensitive anthropological writings of Katherine Verdery (1996) and Gail Kligman, who both concentrate on Romania. Verdery proposes the notion of 'unruly coalitions' as harbingers of populist, nationalist and mythically inclined movements in East Central Europe. These unruly coalitions shape local politics by operating behind the scenes. In the conclusion we will dwell on this intra-regional comparison and on 'unruly coalitions' as an explanation for civic distrust and obstacles for civic democracy.

In this article, we take the city of Wroclaw as a local starting point for a study of civic relations in postsocialist Poland. It shows how waxing waters can reveal the contemporary civic consequences of the communist heritage as the political and sociohistorical context that, by producing overcentralisation, unaccountability of state structures, and deep rivalry among political actors, as well as disrespect among citizens and distrust between citizens and states, explains the incapacity of Wroclaw's citizens to keep control over their city, the Odra, the state organisations and their emotions.

City in the Odra

Wroclaw (640,000 inhabitants) is Poland's fourth city and situated in Lower Silesia (*Dolny Slask*). Its landscape is partly suburban. Around the former German administrative and cultural centre, extensive residential settlements have been erected, consisting of the typical low-quality/low-cost tenement blocks of communism. Its economy, with its wide variety of industries – chemicals, textile, steel/engineering, electrical industries, food and transport – is still a (post) socialist 'update' of an advanced nineteenth-century German industrial location.

Today, Wroclaw is the third most successful transition area of Poland.[4] Capitalist transformation has led to a rapid class differentiation within neighbourhoods, primarily between low-skilled industrial workers, on the one hand, and the higher-educated service class, on the other. Distinctions in wealth, however, have not yet led to residential segregation, except perhaps for the upper ten percent who are now moving to newly developed ex-urban sites of country house development or to gentrified urban apartments. With some exceptions, then, everyone still lives in the same urban ecology of large-scale tenement blocks or badly maintained inner city areas. These areas, nevertheless, are rapidly turning into stages for postsocialist status display, mainly through the medium of cars and other mobile items of conspicuous consumption.

Wroclaw is located in the core of a swamp area where the rivers Bystrzyca, Widawa, Sleza and Olawa pour their waters in the river Odra, the branching arms of which embrace the centre proper. This conjunction of various riverbeds was the cause of the unexpectedly rapid and threatening rising of water levels on 12 July 1997.

The first rumours about the threat of flood started to spread on Wednesday 9 July. That day, the Regional Committee of Flood Control had concluded in its joint meeting that the city could rely on its extensive system of waterworks to channel the excess water safely through the area. Despite the Committee's confidence, or perhaps even as its consequence, rumours about an approaching flood were being raised in tandem with the rising level of the Odra river. On Thursday, a local newspaper on its own account published a doom scenario, self-confidently predicting which neighbourhoods would be flooded. The rumours themselves were a safety valve for the emotions of distrust and anxiety. With its scenario the newspaper created not only a basis for the rumours but also in this way strengthened the cohesion among those who experienced fear and distrust in the local administration and (as is characteristic of rumours as difference of opinions) challenged the local government (Barnard and Spencer 2002: 266–67).

In response to the mounting pressure of public fear, the Regional Committee decided to blow up a dike near Lany to show that it was preparing to spare the city. Angry peasants from Lany, however, prevented miners from doing so and clashed violently with police forces. These farmers circulated a rumour that the dikes from the German times should protect the terrain from much higher waters, and this rumour precisely consolidated their resistance to the idea that the dikes should be purposely destroyed with explosives. The administration willy-nilly retreated and later attempts failed too. Emotional reactions of citizens of Wroclaw were characterised by bitterness towards villagers. According to a 45–year-old male flood victim, whose house stayed under water up to the third floor for days, his plight had all to do with egoistic peasants: 'Our archives and cultural heritage have to go to ruin just because their goddamn potato fields may not get wet.' A dike in the area of Brzeg broke spontaneously, however, which served to postpone the flooding of the urban area.[5]

In the city itself, manifest collective action only started on Saturday afternoon, 12 July. Thousands of volunteers – called on by the popular media – started to reinforce riversides with sandbags. They also blocked off streets and posted guards at critical points. The national government responded by sending military support for the volunteers. The Odra reached its peak-level around midnight. But in the subsequent days fears remained for dikes and bridges, which were under continuous pressure from strong alluvial currents, causing the population to remain on guard.

Except for the nineteenth-century neighbourhood in Traugutta Street (called 'the ghetto'), the old centre was not flooded. The water mainly hit the postwar residential areas in the north and the southeast. Of the city's territory, 26.5 percent was flooded. At some places, the water reached seven metres, such as in the postwar neighbourhood of Kozanow. But the average depth was between thirty and sixty centimetres. There were two casualties in the community, one of whom was drowned.

The flood threw, of course, everyday public life into disarray. Many neighbourhoods were without electricity for many days, and the whole city was without tap water for one and a half weeks. Each day people stood in long lines for pumps and tankers. The telephone network was completely out of order and on 17 July, 30,000 telephone numbers still did not function. For many people it took more than a month to become reconnected. The city centre was completely deserted for one long week, and the reestablishment of daily urban routines took certainly another week. Mountains of litter dominated the street landscape for about a month because the refuse dump was flooded too, and neighbouring communes declined to make space available. It took four months before tramtraffic functioned as before.

The economic damage was considerable: 3,476 buildings were flooded, among which were thousands of apartments, 840 shops and other services.[6] Shortly after the water receded, local authorities claimed that hundreds of apartments should be demolished and replaced. A dilapidated house in Traugutta Street neighbourhood had collapsed. A year later, in this area notorious for its lack of maintenance since the 1930s, several nineteenth-century tenement houses in 'the ghetto' were blown up to prevent the same.

State-citizen Relations in Postcommunism

It is nothing new, that during calamities rumours frequently take over formal media and routine governmental procedures as an informal means of communication and coordination. Wroclaw too, during the flood-episode, was dominated by rumours. But rumours, here, signified something more fundamental than just the cognitive and practical self-organisation of people in the face of danger. They were an (emotional) expression of a basic feature of many postsocialist societies: the profound popular distrust of the purposes and capacities of the authorities, the enduring lack of accountability and transparency of political structures, as well as the deep rivalry and disrespect between contending political factions and between different population segments.

Before, during and after the flood rumours virtually defined citizens' conceptions. They were the effective vehicle of public fear that prepared people for spontaneous action in defiance of the authorities well before the flood reached the city. They kept people mobilised for days during the flood. And almost a week later, on 18 July, a rapidly spreading rumour about a second wave of water motivated many people to barricade themselves in their houses again, incredulous of the authorities' prediction that this second wave would only threaten those areas where dikes had been broken before (as it turned out, the Odra stayed several metres below its former peaklevel).

Rumours reflected a popular anticipation of the state's incapacity to deal with the emerging dangers. Effective local government was made impossible by the lack of reliable and authoritative administrative knowledge, which was, in turn, produced by unclear and overlapping responsibilities, overcentralisation, and political rivalry. Consequently, after spontaneous civic action had initiated the collective rescue of the city, the public administration had a hard job regaining the initiative. Its actions on the two crucial days – 12 and 13 July – were characterised by panic. When the Odra was already well under its maximum, armoured vehicles drove on high alert through the city centre. At the same moment, travellers arriving at the central railway station were ordered back by the police with the warning: 'The whole city is under water! Epidemics are breaking out, it is perilous!' The collective fear for an epidemic was also aired 'from below'. Despite official announcements to the contrary, epidemics were rumoured for over a week. Lack of public confidence was also voiced in the suspicion that tap water, as it became available again, was in fact poisoned industrial water.

Local authorities misjudged situations and panicked because of their fundamental ignorance about the water circulation, the infrastructural systems for its management, and the vulnerability of specific residential areas. As a result, it was completely unclear where the problems would arise and how they could be prevented. The deeper cause of this ignorance had its roots in the communist past. Water management had been treated as an exclusively military domain, information about which was kept at military regional headquarters and in Warsaw, but not at the level of local public authority. The ensuing deficiencies of prediction and management were, moreover, aggravated by rivalry between different governmental agencies, headed by protagonists from opposing political parties, with, on the one side, the city government under leadership of the independent local politician mayor Bogdan Zdrojewski, and, on the other, the Regional Committee of Flood Control headed by the postsocialist regional governor (*voivod*) Janusz Zaleski.

Lack of expertise led to governmental inertia as the floods were approaching the city, causing a temporary power vacuum which was instantly filled up by the local media. Local broadcasting stations (radio and TV) became, for better or for worse, coordination centers for popular mobilisation. Volunteers now took the lead. But, understandably, in the absence of well-defined plans, many things went wrong. For example, dikes of sandbags were erected on places where they were useless or even counterproductive. Local authorities were not capable of removing such obstacles in the next days, fiercely defended as they were by local residents who believed such dams would protect their houses against the upcoming flood, the extent of which no one could really predict.

It was mayor Zdrojewski who understood the crucial importance of local media in this situation. He promptly removed his headquarters to the television station, TD (Telewizja Dolnoslaska), and before long became the hero of the flood, compared in the vernacular with Kordecki, the Prior who in 1655 had led the defence of the Jasna Gora monastery against a Swedish invasion (today a national pilgrimage site near Czestochowa).[7] *Voivod* Zaleski, on the other hand, became the bogeyman, allegedly lacking organisational talents. Zaleski's failure on 13 July to blow up a dike near Lany was expatiated upon in the press and his reputation was thoroughly destroyed.[8]

But more than lack of personal talent, it was political rivalry that aggravated governmental incapacity. The regional administration was appointed by the national government, at that moment a coalition of postsocialist and peasant parties. The regional governor Zaleski was a postsocialist. The town council, however, was controlled by a coalition of local and opposition parties, and mayor Zdrojewski – chosen by the council – was an independent politician. Conflicting political (and electoral) interests between, on the one hand, the postsocialist central government and its representative the *voivod*, and, on the other, oppositional politicians in control of the local administration, certainly, in the atmosphere of deep and profound disrespect of political rivals characteristic of the nation of Poland with its long years of people's protest, frustrated any cooperation between the administrative levels and obstructed all possible action.

The structure of regional governments, moreover, was inherited from the communist regime, and its set-up reflected the centralising plus fragmenting aims of the Politburo vis-à-vis the provinces. In 1975 the regime changed the administrative division from twenty-two into forty-nine *voivod*ships – the region of Wroclaw, for example, was divided into four different *voivod*ships.[9] This policy of centralisation through fragmentation was meant to strengthen the vertical lines within the command economy by cutting off lower-level communication between districts and allowing optimal local penetration by the centre. The organised lack of contacts between adjacent local units is a basic and little recognised administrative feature of (ex-) communist societies, as the former Polish deputy Minister of Housing, Irena Herbst, emphasised in an interview.[10] During the flood, this administrative heritage obstructed the transmission of information between local public authorities and inhibited any effective 'voice' from below, which, needless to say, should not be identified with direct popular action.

Dutch and Polish Policy-making

It seems interesting to compare this situation with the grassroots information and coordination system characteristic of 'civic' systems of water control in the Netherlands, a country deeply dependent on the effectiveness of these social structures. In this river-delta country, control of waterworks lies in the hands of decentralised district water boards with democratically elected board-members and a professional chair (dike warden) appointed by the crown. These boards have great professional autonomy, and short communication lines with higher executive levels. Board members are regularly recruited from local interests with intimate knowledge of, and high dependence on, local river landscapes, such as farmers and landlords, who have extensive democratic rights (voting, information, etc.) vis-à-vis the dike warden.[11] As the water rises – for instance in February 1995, when 200,000 people were evacuated – district water boards install warning systems and inform and advise higher public authorities, i.e., mayors and provincial governors who are in charge during such operations. The role and influence of the national government is a minor and supportive one. Of course, this system can bring about conflicts, as it did in 1995, but such conflicts are typically triggered by excess of power and autonomy on the part of the boards and the professional water-managers as compared to other civic interests, such as those of the village inhabitants, rather than by their weakness/dependence.

It should be stressed that organisations and administrators worked with the assistance of previously elaborated scenarios providing, for example, for evacuation of hundreds of thousands people. Such a strategy is responsible also for the regulation of rumour. Rumours were not eliminated but they functioned first of all as an emotional safety valve, and did not influence management. Daily press conferences provided the public and media with information. Various media spread and interpreted this governmental information, producing at the same time coverage of the *couleur locale* (flooded living rooms, drowning animals, cars and people loaded at evacuation centres), which contributed to expression and regulation of emotions.

Ideologies of state policy-making in postsocialist Poland also worked to disqualify governmental responses. Initially, the national postsocialist government saw the flood as an alibi for regional claimmaking. It tried to play it down just like it would have done with other popular claims on its highly conservative public budget. This response was firmly rooted in the ideological conditions of postsocialism. In East Central European citizenship-discourse, a sharp demarcation is nowadays drawn between 'real citizenship' on the one hand, which is held to be highly 'self-responsible', and 'ordinary claim-making' on the other, which is negatively associated with the communist heritage of popular distributive demands vis-à-vis a state with which nobody in the end would identify. Surely, in historical and comparative perspectives this is a dubious and moralistic contrast. It overlooks the origins of contemporary citizenship practices in eighteenth- and nineteenth-century popular contestation with states, and it suppresses the question under which circumstances of governance people can become 'self-responsible' citizens rather than egoistic and non-committed claimants. But the distinction between self-responsibility and claim-making is of course political rather than scientific. It serves to bring citizenship-discourse, with its roots in the dissident culture of the 1970s and 1980s and its powerful mythical and legitimating functions for the new democratic state, in line with the requirements of conservative social policies and neoliberal public finances such as those demanded by the international institutions.

In the case of the flood, this ideological predisposition led to politically self-defeating rhetoric. Prime Minister Cimoszewicz aroused country-wide fierce emotional reactions when he first remarked from a typical political 'ethic of responsibility' that the number of the flood's casualties was far below the daily average in Polish traffic. In the second instance, when it became clear that this was a serious event, the government started to blame the neighbours. According to a government spokesman, the situation was made worse by the Czech Republic emptying its water reservoirs. That same day, 12 July, Prime Minister Cimoszewicz visited some flooded areas and declared that farmers would not receive any restitution for destroyed crops, by saying: 'You have to take precautions, and get insured for eventual disasters. But unfortunately this has not been a popular attitude.' This pronouncement also raised emotionally charged discussions, with the result that the regulation was cancelled by the Polish parliament.[12]

Next, on 9 July, local authorities incapable of managing the approaching water masses, begged the national government to announce a state of emergency, but the Ministry of Internal Affairs deemed such a step unconstitutional and claimed that regional governors had all the means at hand to tackle the problems. Remarkably enough, the Polish army had earlier declared that it was ready for action, but the authorities did not ask for systematic help, even though all knowledge of waterworks had been under military control for decades.[13]

There are Polish ways to solve such a situation of governmental unaccountability. In Wroclaw, during the night in which the waters reached their peak, as we were told, a pensioned military officer came to the town hall and offered his help. He was active there for a couple of days, and when he suddenly disappeared local administrators understood that 'the flood was over' (evidently, his name was not known then or now).

Centralism, rivalry, unaccountability, and the political rejection of state responsibilities fed back and forth into a profound lack of trust and cooperation among citizens. Some towns suffered from large-scale and, in some cases, clearly organised plundering, a problem bluntly denied by the national government. Many people anticipated this and refused to be evacuated. Problems with enforcing authority also surfaced in the attempts to blow-up dikes upstream from Wroclaw. *Voivod* Zaleski personally mediated with the inhabitants of Lany and offered them financial compensation. However, he had to be rescued by a police escort in an 'atmosphere of threat' (Wrzesinski 1997: 39). Months later it turned out that he had been taken hostage for some hours. The countryside especially was rebellious. Inhabitants of Siechnice – a village a few kilometers from Wroclaw – changed the nameplates of their village into: 'Welcome into water reservoir Siechnice.' Inhabitants of Siechnice then turned to less frivolous protest, throwing up road-blocks to add strength to their demand for the construction of a canal to empty their village of water.[14]

To disguise the fact that there was no effective government in Wroclaw for at least two days, President Aleksander Kwasniewski complimented the citizens of Wroclaw for their 'excellent rescue operations', but at the same time emphasised: 'I don't want to talk about responsibilities in an emotionally charged atmosphere.'

In complimenting Wroclaw's citizens, Kwasniewski was followed by mayor Zdrojewski,[15] whose growing popularity was founded upon the fact that he chose not to let his council, civil service or other professionals do the job but the local population at large. By doing so, and by using the local media for this purpose, he turned the lack of administrative capacities into populist electoral advantage. During the national elections of 21 September 1997, he was easily elected to the senate. The election campaign – also for parliament (*Sejm*) – was a tough and expensive one. But on the eve of the elections Mayor Zdrojewski announced that his budget had been zero. His campaign had taken place during the flood.

Because the governmental coalition lost the elections, *voivod* Zaleski had to resign. The new national government – a coalition of Solidarnosc parties and Unia Wolnosci (Freedom Union) – appointed new regional governments and immediately prepared the ground for the reorganisation of local and regional administrations. Since August 1998, the former forty-eight *voivod*ships have been negotiated down to sixteen.

New Mythologies

The flood and the social events that accompanied it exerted a powerful, unique impression upon Wroclaw's citizens. In the late summer and in the autumn of 1997 two large photo exhibitions were staged for months, which were visited by thousands of people. Five illustrated books on the flood have to date been published, as well as a video entitled 'Historical Catastrophe'. These facts should be interpreted as reconstructions of traumatic experiences, which are essential in the collective process of recovery and the recognition of individual traumas. Such representations 'firmly place emotions in the cultural, political, and socio-historical context in which they are evoked, felt, framed, expressed and contested' (Svašek 2002: 12).

Understandably, the flood was a special expression of an inability of governmental institutions and provincial as well as national politics. The already existing civic distrust found a confirmation and expression in the citizens' fear (of the yet to come floods, infectious diseases, and poisoned running water) and anger (squabbles, blockades and even a temporary kidnapping of a local politician in the country). In fact, the interactions between emotions and politics, and the power structures they generated (the rising political star of mayor Zdrojewski) found their expression during, and, even more so after the flood.

In Wroclaw a new mythology arose in the period that followed the calamity. It was characterised by two interrelated exaggerations: one concerning the extent of danger and damage and the other concerning the supposedly close spontaneous cooperation among citizens protecting their collective safety. In a special issue of The Warsaw Voice (31 August 1997), mayor Zdrojewski claimed one-third of the city to have been flooded. The sociologist Wojciech Sitek even writes in his book *Wspolnota i Zagrozenie* (Community and Danger) (1997) that half the city had stood under water. In reality, 26.5 percent of the commune's territory, the larger part of it undeveloped, had been inundated. While we do not want to deny that spontaneous civic cooperation was widespread, there was also self-seeking behaviour, plain sabotage and plundering, and a remarkably non-collaborative attitude vis-à-vis public authorities trying to coordinate collective action.

Myth-making in Wroclaw served a populist and mildly redemptive function. To be sure, it did not posit any internal enemy to be deported nor did it envision any final solution, as redemptive myths, also in postsocialist Europe, regularly do (Tismaneanu 1998). But it helped to reactivate and remind people of a basic mythic aspect of Polish nationalism: the whole nation's fight against an alien and intrusive state in order to protect its integrity.

A similar vision of 'the people against the state' had been wrapped into the idea of anti-politics, the well-known cultural banner of the Polish and Central European opposition under communism, an idea which has itself grown into a founding myth for the new democratic state after 1989. Anti-politics was about the liberation from communism by civic self-organisation, a self-organisation that was not primarily meant to lead to the conquering of the state. Rather, it was a goal in itself, an everyday practice that should lead to a 'parallel polis'. This parallel polis could perhaps (gradually) be substituted for the state. But more importantly, precisely as a consequence of its state-abstinence, it would remain authentic, spontaneous and personalistic rather than bureaucratic and artificial.

Linz and Stepan, in their recent comparative work on consolidating democracies (1996), have rightly called attention to the potential incompatibility of this populist cultural configuration with the ideological requirements for the consolidation of democracy in Poland. They have shown how a perceived inevitable incongruity between the nation and the state prevented Walesa himself, the embodiment of Polish populism, but also many other Solidarity intellectuals, from playing the careful, constructive, and responsible role in relation to the state's institutions that is required to help instil trust, justice and transparency of public governance. Instead, their actions following 1989 often reproduced civic distrust and institutional unreliability (Gross 1992; Linz and Stepan 1996: 255–93). Polish populist nationalism apparently does not transform itself easily into the mindscape of a nation-state.

The particularities of the Polish path out of communism mattered. After 1989, the Polish opposition, and certainly Adam Michnik, the editor-in-chief of the *Gazeta Wyborcza*, has accepted and argued in favour of the policy of the Thick Line. Ex-communists would be forgiven for their earlier practices and would face no revenge in the new Polish state. Although many postsocialist states have adopted the same stance (the Czech Republic is a partial exception, as is, of course, East Germany), there was a special involuntary reason for this in the Polish case, creating a situation not particularly conducive to the consolidation of civic democracy.[18] The new Polish democracy was squeezed between popular anti-communism on the one side and its own provisional constitution and the policy of the Thick Line on the other.

It was precisely this contradictory heritage of popular anti-communism caged in by the constitutionally enshrined Thick Line that allowed the populist idea of the Polish self-organising nation, in its qualities clearly distinct from, distrustful of, and somehow against the state, to be reproduced under post-1989 circumstances. The flood of 1997 helped to reactivate, relive and remind people of this fundamental contradiction. The popular self-defence against the flood was felt to signal the people's superiority over, and defiance of, the state and its ex-communist ruling party. Mayor Zdrojewski successfully rode this sentiment in his victorious assault on the ex-communist statebureaucrats and governors. This relived sentiment subsequently helped the opposition to regain power in the next election.

Conclusion: 'Unruly Coalitions'

In the present paper we have tried to perform a descriptive analysis of interactions between distrust (expresssed through anger, panic, fear and rumours) of citizens and politicians, and the repercussions they have upon politics itself. In line with other authors (Leavitt 1996), our study suggests that basic emotions such as trust and distrust are formed through specific cirtcumstances. Emotions are, as shown in this paper, embedded in sociocultural, political-economic practices, and produced within discourses which define what they are and how they operate. In postsocialist landscapes, trust and mistrust are basic in political practices on local, regional and national levels, and they play important roles in the perception and shaping and reshaping of these political practices.

In the case of the inhabitants of Wroclaw, their trust/distrust and meanings they ascribe to them are largely determined through local and national political-historical circumstances, complemented by their new experiences during the flood, which constitute part of their cognitive map – one that displays a certain family resemblance to those of citizens in other parts of postsocialist Europe. These kinds of cognitive maps are naturally built upon experiences, both historical and recent, constituted by interpreted and constructed memories, just as mythologies created around this flood suggest. But apart from reminding functions, mythmaking also served at least three 'misrecognising' functions. First, it helped to repress public awareness of the fact that the flooding of Wroclaw was not the consequence of ex-communist undeserved leadership, but rather of inadequate public attention to governmental organisation and institutions compounded by deep political rivalry and mistrust expressed in identity politics. Secondly, it took away from view the unhappy insight that still, after ten years of democratisation and liberalisation in the name of citizenship, state-citizen relations in Poland are not yet transparent, reliable or trust-invoking. And third, it served to celebrate and remember Polish popular unity and *communitas* (Turner 1974) in a situation of rapidly increasing and visible social differentiation, inequalities, widespread status anxiety, and frequently surfacing group conflict.

In her essay on pyramid schemes in Romania, Katherine Verdery (1996) has proposed the notion of 'unruly coalitions', which are locally or regionally based and which shape local politics by operating behind the scenes, potentially through violence, and usually including local nomenklatura, ex-security agents, large proprietors, managers and members of the judiciary. Now, it makes sense to see the Polish flood as having occasioned an unruly coalition in the Silesian region with mayor Zdrojewski as its centre. Unruly coalitions are certainly not limited to network politics in the Balkans or the ex-Soviet 'inner empire'. Nor are they necessarily mafia-like. Rather, we would suggest, they are the consequence of the absence of well-defined and well structured local party organisations and grassroots political platforms. Political parties everywhere in ECE countries are very thin institutions, with few members, little formal organisation, high visibility of key personalities, and a heavy emphasis on capital cities and national politics. In such a situation, unruly coalitions among local elites necessarily emerge to organise interests behind local policy. They are unruly, not because they may be mafia-like, but rather because of the absence of clear programmes, explicit procedures, the weakness of local democracy, and the, as yet, unstable relations between governmental hierarchies. This kind of coalition not only channels and exploits such emotions as anger, fear and distrust, but does so with an unarticulated promise that the 'ethic of responsibility' will be turned into a popular 'ethic of conviction' rooted in absolute and ultimate ends.

This case study of floods, populism and the state in a Polish city indicates that unruly coalitions may be an inevitable region-wide phenomenon associated with the problems of establishing democratic politics in postsocialist societies. It suggests that their specific form, function and content will be largely a product of their wider environment. This particular unruly coalition in Wroclaw decisively helped to bring the issue of regional government and decentralisation to the public agenda and facilitated a new chance to govern for the two parties that came out of the ex-opposition movement. It thereby helped to create new chances for civic consolidation rather than for mafia-type developments. The difference resides in the wider political society and its path of extrication from the communist past.

Notes

1. The Odra river flows from the south to the Baltic Sea and the flood also struck parts of northeast Germany such as the Frankfurt (Oder) area.
2. See Cono-Foniol et al. (1997: 115; 120).
3. *The Warsaw Voice. Polish and Central European Review*, 27 July 1997, p. 5.
4. *Polityka,* 22 August 1998, no. 44.
5. Cf. Wrzesinski (1997: 12, 16–19).
6. ibid.: pp. 72, 137.
7. Kordecki led the defence against a Swedish invasion (cf. Davies 1982 Vol. I: 452) and is as an historical hero, known among the people, among other reasons, because of the historical novel *Potop* (Flood) of H. Sienkiewicz (1868), prescribed reading in secondary schools.
8. Cf. Sitek (1997: 43).
9. Until 3 May, 1975 the three-tier administrative division counted twenty-two *voivod*ships (with five special-status cities) and was changed into forty-nine *voivod*ships (and three urban agglomerations); 2,345 communes and 814 towns/cities.
10. Interview on Soco-financed research with Don Kalb, 19 June, 1998.
11. For information about Dutch district water boards, see *Winkler Prins Encyclopedie* (1984 Vol. 24: 5).
12. This is a good example of the generally pedagogic citizenship-discourse that ECE governments hold before their constituencies. As with his judgement about the first victims of the flood, Prime Minister Cimoszewicz had to withdraw his remarks about damages because of fierce public protest. On 15 July the government decided to compensate farmers whose harvests were devastated, and every household hit by the flood was to get 2,000 zl, an amount that was raised to 3,000 zl by the Polish parliament two days later (cf. Cebo-Fonoil et al. 1997: 71; 89).

13. Cf. Cebo-Foniol et al. (1997: 10,18–19, 24).
14. ibid.: pp. 18, 24, 40, 101.
15. Cf. Wrzesinski (1997: 70).
16. Since Poland was the first nation to take decisive steps out of communism, develop the Round Table and agree to elections, nobody could be certain how the Soviet Union would react. Moreover, the Communist Party in Poland had moved towards negotiations on its own during 1988. Contrary to a widespread and important myth, it was not primarily pressed by popular protest. Rather it initiated the pact with the opposition itself, as a deliberate way out of economic crisis and social stagnation (see above all Staniszkis 1992). This created a special heritage: the birth of the new Polish national and democratic state, the outcome of the Round Table, was not the product of democratic concertation, certainly not the constitutionally enshrined enduring position in state and economy of the ex-communists. At the same time, Poland had been the only East European nation with a heritage of large-scale and tenacious popular protest against, and non-acceptance of, the communist state, which was not unreasonably perceived as an alien Soviet-imposed intrusion. The almost general rejection of communism expressed itself again in the 1989 elections. Against all predictions and expectations, and unintentionally allowed by the technicalities of the voting procedure which were expressly designed to guarantee a planned communist majority in the *Sejm*, people expressed their own idea of a Thick Line: eliminating all the names of the communists from the voting lists and with this trick allowing Solidarity a great victory. But here the paradoxes of the first postsocialist elections came immediately to the fore: the victory was unconstitutional (because not planned during the Round Table) and Solidarity decided it would allow the communists their pre-planned seats.

Bibliography

Banfield, E.C. 1967 (1958). *The Moral Basis of a Backward Society*. New York: Free Press.

Barnard, A. and Spencer, J. 2002. *Encyclopedia of Social and Cultural Anthropology*. London and New York: Routledge.

Cebo-Foniol, M., Zbigniew, F., Turczynska, E., Rzetecki, P., Witkowski, A., Golembnik, B., Kutla, J., Rzadkowski, T., Tkaczyk, M. and Wisniewski, D. eds. 1997. *Powʌdz*. Warszawa: Amber.

Davies, N. 1982. *God's Playground. A History of Poland*. Volume I. *The Origins to 1795*; Volume II: *1795 to the Present*. New York: Columbia University Press.

Giddens, A. 1990. *The Consequences of Modernity*. Stanford, CA: Stanford Univerity Press.

Gross, J. 1992. 'Poland: From Civil Society to Political Nation', in *Eastern Europe in Revolution*, ed. I. Banac. Ithaca, NY: Cornell University Press.

Handelman, D. 1996. 'Microhistorical Anthropology: Atemporal, Retrospective, Prospective', *Focaal. European Journal of Anthropology* 26/27: 135–48.

Jowitt, K. 1992. *New World Disorder. The Leninist Extinction*. Berkeley: California University Press.

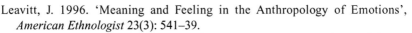

Leavitt, J. 1996. 'Meaning and Feeling in the Anthropology of Emotions', *American Ethnologist* 23(3): 541–39.

Linz, J. and Stepan, A. 1996. *Problems of Democratic Transition and Consolidation. Southern Europe, South America, and Post-communist Europe*. Baltimore, MD: Johns Hopkins University Press.

Milton, K. 2002. *Loving Nature. Towards an Ecology of Emotions*. London and New York: Routledge.

Niedermüller, P. 1999. 'Rethinking History: Time, Past and Nation in Post-Socialism', *Focaal. European Journal of Anthropology* 33.

Offe, C. 1996. *Varieties of Transition. The East European and East German Experience*. Cambridge: Polity Press.

Sitek, W. 1997. *Wspolnota i Zagrozenie. Socjologiczny Przyczynek do Analizy Krotkotrwalej Wspolnoty*. Wroclaw: Wydawnictwo Uniwersytetu Wroclawskiego.

Staniszkis, J. 1992. *The Dynamics of Breakthrough in Eastern Europe. The Polish Experience*. Berkeley: California University Press.

Svašek, M. 2002. 'The Politics of Emotions. Emotional Discourses and Displays in Post-Cold War Contexts', *Focaal. European Journal of Anthropology* 39: 7–27.

Sztompka, P. 1999. *Trust. A Sociological Theory*. Cambridge: Cambridge University Press.

Tismaneanu, V. 1998. *Fantasies of Salvation. Democracy, Nationalism and Myth in Post-communist Europe*. Princeton: Princeton University Press.

Turner, V. 1974. *Dramas, Fields, and Metaphors. Symbolic Action in Human Society*. Ithaca and London: Cornell University Press.

Verdery, K. 1996. *What Was Socialism, and What Comes Next?* Princeton, Princeton University Press.

Winkler Prins Encyclopedie (25 volumes) 1979–1984. Amsterdam: Elsevier.

Wrzesinski, W., ed. 1997. *Wroclawska Kronika Wielkiej Wody. 10 lipca–18 sierpnia 1997*. Wroclaw: Instytut Historyczny Uniwersytetu Wroclawskiego.

Afterword

Alaina Lemon

After reading these essays, it might seem crudely commonsensical for me to repeat their point that politics are sentimental: they lucidly demonstrate this many times over. Moreover, the specific cases taken up by each one deliver conclusions that should not be limited to understanding change in East Europe after state socialism. They should render it almost absurd to argue that politics anywhere actually are maintained indifferently, rationally, or through calculations even of enlightened interest. However, rather than reiterate these contributions, in this afterword I will take a different tack, and look in directions the essays point to but do not follow here. Rather than summarise each chapter individually, I will address themes evoked by the collection as a whole, referring impressionistically to a few chapters.

The authors, in order to demonstrate that the political is emotional and that emotions have politics, had first to bring together analytic categories that have most often been separated by centuries of intellectual practice. The introduction to this book nicely illuminates these traditions, tracing social thinking in anthropology and in other disciplines that has attempted to bridge or to transcend those traditions. I will not rehearse those insights here, except to note that because they are working against the current in so many ways, it seems unavoidable that the authors bring together the sentimental and the political by first treating them as ontologically separate modalities of experience. One way to do this is by depicting an expression of feeling as it is channelled to serve within a political discourse. Another is for the scholar to privilege the political modality as the key frame for a sphere of social action within which to distinguish a relevant or active emotion. But what would happen if, instead, we reversed the methodological direction in which to track this intersection? If we were first to position and interpret phenomena that people identify as 'emotional', and only then trace those across arenas or actions defined as 'political'? And perhaps to relinquish assuming that we already know what emotions – or politics – 'are' in the first place, or that they always already exist (I will return to this question at the end)?

It occurs to me that what I am proposing is less clever and more reactionary than what these scholars have achieved. They have made the counterintuitive move to unmask the feeling in and around ostensibly rational policy or political action. But I hope, if not to suggest anything new for social thought, at least to propose alternative trajectories within study of the 'postsocialist' regions. Like scholars conducting research in other, variously bounded world areas, we encounter limitations and judgements (reinforced by granting agencies, academic circles and local gatekeepers) about what constitutes relevant and appropriate research sites, evidence and questions. Certainly, scholars of East Europe and of the former Soviet states focus on property redistribution after state socialism, wartime trauma and postwar resettlements, shifting national and transnational alignments and loyalties because these *are* processes that acutely affect people across a vast region. But it is also clear that these foci are of immediate interest to Western states, Eastern states, financial institutions, corporations and NGOs. Yet, Leutloff-Grandits' piece discusses alternatives to state pressure to think in national categories: if there are still other kinds of alternatives that are equally important, how can we find them?

The majority of the scholars writing for this collection are anthropologists, as am I. We seek intersections of discourses and practices in specific sites and events, in interactions, texts, spaces, performances and displays. We look for patterns, relations, and contradictions across such sites and events. Or we look for connections from fleeting moments to broader processes, from particular things to their trajectories through larger circulations. The trouble we face, however, in establishing our observations as relevant is that significant 'sites' and 'events' are largely framed *as such* by forces other than those that the people we are talking to can marshal and control. These essays, by taking up a particular kind of intersection of feeling and politics, may inspire more readers to think of ways to reach outside these practical paradigms, outside the doxa of 'Transition studies.' I want to mention a few possibilities for future research that came to my mind, and have no doubt already occurred to the authors.

For instance, a future project might, rather than delineating affects displayed around an already polarised political issue, begin by sweeping the field in search for sentimental expressions of any kind – to find also 'positive' pleasures and feelings that call for explanation. Skrbiš points in this direction by highlighting the pleasures Slovenian diaspora nationalists take in making their own small discoveries that support Venetological arguments. Svašek carefully teases apart and weaves back together the angers and resentments that Czech villagers, Sudeten Germans, and foreign estate holders express about property loss with the embodied and aesthetic pleasures they took in extending their sense of identity – both through property they owned and through that they did not own. Such approaches do not brush aside suffering, or the effects of displacement and instability; perhaps such a Foucauldian touch could allow lingering longer at sites and events that may not be framed as overtly political. Or perhaps one might begin with expressions of cosy belonging in the present: might they connect to 'nostalgia' in unexpected ways? Are they produced by larger processes and powers? How? Do they serve to scaffold and reproduce them? What to make of infatuation, respect, hilarity, irony, of 'feeling groovy' (Russian slang: *kaif, kruto…*):

> Once again, my man messed around,
> got in a fight, swallowed pills.
> I felt so low I threw him out,
> and now – I want a man like Putin!
> A man like Putin, full of strength,
> a man like Putin, who doesn't drink,
> a man like Putin, who doesn't swear,
> a man like Putin, who won't run off!
> (Russian airwaves, 2002)

Is this song an expression of humour, admiration, the Blues, or orchestrated PR? No one commenting in the press, whether in Russian, U.S., German, or Japanese publications, seemed quite sure what to make of this pop recording, much less of its singers' (the girl group, Singing Together) intentions.

The essays in this anthology all describe much clearer connections between emotional and political modalities and the motives driving deployments of affect than we might make of the feelings colouring the Putin song. They take up cases where subjects were able to transpose or articulate affects in ways that generated specific political effects. But in doing so the authors also thereby suggest a converse possibility: in future studies, and in order to better understand those cases where emotions are politically effective, we need also to attend to cases where they do not. For instance, when do people domesticate political trauma, fear or organised victimisation in ways that render discussion of structural or political change inaccessible or inappropriate? When do particular means for mourning, as for symbolising war losses and separations, bracket sorrow as a family affair in ways that position criticism of the state or protests against the specific war as attacks on the soldier or on the family? Why then do people or collectives act or express affect about these matters in one manner and not in another? What institutional, cultural or other forces, or patterns, constrain such choices?

To this end, it might be worth while in further work that links emotions and politics to begin neither with categories of 'emotions' nor those of 'politics', but with salient forms, methods and media. Zerilli convincingly argues that public songs mediate the shedding of tears, transforming them into symbols of legitimacy. But what other emotions, positions or identities can this or similar local song genres mediate – and how could knowing that tell us more about this particular transformation? A similar example: Golanska-Ryan compellingly demonstrates that the UPR in Poland deploys the register of informational speech to respond to and to stir up fears, without admitting that this is what they are doing. How might we juxtapose this usage of 'informational' speech to other uses of that register? Or, in parallel, in what formal ways are UPR communications that are delivered as 'information' different from or similar to UPR slogans, especially since the latter formally recall and index socialist slogans? By suggesting questions at this level of detail I am not trying to invest media or forms of communication with special powers in themselves. Rather, I want to draw attention to analytic benefits when expressive media for and styles of affect are thereby located in particular and in context, rather than evoked in general.

There are powerful metaphors that seem to explain the force of emotion, and that seem difficult to think without. Familiar tropes underlie generalised notions of symbolic forms or mediums, depicting them as if they were conduits for feelings, conduits whose exerted pressure creates social and political effects. Poems *amplify* feelings of being ignored and of being manipulated into hatred, as Müller illustrates, while also *diffusing* responsibility for their expression. Kalb and Tak explore the complex ways in which rumours both *focus* distrust in the state and act as a *safety valve* for anxiety and distrust. Yet, as Svašek notes in her introduction, as social thinkers we have become as haunted by the Marxian metaphor of circulating emotional 'capital' as we are troubled by this Freudian one of flowing emotional 'hydraulics'. How might our future research add facets and dimensions to the insights made here by making room for additional ways of picturing feeling? I do not have a new answer in the form of a new metaphor. I can only press a few specific questions about how scholars might write about feeling to see if they yield anything.

First: How can we distinguish in our writing between (1) embodied feelings, (2) conventional forms or displays of feelings (sentiments or affects), and (3) images *of* feelings and uses of feeling terms or categories, whether in discourse *about* appropriate displays of affect, or in discourse describing emotional effects? It seems important not to collapse these distinct levels, even while allowing for ways they each can leak into and influence the others.

Second: What are the local contents of emotion categories such as 'nostalgia', 'anger', 'bitterness', 'guilt'? How do they overlap and conflict? Mihaylova begins to trace some of this local content in fascinating ways by connecting usages of expressions of 'suffering' to recent, historically specific, and embodied experiences of 'silence' and 'emptiness' after the withdrawal of the state. Heady and Miller imply that 'nostalgia' hooks to different referents, or at least it hooks to them to different degrees in different places across Russia – and they show where the content of 'nostalgia' may and may not have real or material referents. Whether bodily 'emotions' exist without histories of such specific referents is not something I can answer. But certainly modes of expressing affects as well as the general terms and categories for feelings circulate through changing fields. I think it is precisely to follow this moving history of specific modalities and references that is most interesting, as an anthropologist. Attention to changing histories and particulars seems even more crucial for understanding those sentiments mentioned in the essays that could hardly be even potentially universal, but that hook onto specific identities, or that index those specificities through compounded emotion categories. What constitutes an 'anti-Gypsy feeling', a 'national sentiment', an 'anti-communist feeling', a 'sense of authenticity', or a 'desire for revenge'?

Third: How and why are certain emotion categories deployed for certain ends? Why not some alternative affect? The essays are very strong in showing the political uses of affect-laden terms such as 'crimes against humanity', and 'deportation'. However, I do think that in order to communicate to scholars outside our area, we need to answer: why do people in these places use these categories and not other ones? Clearly, recent experience is part of the answer, but is there more to the story?

Fourth (and related): How have these emotion categories and expressions of affect come to be socially positioned and valued? What *else* does 'anger' index besides a 'feeling', even a feeling about an injustice? Weakness or strength? Masculinity or femininity? Racial categories? Does that 'something else' matter to its perceived value or force? What *else* does nostalgia point to besides a relation to memory or to the past? Ideas about class positions or about 'the West'? Do certain affects *also* point to identities formed by experience in particular occupations or roles (the military, service work, bureaucratic work, wife etc.?) Who is entitled to express which affects, or to speak about them, and how?

In conclusion, I want to stress again the value of the works brought together here for the larger field of studies of this area. Several scholars have questioned the utility of terms such as 'transition' and 'postsocialist' to account for what has been happening since about 1989 across former socialist states of East Europe and Eurasia. They have proposed that we seek other rubrics and ways of asking questions. This call is one that has repeatedly stymied many of us as we rack our brains for substitutes. But perhaps one way to ask new questions is to bracket the issue of general rubrics and terms (for now), and instead to take up particular, counterintuitive intersections, as these papers do. Inspired by them, and turning them inside out, we arrive somewhere else.

Notes on Contributors

Liesl L. Gambold Miller received her Ph.D. from the University of California, Los Angeles, Department of Anthropology for research on farm reorganisation in Russia. She has been a visiting scholar at the Max Planck Institute for Social Anthropology, Halle, Germany, and is currently assistant professor in the department of Sociology and Social Anthropology at Dalhousie University, Nova Scotia, Canada, where she continues her research on Russia. Her publications include 'Communal Coherence and Barriers to Reform', in *Rural Reform in Post-soviet Russia,* D.J. O'Brien and S. Wegren (eds), Baltimore: Johns Hopkins University Press, 2002, pp. 221–42, and *Interdependence in Rural Russia: The Post-socialist Mixed Feudal Economy,* Max Planck Institute for Social Anthropology Working paper No. 51, 2003.

Justine Golanska-Ryan received her M.A. in social anthropology from the School of Anthopological Studies, Queens University in Belfast, on the basis of the thesis 'Discursive Strategies of Resistance in the Polish Campaign against EU Membership'. She also studied theory of anthropology in the Department of Theory and History of Culture, University of Silesia, Katowice, Poland. Her major research interests include transition in Poland and other postsocialist states, border studies (Ireland and Poland), anthropology of space, postmodernity and transgression. She conducted fieldwork in Poland on the sense of space, cultural borders between Silesia and Zagłę bie and on Polish attitudes towards EU membership. Her Ph.D. plans focus on the study of borders and cultural change.

Patrick Heady is a senior research fellow at the Max Planck Institute for Social Anthropology in Halle, Germany, with whom he has carried out fieldwork in Russia. He obtained his Ph.D. from the London School of Economics on the basis of fieldwork in the Italian Alps, described in *The Hard People: Rivalry, Sympathy and Social Structure in an Alpine Valley* (Amsterdam: Harwood Academic, 1999). He is joint editor of *Conceiving*

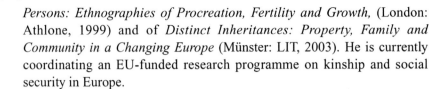

Persons: Ethnographies of Procreation, Fertility and Growth, (London: Athlone, 1999) and of *Distinct Inheritances: Property, Family and Community in a Changing Europe* (Münster: LIT, 2003). He is currently coordinating an EU-funded research programme on kinship and social security in Europe.

Don Kalb is associate professor of sociology and social anthropology at Central European University, Budapest, and researcher at the department of anthropology, Utrecht University, the Netherlands. He was a senior fellow at the Institute for Human Sciences, IWM, Vienna, and directed IWM's SOCO programme (Social Consequences of Economic Transformation in East Central Europe) between 1998 and 2000. His publications include *Expanding Class: Power and Everyday Politics in Industrial Communities, The Netherlands, 1850–1950* (Durham and London: Duke University Press, 1997); (ed.) *The Ends of Globalization. Bringing Society Back In*, (Boulder and London: Rowman and Littlefield Publishers, 2000); (ed.) *Globalization and Development: Themes and Concepts in Current Research* (Dordrecht: Kluwer, 2004); (ed.) *Critical Junctions: Pathways beyond the Cultural Turn* (New York and Oxford: Berghahn Books, 2005). His recent research focuses on problems of economic restructuring, culture, class and citizenship in Eastern Europe; see also his Afterword to Chris Hann (ed*.), Postsocialism; Ideals, Ideologies and Practices in Eurasia* (London: Routledge, 2002). He is the (founding) Editor of *Focaal. European Journal of Anthropology.*

Alaina Lemon is associate professor in the Department of Anthropology at the University of Michigan, and is associated with the Center for Russian and East European Studies. Her research focuses on Russia and the CIS, and links discourse and performance to state bureaucracies, exchange practices, and institutions for cultural production and for the production of memory. Her current project investigates how criteria for and claims to discursive values such as 'transparency/opacity' or 'sincerity/dissimulation' both presuppose and produce social hierarchies. Crucial to her research are transformations and continuities of power and person; in her most recent publications, as they involve racialised or gendered categories in formerly socialist states. Her publications include *Between Two Fires: Gypsy Performance and Romani Memory from Pushkin to Post-Socialism* (Duke University Press, 2000, Winner 2001 AAASS Wayne Vucinich Prize), '"Dealing Emotional Blows": Realism and Verbal "Terror" at the Russian State Theatrical Academy', in *Language and Communication* 24(4):

313–37, 'Talking Transit and Spectating Transition: The Moscow Metro,' in *Altering States: Anthropology in Transition*, eds. Daphne Berdahl, Matti Bunzl and Martha Lampland (University of Michigan Press, 2000), and 'Your Eyes are Green Like Dollars: Counterfeit Cash, National Substance, and Currency Apartheid in 1990s' Russia', in *Cultural Anthropology* 13(1): 22–55 (1998).

Carolin Leutloff-Grandits is currently completing her Ph.D. thesis at the Max Planck Institute for Social Anthropology in Halle/Saale. Her thesis focuses on ethnic property conflicts and the transformation of property relations in postwar Croatia. Recent publications are 'Coping with Economic Devastation. Agriculture in Post-war Knin, Croatia', in C. Hann and the Property Relations Group (eds), *The Postsocialist Agrarian Question: Property Relations and the Rural Condition* (Münster: LIT, 2003), and 'Houses without Owners? Historical Insights into Missing Ownership Documents of Houses in Rural Croatia in the 1990s', in H. Grandits and P. Heady (eds), *Distinct Inheritances: Property, Family, and Community in a Changing Europe* (Münster: Lit, pp. 371–88)

Dimitrina Mihaylova is a post doctoral fellow at COMPAS (Centre on Migration, Policy and Society), University of Oxford, who has recently completed a D.Phil. in Social Anthropology about the transformations of Pomak political subjectivity at the Bulgarian-Greek border. She has an M.A. in Race and Ethnic Studies, University of Warwick, and an M.Sc. in History and Ethnology from the University of Sofia, and was a 2003 Marie Curie Research Fellow at MIGRINTER, University of Poitiers, France. Dimitrina has been involved in academic and applied projects in Bulgaria, Macedonia, Greece, Turkey and the U.K. She has conducted research on postsocialist transitions, post-Cold War Balkan borders, trust and social networks, migration, community development, and religious, ethnic and national identity in the Balkans. Her publications include: 'Categories at Cross-Purposes: Redefining Ethnic Stereotypes at the Bulgarian-Greek Border', in Dimitris Theodossopoulous and Keith Brown (eds), *Journal of Mediterranean Studies* (2005), and 'Between the Rock and the Hard Place: Bulgarian Muslims on the Bulgarian Greek Border', *Focaal. European Journal of Anthropology* 41: 45–58 (2003).

Birgit Müller is senior researcher at the LAIOS (Laboratoire de l'anthropologie des institutions et organisations sociales), CNRS in Paris. She has worked extensively on social movements and societies in rapid transformation: on riots in colonial Nigeria, on alternative movements in West Germany (*Toward an Alternative Culture of Work. Political Idealism and Economic Practices in West Berlin Collective Enterprises*, Westview Press, 1991), in Nicaragua during and after the Sandinista period, and on postsocialist transformations in East Germany (*Die Entzauberung der Marktwirtschaft – Ethnologische Erkundungen in Ostberliner Betrieben*, Campus, 2002), the Czech Republic and Russia (*Political and Institutional Change in Post-communist Eastern Europe* CSA, 1999). Her focus is on institutional change, mechanisms of domination and the unintended and intended consequences brought about by political and cultural contestation and economic struggles.

Zlatko Skrbiš lectures in sociology at University of Queensland. His main research interest concerns questions of diasporic imagination, migrations and nationalism in a transnational context. His book titled *Long-Distance Nationalism* was published in 1999 by Ashgate. His other publications include papers on gender (with Maria Pallotta-Chiarolli in the *Australian and New Zealand Journal of Sociology*), diasporic imagination and transnationalism (*Cultural Studies, Focaal: European Journal of Anthropology, Asian and Pacific Migration Journal*), cosmopolitanism (with Gavin Kendall and Ian Woodward in *Theory, Culture and Society*) and religious apparitions and nationalism (*Nations and Nationalism*). He is the Vice-president of the Australian Sociological Association and the vice-president of the International Sociological Association Research Committee on Ethnic, Race and Minority Relations.

Maruška Svašek is lecturer at the School of Anthropological Studies, Queens University, Belfast. Her main research interests include postsocialism, border issues, emotions, and the politics of art. She has published numerous papers in journals and edited collections on these issues, including 'Narratives of "Home" and "Homeland". The Symbolic Construction of the Sudeten German Heimat', *Identities. Global Studies in Culture and Power*, 9: 495–518' (2002), and 'Borders and Emotions. Hope and Fear in the Bohemian-Bavarian Frontier Zone' *Ethnologia Europaea* (2000). She is coeditor (with Kay Milton) of *Mixed Emotions. Anthropological Studies of Feeling* (Oxford: Berg, 2005), and is currently working on a book on the anthropology of art for Pluto. She is also editor of *Focaal. European Journal of Anthropology* and assistant editor of *Identities. Global Studies in Culture and Power*. Her current research focuses on the emotional dimensions of post-Cold War transformations in the Czech–German border region, and on artefacts and emotional agency.

Herman Tak is associate professor of Social Sciences at Utrecht University and University College Utrecht, the Netherlands. He published *South Italian Festivals. A Local History of Ritual and Change* (Amsterdam: Amsterdam University Press, 2000), *Feste in Italia meridionale* (Potenza: Edizioni Ermes, 2000), and coedited *Critical Junctions: Pathways beyond the Cultural Turn*, (Oxford: Berghahn Books, 2005). He is editor of *Focaal. European Journal of Anthropology* (Berghahn Books).

Filippo M. Zerilli is researcher and lecturer at the University of Cagliari, Italy. His main research interests include the history of anthropology, postsocialism, changing property relations, and the emotional and moral dimension of ownership claims. He is the author of *Il lato oscuro dell'etnologia* (Rome: CISU, 1998) and is the editor of *Dalle "Regole" al "Suicidio". Percorsi durkheimiani* (Lecce: Argo, 2001). He is co-editor of *Incontri di etnologia europea. European Ethnology Meetings* (Naples: ESI, 1998) and of *La ricerca antropologica in Romania. Prospettive storiche ed etnografiche* (Naples: ESI, 2003). He is currently preparing a book on the property restitution debate in postsocialist Romania.

Index

Printed in the United Kingdom
by Lightning Source UK Ltd.
126583UK00001B/238-291/P